MW00788603

The Story of Redemption

The Great Controversy illustrated since the war in
heaven until the days of the new heaven.

Ellen G. White

LS COMPANY

ISBN: 978-1-0879-0291-3

Content:

God's Love Triumphant at Last

The story of redemption, by the gifted author Ellen G. White, is a book written for these times. As we approach the year 2000, world events leave a question mark hanging on the horizon. Are we, a race of tormented human beings, doomed to more trouble and worries, or will the vision of tomorrow change for the better?

Some hope is held out by political and scientific leaders, but the voices of most philosophers, statesmen, and clergymen seem pitched in a minor key.

Is there hope and reassurance anywhere? Yes, for those who refuse to despair and who reason that God must surely know about the human predicament and will act dramatically to change the course of events—for them there will be a way out. But the reader of this volume will find more than human reasoning to support the optimistic view. Faith will spring up in his heart as he reads this enlightening and powerful account of mankind's passionate struggles against the dark powers of evil. The narrative is based upon the scriptural theme of the age-long conflict between divine and Satanic agencies for the control of man's will and destiny. Here is reviewed the story of man's creation and his fall into sin, also of the demonic control that has inspired wars and instigated crime and universal suffering and tragedy. At the heart of the book is the redemption of man wrought by Christ on the cross.

Each page in this narrative provides insights into history rarely attempted by any author except by the writers of the Holy Scriptures. The story of redemption is a true war story—the story of God and demons and man in conflict. It culminates in a triumphant denouement, with peace and restoration for all who follow Jesus Christ, the King of kings, who returns to earth triumphantly.

The compilers of this volume have extracted choice selections from four previous books by Ellen G. White on this commanding theme. These excerpts have been placed together in the order of historical development. The narrative encompasses the entire span of human existence and provides most comprehensive and revealing chapters on the subject.

Time is precious. Time is running out. Eternity beckons all of us. The reader of this book will discover that the future is bright. God and the forces of right will gain the final victory.

The Publishers

Chapter 1—The Fall of Lucifer

Lucifer in heaven, before his rebellion, was a high and exalted angel, next in honor to God's dear Son. His countenance, like those of the other angels, was mild and expressive of happiness. His forehead was high and broad, showing a powerful intellect. His form was perfect; his bearing noble and majestic. A special light beamed in his countenance and shone around him brighter and more beautiful than around the other angels; yet Christ, God's dear Son, had the pre-eminence over all the angelic host. He was one with the Father before the angels were created. Lucifer was envious of Christ, and gradually assumed command which devolved on Christ alone.

The great Creator assembled the heavenly host, that He might in the presence of all the angels confer special honor upon His Son. The Son was seated on the throne with the Father, and the heavenly throng of holy angels was gathered around them. The Father then made known that it was ordained by Himself that Christ, His Son, should be equal with Himself; so that wherever was the presence of His Son, it was as His own presence. The word of the Son was to be obeyed as readily as the word of the Father. His Son He had invested with authority to command the heavenly host. Especially was His Son to work in union with Himself in the anticipated creation of the earth and every living thing that should exist upon the earth. His Son would carry out His will and His purposes but would do nothing of Himself alone. The Father's will would be fulfilled in Him.

Lucifer was envious and jealous of Jesus Christ. Yet when all the angels bowed to Jesus to acknowledge His supremacy and high authority and rightful rule, he bowed with them; but his heart was filled with envy and hatred. Christ had been taken into the special counsel of God in regard to His plans, while Lucifer was unacquainted with them. He did not understand, neither was he permitted to know, the purposes of God. But Christ was acknowledged sovereign of heaven, His power and authority to be the same as that of God Himself. Lucifer thought that he was himself a favorite in heaven among the angels. He had been highly exalted, but this did not call forth from him gratitude and praise to his Creator. He aspired to the height of God Himself. He gloried in his loftiness. He knew that he was honored by the angels. He had a special mission to execute. He had been near the great Creator, and the ceaseless beams of glorious light enshrouding the eternal God had shone especially upon him. He thought how angels had obeyed his command with pleasurable alacrity. Were not his garments light and beautiful? Why should Christ thus be honored before himself?

He left the immediate presence of the Father, dissatisfied and filled with envy against Jesus Christ. Concealing his real purposes, he assembled the angelic host. He introduced his subject, which was himself. As one aggrieved, he related the preference God had given Jesus to the neglect of himself. He told them that henceforth all the sweet liberty the angels had enjoyed was at an end. For had not a ruler been appointed over them, to whom they from henceforth must yield servile honor? He stated to them that he had called them together to assure them that he no longer would submit to this invasion of his rights and theirs; that never would he again bow down to Christ; that he would take the honor upon himself which should have been conferred upon him, and would be the commander of all who would submit to follow him and obey his voice.

There was contention among the angels. Lucifer and his sympathizers were striving to reform the government of God. They were discontented and unhappy because they could not look into His unsearchable wisdom and ascertain His purposes in exalting His Son, and endowing Him with such unlimited power and command. They rebelled against the authority of the Son.

Angels that were loyal and true sought to reconcile this mighty, rebellious angel to the will of his Creator. They justified the act of God in conferring honor upon Christ, and with forcible reasoning sought to convince Lucifer that no less honor was his now than before the Father had proclaimed the honor which He had conferred upon His Son. They clearly set forth that Christ was the Son of God, existing with Him before the angels were created; and that He had ever stood at the right hand of God, and His mild, loving authority had not heretofore been questioned; and that He had given no commands but what it was joy for the heavenly host to execute. They urged that Christ's receiving special honor from the Father, in the presence of the angels, did not detract from the honor that Lucifer had heretofore received. The angels wept. They anxiously sought to move him to renounce his wicked design and yield submission to their Creator; for all had heretofore been peace and harmony, and what could occasion this dissenting, rebellious voice?

Lucifer refused to listen. And then he turned from the loyal and true angels, denouncing them as slaves. These angels, true to God, stood in amazement as they saw that Lucifer was successful in his effort to incite rebellion. He promised them a new and better government than they then had, in which all would be freedom. Great numbers signified their purpose to accept him as their leader and chief commander. As he saw his advances were met with success, he flattered himself that he should yet have all the angels on his side, and that he would be equal with God Himself, and his voice of authority would be heard in commanding the entire host of heaven. Again the loyal angels warned him, and assured him what must be the consequences if he persisted; that He who could create the angels could by His power overturn all their authority and in some signal manner punish their audacity and terrible rebellion. To think that an angel should resist the law of God which was as sacred as Himself! They warned the rebellious to close their ears to Lucifer's deceptive reasonings, and advised him and all who had been affected by him to go to God and confess their wrong for even admitting a thought of questioning His authority.

Many of Lucifer's sympathizers were inclined to heed the counsel of the loyal angels and repent of their dissatisfaction and be again received to the confidence of the Father and His dear Son. The mighty revolter then declared that he was acquainted with God's law, and if he should submit to servile obedience, his honor would be taken from him. No more would he be intrusted with his exalted mission. He told them that himself and they also had now gone too far to go back, and he would brave the consequences, for to bow in servile worship to the Son of God he never would; that God would not forgive, and now they must assert their liberty and gain by force the position and authority which was not willingly accorded to them. [Thus it was that Lucifer, "the light-bearer," the sharer of God's glory, the attendant of his throne, by transgression became Satan, "the adversary."—*Patriarchs and Prophets, 40.*]

The loyal angels hastened speedily to the Son of God and acquainted Him with what was taking place among the angels. They found the Father in conference with His beloved Son, to determine the means by which, for the best good of the loyal angels, the assumed authority of Satan could be forever put down. The great God could at once have hurled this archdeceiver from heaven; but this was not His purpose. He would give the rebellious an equal chance to measure strength and might with His own Son and His loyal angels. In this battle every angel would choose his own side and be manifested to all. It would not have been safe to suffer any who united with Satan in his rebellion to continue to occupy heaven. They had learned the lesson of genuine rebellion against the unchangeable law of God, and this is incurable. If God had exercised His power to punish this chief rebel, disaffected angels would not have been manifested; hence, God took another course, for He would manifest distinctly to all the heavenly host His justice and His judgment.

War in Heaven

It was the highest crime to rebel against the government of God. All heaven seemed in commotion. The angels were marshaled in companies, each division with a higher commanding angel at its head. Satan was warring against the law of God, because ambitious to exalt himself and unwilling to submit to the authority of God's Son, heaven's great commander.

All the heavenly host were summoned to appear before the Father, to have each case determined. Satan unblushingly made known his dissatisfaction that Christ should be preferred before him. He stood up proudly and urged that he should be equal with God and should be taken into conference with the Father and understand His purposes. God informed Satan that to His Son alone He would reveal His secret purposes, and He required all the family in heaven, even Satan, to yield Him implicit, unquestioned obedience; but that he (Satan) had proved himself unworthy of a place in heaven. Then Satan exultingly pointed to his sympathizers, comprising nearly one half of all the angels, and exclaimed, "These are with me! Will you expel these also, and make such a void in heaven?" He then declared that he was prepared to resist the authority of Christ and to defend his place in heaven by force of might, strength against strength.

Good angels wept to hear the words of Satan and his exulting boasts. God declared that the rebellious should remain in heaven no longer. Their high and happy state had been held upon condition of obedience to the law which God had given to govern the high order of intelligences. But no provision had been made to save those who should venture to transgress His law. Satan grew bold in his rebellion, and expressed his contempt of the Creator's law. This Satan could not bear. He claimed that angels needed no law but should be left free to follow their own will, which would ever guide them right; that law was a restriction of their liberty; and that to abolish law was one great object of his standing as he did. The condition of the angels, he thought, needed improvement. Not so the mind of God, who had made laws and exalted them equal to Himself. The happiness of the angelic host consisted in their perfect obedience to law. Each had his special work assigned him, and until Satan rebelled, there had been perfect order and harmonious action in heaven.

Then there was war in heaven. The Son of God, the Prince of heaven, and His loyal angels engaged in conflict with the archrebel and those who united with him. The Son of God and true, loyal angels prevailed; and Satan and his sympathizers were expelled from heaven. All the heavenly host acknowledged and adored the God of justice. Not a taint of rebellion was left in heaven. All was again peaceful and harmonious as before. Angels in heaven mourned the fate of those who had been their companions in happiness and bliss. Their loss was felt in heaven.

The Father consulted His Son in regard to at once carrying out their purpose to make man to inhabit the earth. He would place man upon probation to test his loyalty before he could be rendered eternally secure. If he endured the test wherewith God saw fit to prove him, he should eventually be equal with the angels. He was to have the favor of God, and he was to converse with angels, and they with him. He did not see fit to place them beyond the power of disobedience.

Chapter 2—The Creation

This chapter is based on Genesis 1

The Father and the Son engaged in the mighty, wondrous work they had contemplated—of creating the world. The earth came forth from the hand of the Creator exceedingly beautiful. There were mountains and hills and plains; and interspersed among them were rivers and bodies of water. The earth was not one extensive plain, but the monotony of the scenery was broken by hills and mountains, not high and ragged as they now are, but regular and beautiful in shape. The bare, high rocks were never seen upon them, but lay beneath the surface, answering as bones to the earth. The waters were regularly dispersed. The hills, mountains, and very beautiful plains were adorned with plants and flowers and tall, majestic trees of every description, which were many times larger and much more beautiful than trees now are. The air was pure and healthful, and the earth seemed like a noble palace. Angels beheld and rejoiced at the wonderful and beautiful works of God.

After the earth was created, and the beasts upon it, the Father and Son carried out their purpose, which was designed before the fall of Satan, to make man in their own image. They had wrought together in the creation of the earth and every living thing upon it. And now God said to His Son, "Let us make man in our image." As Adam came forth from the hand of his Creator he was of noble height and of beautiful symmetry. He was more than twice as tall as men now living upon the earth, and was well proportioned. His features were perfect and beautiful. His complexion was neither white nor sallow, but ruddy, glowing with the rich tint of health. Eve was not quite as tall as Adam. Her head reached a little above his shoulders. She, too, was noble, perfect in symmetry, and very beautiful.

This sinless pair wore no artificial garments. They were clothed with a covering of light and glory, such as the angels wear. While they lived in obedience to God, this circle of light enshrouded them. Although everything God had made was in the perfection of beauty, and there seemed nothing wanting upon the earth which God had created to make Adam and Eve happy, yet He manifested His great love to them by planting a garden especially for them. A portion of their time was to be occupied in the happy employment of dressing the garden, and a portion in receiving the visits of angels, listening to their instruction, and in happy meditation. Their labor was not wearisome but pleasant and invigorating. This beautiful garden was to be their home.

In this garden the Lord placed trees of every variety for usefulness and beauty. There were trees laden with luxuriant fruit, of rich fragrance, beautiful to the eye, and pleasant to the taste, designed of God to be food for the holy pair. There were the lovely vines which grew upright, laden with their burden of fruit, unlike anything man has seen since the fall. The fruit was very large and of different colors; some nearly black, some purple, red, pink, and light green. This beautiful and luxuriant growth of fruit upon the branches of the vine was called grapes. They did not trail upon the ground, although not supported by trellises, but the weight of the fruit bowed them down. It was the happy labor of Adam and Eve to form beautiful bowers from the branches of the vine and train them, forming dwellings of nature's beautiful, living trees and foliage, laden with fragrant fruit.

The earth was clothed with beautiful verdure, while myriads of fragrant flowers of every variety and hue sprang up in rich profusion around them. Everything was tastefully and gloriously arranged. In the midst of the garden stood the tree of life, the glory of which surpassed all other trees. Its fruit looked like apples of gold and silver, and was to perpetuate immortality. The leaves contained healing properties.

Adam and Eve in Eden

Very happy were the holy pair in Eden. Unlimited control was given them over every living thing. The lion and the lamb sported peacefully and harmlessly around them, or slumbered at their feet. Birds of every variety of color and plumage flitted among the trees and flowers and about Adam and Eve, while their mellow-toned music echoed among the trees in sweet accord to the praises of their Creator.

Adam and Eve were charmed with the beauties of their Eden home. They were delighted with the little songsters around them, wearing their bright yet graceful plumage, and warbling forth their happy, cheerful music. The holy pair united with them and raised their voices in harmonious songs of love, praise, and adoration to the Father and His dear Son for the tokens of love which surrounded them. They recognized the order and harmony of creation, which spoke of wisdom and knowledge that were infinite. Some new beauty and additional glory of their Eden home they were continually discovering, which filled their hearts with deeper love and brought from their lips expressions of gratitude and reverence to their Creator.

Chapter 3—Consequences of Rebellion

In the midst of the garden, near the tree of life, stood the tree of knowledge of good and evil. This tree was especially designed of God to be the pledge of their obedience, faith, and love to Him. Of this tree the Lord commanded our first parents not to eat, neither to touch it, lest they die. He told them that they might freely eat of all the trees in the garden except one, but if they ate of that tree they should surely die.

When Adam and Eve were placed in the beautiful garden they had everything for their happiness which they could desire. But God chose, in His all-wise arrangements, to test their loyalty before they could be rendered eternally secure. They were to have His favor, and He was to converse with them and they with Him. Yet He did not place evil out of their reach. Satan was permitted to tempt them. If they endured the trial they were to be in perpetual favor with God and the heavenly angels.

Satan stood in amazement at his new condition. His happiness was gone. He looked upon the angels who, with him, were once so happy, but who had been expelled from heaven with him. Before their fall not a shade of discontent had marred their perfect bliss. Now all seemed changed. Countenances which had reflected the image of their Maker were gloomy and despairing. Strife, discord, and bitter recrimination were among them. Previous to their rebellion these things had been unknown in heaven. Satan now beheld the terrible results of his rebellion. He shuddered, and feared to face the future and to contemplate the end of these things.

The hour for joyful, happy songs of praise to God and His dear Son had come. Satan had led the heavenly choir. He had raised the first note; then all the angelic host had united with him, and glorious strains of music had resounded through heaven in honor of God and His dear Son. But now, instead of strains of sweetest music, discord and angry words fall upon the ear of the great rebel leader. Where is he? Is it not all a horrible dream? Is he shut out of heaven? Are the gates of heaven never more to open to admit him? The hour of worship draws nigh, when bright and holy angels bow before the Father. No more will he unite in heavenly song. No more will he bow in reverence and holy awe before the presence of the eternal God.

Could he be again as he was when he was pure, true, and loyal, gladly would he yield up the claims of his authority. But he was lost! beyond redemption, for his presumptuous rebellion! And this was not all; he had led others to rebellion and to the same lost condition with himself—angels, who had never thought to question the will of Heaven or refuse obedience to the law of God till he had put it into their minds, presenting before them that they might enjoy a greater good, a higher and more glorious liberty. This had been the sophistry whereby he had deceived them. A responsibility now rests upon him from which he would fain be released.

These spirits had become turbulent with disappointed hopes. Instead of greater good, they were experiencing the sad results of disobedience and disregard of law. Never more would these unhappy beings be swayed by the mild rule of Jesus Christ. Never more would their spirits be stirred by the deep, earnest love, peace, and joy which His presence had ever inspired in them, to be returned to Him in cheerful obedience and reverential honor.

Satan Seeks Reinstatement

Satan trembled as he viewed his work. He was alone in meditation upon the past, the present, and his future plans. His mighty frame shook as with a tempest. An angel from heaven was passing. He called him and entreated an interview with Christ. This was granted him. He then related to the Son of God that he repented of his rebellion and wished again the favor of God. He was willing to take the place God had previously assigned him, and be under His wise command. Christ wept at Satan's woe but told him, as the mind of God, that he could never be received into heaven. Heaven must not be placed in jeopardy. All heaven would be marred should he be received back, for sin and rebellion originated with him. The seeds of rebellion were still within him. He had, in his rebellion, no occasion for his course, and he had hopelessly ruined not only himself but the host of angels also, who would then have been happy in heaven had he remained steadfast. The law of God could condemn but could not pardon.

He repented not of his rebellion because he saw the goodness of God which he had abused. It was not possible that his love for God had so increased since his fall that it would lead to cheerful submission and happy obedience to His law which had been despised. The wretchedness he realized in losing the sweet light of heaven, and the sense of guilt which forced itself upon him, and the disappointment he experienced himself in not finding his expectation realized, were the cause of his grief. To be commander out of heaven was vastly different from being thus honored in heaven. The loss he had sustained of all the privileges of heaven seemed too much to be borne. He wished to regain these.

This great change of position had not increased his love for God, nor for His wise and just law. When Satan became fully convinced that there was no possibility of his being reinstated in the favor of God, he manifested his malice with increased hatred and fiery vehemence.

God knew that such determined rebellion would not remain inactive. Satan would invent means to annoy the heavenly angels and show contempt for His authority. As he could not gain admission within the gates of heaven, he would wait just at the entrance, to taunt the angels and seek contention with them as they went in and out. He would seek to destroy the happiness of Adam and Eve. He would endeavor to incite them to rebellion, knowing that this would cause grief in heaven.

The Plot Against the Human Family

His followers were seeking him, and he aroused himself and, assuming a look of defiance, informed them of his plans to wrest from God the noble Adam and his companion Eve. If he could in any way beguile them to disobedience, God would make some provision whereby they might be pardoned, and then himself and all the fallen angels would be in a fair way to share with them of God's mercy. If this should fail, they could unite with Adam and Eve, for when once they should transgress the law of God they would be subjects of God's wrath, like themselves. Their transgression would place them, also, in a state of rebellion, and they could unite with Adam and Eve, take possession of Eden, and hold it as their home. And if they could gain access to the tree of life in the midst of the garden, their strength would, they thought, be equal to that of the holy angels, and even God Himself could not expel them.

Satan held a consultation with his evil angels. They did not all readily unite to engage in this hazardous and terrible work. He told them that he would not entrust any one of them to accomplish this work, for he thought that he alone had wisdom sufficient to carry forward so important an enterprise. He wished them to consider the matter while he should leave them and seek retirement, to mature his plans. He sought to impress upon them that this was their last and only hope. If they failed here, all prospect of regaining and controlling heaven, or any part of God's creation, was hopeless.

Satan went alone to mature plans that would most surely secure the fall of Adam and Eve. He had fears that his purposes might be defeated. And again, even if he should be successful in leading Adam and Eve to disobey the commandment of God, and thus become transgressors of His law, and no good come to himself, his own case would not be improved; his guilt would only be increased.

He shuddered at the thought of plunging the holy, happy pair into the misery and remorse he was himself enduring. He seemed in a state of indecision: at one time firm and determined, then hesitating and wavering. His angels were seeking him, their leader, to acquaint him with their decision. They would unite with Satan in his plans, and with him bear the responsibility and share the consequences.

Satan cast off his feelings of despair and weakness, and, as their leader, fortified himself to brave out the matter and do all in his power to defy the authority of God and His Son. He acquainted them with his plans. If he should come boldly upon Adam and Eve and make complaints of God's own Son, they would not listen to him for a moment but would be prepared for such an attack. Should he seek to intimidate them because of his power, so recently an angel in high authority, he could accomplish nothing. He decided that cunning and deceit would do what might, or force, could not.

Adam and Eve Warned

God assembled the angelic host to take measures to avert the threatened evil. It was decided in heaven's council for angels to visit Eden and warn Adam that he was in danger from the foe. Two angels sped on their way to visit our first parents. The holy pair received them with joyful innocence, expressing their grateful thanks to their Creator for thus surrounding them with such a profusion of His bounty. Everything lovely and attractive was theirs to enjoy, and everything seemed wisely adapted to their wants; and that which they prized above all other blessings, was the society of the Son of God and the heavenly angels, for they had much to relate to them at every visit, of their new discoveries of the beauties of nature in their lovely Eden home, and they had many questions to ask relative to many things which they could but indistinctly comprehend.

The angels graciously and lovingly gave them the information they desired. They also gave them the sad history of Satan's rebellion and fall. They then distinctly informed them that the tree of knowledge was placed in the garden to be a pledge of their obedience and love to God; that the high and happy estate of the holy angels was to be retained upon condition of obedience; that they were similarly situated; that they could obey the law of God and be inexpressibly happy, or disobey and lose their high estate and be plunged into hopeless despair.

They told Adam and Eve that God would not compel them to obey—that He had not removed from them power to go contrary to His will; that they were moral agents, free to obey or disobey. There was but one prohibition that God had seen fit to lay upon them as yet. If they should transgress the will of God they would surely die. They told Adam and Eve that the most exalted angel, next in order to Christ, refused obedience to the law of God which He had ordained to govern heavenly beings; that this rebellion had caused war in heaven, which resulted in the rebellious being expelled therefrom, and every angel was driven out of heaven who had united with him in questioning the authority of the great Jehovah; and that this fallen foe was now an enemy to all that concerned the interest of God and His dear Son.

They told them that Satan purposed to do them harm, and it was necessary for them to be guarded, for they might come in contact with the fallen foe; but he could not harm them while they yielded obedience to God's command, for, if necessary, every angel from heaven would come to their help rather than that he should in any way do them harm. But if they disobeyed the command of God, then Satan would have power to ever annoy, perplex, and trouble them. If they remained steadfast against the first insinuations of Satan, they were as secure as the heavenly angels. But if they yielded to the tempter, He who spared not the exalted angels would not spare them. They must suffer the penalty of their transgression, for the law of God was as sacred as Himself, and He required implicit obedience from all in heaven and on earth.

The angels cautioned Eve not to separate from her husband in her employment, for she might be brought in contact with this fallen foe. If separated from each other they would be in greater danger than if both were together. The angels charged them to closely follow the instructions God had given them in reference to the tree of knowledge, for in perfect obedience they were safe, and this fallen foe could then have no power to deceive them. God would not permit Satan to follow the holy pair with continual temptations. He could have access to them only at the tree of knowledge of good and evil.

Adam and Eve assured the angels that they should never transgress the express command of God, for it was their highest pleasure to do His will. The angels united with Adam and Eve in holy strains of harmonious music, and as their songs pealed forth from blissful Eden, Satan heard the sound of their strains of joyful adoration to the Father and Son. And as Satan heard it his envy, hatred, and malignity increased, and he expressed his anxiety to his followers to incite them (Adam and Eve) to disobedience and at once bring down the wrath of God upon them and change their songs of praise to hatred and curses to their Maker.

Chapter 4—Temptation and Fall

This chapter is based on Genesis 3.

Satan assumes the form of a serpent and enters Eden. The serpent was a beautiful creature with wings, and while flying through the air his appearance was bright, resembling burnished gold. He did not go upon the ground but went from place to place through the air and ate fruit like man. Satan entered into the serpent and took his position in the tree of knowledge and commenced leisurely eating of the fruit.

Eve, unconsciously at first, separated from her husband in her employment. When she became aware of the fact she felt that there might be danger, but again she thought herself secure, even if she did not remain close by the side of her husband. She had wisdom and strength to know if evil came, and to meet it. This the angels had cautioned her not to do. Eve found herself gazing with mingled curiosity and admiration upon the fruit of the forbidden tree. She saw it was very lovely, and was reasoning with herself why God had so decidedly prohibited their eating or touching it. Now was Satan's opportunity. He addressed her as though he was able to divine her thought: "Yea, hath God said, Ye shall not eat of every tree of the garden?" Thus, with soft and pleasant words, and with musical voice, he addressed the wondering Eve. She was startled to hear a serpent speak. He extolled her beauty and exceeding loveliness, which was not displeasing to Eve. But she was amazed, for she knew that to the serpent God had not given the power of speech.

Eve's curiosity was aroused. Instead of fleeing from the spot, she listened to hear a serpent talk. It did not occur to her mind that it might be that fallen foe, using the serpent as a medium. It was Satan that spoke, not the serpent. Eve was beguiled, flattered, infatuated. Had she met a commanding personage, possessing a form like the angels and resembling them, she would have been upon her guard. But that strange voice should have driven her to her husband's side to inquire of him why another should thus freely address her. But she entered into a controversy with the serpent. She answered his question, "We may eat of the fruit of the trees of the garden. But of the fruit of the tree which is in the midst of the garden, God hath said, Ye shall not eat of it, neither shall ye touch it, lest ye die." The serpent answered, "Ye shall not surely die: for God doth know that in the day ye eat thereof, then your eyes shall be opened, and ye shall be as gods, knowing good and evil."

Satan would convey the idea that by eating of the forbidden tree they would receive a new and more noble kind of knowledge than they had hitherto attained. This has been his special work, with great success, ever since his fall—to lead men to pry into the secrets of the Almighty and not to be satisfied with what God has revealed, and not careful to obey that which He has commanded. He would lead them to disobey God's commands, and then make them believe that they are entering a wonderful field of knowledge. This is purely supposition, and a miserable deception. They fail to understand what God has revealed, and disregard His explicit commandments and aspire after wisdom, independent of God, and seek to understand that which He has been pleased to withhold from mortals. They are elated with their ideas of progression and charmed with their own vain philosophy, but grope in midnight darkness relative to true knowledge. They are ever learning and never able to come to the knowledge of the truth.

It was not the will of God that this sinless pair should have any knowledge of evil. He had freely given them the good but withheld the evil. Eve thought the words of the serpent wise, and she received the broad assertion, "Ye shall not surely die: for God doth know that in the day ye eat thereof, then your eyes shall be opened, and ye shall be as gods, knowing good and evil"—making God a liar. Satan boldly insinuated that God had deceived them to keep them from being exalted in knowledge equal with Himself. God said: If ye eat ye shall surely die. The serpent said, If ye eat, "ye shall not surely die."

The tempter assured Eve that as soon as she ate of the fruit she would receive a new and superior knowledge that would make her equal with God. He called her attention to himself. He ate freely of the tree and found it not only perfectly harmless but delicious and exhilarating, and told her that it was because of its wonderful properties to impart wisdom and power that God had prohibited them from tasting or even touching it, for He knew its wonderful qualities. He stated that his eating of the fruit of the tree forbidden to them was the reason he had attained the power of speech. He intimated that God would not carry out His word. It was merely a threat to intimidate them and keep them from great good. He further told them that they could not die. Had they not eaten of the tree of life which perpetuates immortality? He said that God was deceiving them to keep them from a higher state of felicity and more exalted happiness. The tempter plucked the fruit and passed it to Eve. She took it in her hand. Now, said the tempter, you were prohibited from even touching it lest you die. He told her that she would realize no more sense of evil and death in eating than in touching or handling the fruit. Eve was emboldened because she felt not the immediate signs of God's displeasure. She thought the words of the tempter all wise and correct. She ate, and was delighted with the fruit. It seemed delicious to her taste, and she imagined that she realized in herself the wonderful effects of the fruit.

Eve Becomes a Tempter

She then plucked for herself of the fruit and ate, and imagined she felt the quickening power of a new and elevated existence as the result of the exhilarating influence of the forbidden fruit. She was in a strange and unnatural excitement as she sought her husband with her hands filled with the forbidden fruit. She related to him the wise discourse of the serpent and wished to conduct him at once to the tree of knowledge. She told him she had eaten of the fruit, and instead of her feeling any sense of death, she realized a pleasing, exhilarating influence. As soon as Eve had disobeyed she became a powerful medium through which to occasion the fall of her husband.

I saw a sadness come over the countenance of Adam. He appeared afraid and astonished. A struggle appeared to be going on in his mind. He told Eve he was quite certain that this was the foe that they had been warned against, and if so, that she must die. She assured him she felt no ill effects but rather a very pleasant influence, and entreated him to eat.

Adam quite well understood that his companion had transgressed the only prohibition laid upon them as a test of their fidelity and love. Eve reasoned that the serpent said they should not surely die, and his words must be true, for she felt no signs of God's displeasure, but a pleasant influence, as she imagined the angels felt.

Adam regretted that Eve had left his side, but now the deed was done. He must be separated from her whose society he had loved so well. How could he have it thus? His love for Eve was strong. And in utter discouragement he resolved to share her fate. He reasoned that Eve was a part of himself, and if she must die, he would die with her, for he could not bear the thought of separation from her. He lacked faith in his merciful and benevolent Creator. He did not think that God, who had formed him out of the dust of the ground into a living, beautiful form, and had created Eve to be his companion, could supply her place.

After all, might not the words of this wise serpent be correct? Eve was before him, just as lovely and beautiful, and apparently as innocent, as before this act of disobedience. She expressed greater, higher love for him than before her disobedience, as the effects of the fruit she had eaten. He saw in her no signs of death. She had told him of the happy influence of the fruit, of her ardent love for him, and he decided to brave the consequences. He seized the fruit and quickly ate it, and like Eve, felt not immediately its ill effects.

Eve had thought herself capable of deciding between right and wrong. The flattering hope of entering a higher state of knowledge had led her to think that the serpent was her especial friend, possessing a great interest in her welfare. Had she sought her husband, and they had related to their Maker the words of the serpent, they would have been delivered at once from his artful temptation. The Lord would not have them investigate the fruit of the tree of knowledge, for then they would be exposed to Satan masked. He knew that they would be perfectly safe if they touched not the fruit.

Man's Freedom of Choice

God instructed our first parents in regard to the tree of knowledge, and they were fully informed relative to the fall of Satan, and the danger of listening to his suggestions. He did not deprive them of the power of eating the forbidden fruit. He left them as free moral agents to believe His word, obey His commandments, and live, or believe the tempter, disobey, and perish. They both ate, and the great wisdom they obtained was the knowledge of sin and a sense of guilt. The covering of light about them soon disappeared, and under a sense of guilt and loss of their divine covering, a shivering seized them, and they tried to cover their exposed forms.

Our first parents chose to believe the words, as they thought, of a serpent; yet he had given them no tokens of his love. He had done nothing for their happiness and benefit, while God had given them everything that was good for food and pleasant to the sight. Everywhere the eye might rest was abundance and beauty; yet Eve was deceived by the serpent, to think that there was something withheld which would make them wise, even as God. Instead of believing and confiding in God, she basely distrusted His goodness and cherished the words of Satan.

After Adam's transgression he at first imagined that he felt the rising to a new and higher existence. But soon the thought of his transgression terrified him. The air, that had been of a mild and even temperature, seemed to chill them. The guilty pair had a sense of sin. They felt a dread of the future, a sense of want, a nakedness of soul. The sweet love and peace and happy contented bliss seemed removed from them, and in its place a want of something came over them that they had never experienced before. They then for the first time turned their attention to the external. They had not been clothed but were draped in light as were the heavenly angels. This light which had enshrouded them had departed. To relieve their sense of lack and nakedness which they realized, their attention was directed to seek a covering for their forms, for how could they meet the eye of God and angels unclothed?

Their crime is now before them in its true light. Their transgression of God's express command assumes a clearer character. Adam censured Eve's folly in leaving his side and being deceived by the serpent. They both flattered themselves that God, who had given them everything to make them happy, might yet excuse their disobedience because of His great love to them and that their punishment would not be so dreadful after all.

Satan exulted in his success. He had now tempted the woman to distrust God, to question His wisdom, and to seek to penetrate His all-wise plans. And through her he had also caused the overthrow of Adam, who, in consequence of his love for Eve, disobeyed the command of God and fell with her.

The news of man's fall spread through heaven—every harp was hushed. The angels cast their crowns from their heads in sorrow. All heaven was in agitation. The angels were grieved at the base ingratitude of man in return for the rich bounties God had provided. A council was held to decide what must be done with the guilty pair. The angels feared that they would put forth the hand and eat of the tree of life, and thus perpetuate a life of sin.

The Lord visited Adam and Eve, and made known to them the consequence of their disobedience. As they heard God's majestic approach they sought to hide themselves from His inspection, whom they delighted, while in their innocence and holiness, to meet. "And the Lord God called unto Adam, and said unto him, Where art thou? And he said, I heard Thy voice in the garden, and I was afraid, because I was naked; and I hid myself. And He said, Who told Thee that thou wast naked? Hast thou eaten of the tree, whereof I commanded thee that thou shouldest not eat?" This question was asked by the Lord, not because He needed information, but for the conviction of the guilty pair. How didst thou become ashamed and fearful? Adam acknowledged his transgression, not because he was penitent for his great disobedience, but to cast reflection upon

God. "The woman whom Thou gavest to be with me, she gave me of the tree, and I did eat." The woman was then addressed: "What is this that thou hast done?" Eve answered, "The serpent beguiled me, and I did eat."

The Curse

The Lord then addressed the serpent: "Because thou hast done this, thou art cursed above all cattle, and above every beast of the field: upon thy belly shalt thou go, and dust shalt thou eat all the days of thy life." As the serpent had been exalted above the beasts of the field, he should be degraded beneath them all, and be detested by man, inasmuch as he was the medium through which Satan acted. "And unto Adam He said, Because thou hast hearkened unto the voice of thy wife, and hast eaten of the tree, of which I commanded thee, saying, Thou shalt not eat of it: cursed is the ground for thy sake; in sorrow shalt thou eat of it all the days of thy life; thorns also and thistles shall it bring forth to thee; and thou shalt eat the herb of the field; in the sweat of thy face shalt thou eat bread, till thou return unto the ground."

God cursed the ground because of their sin in eating of the tree of knowledge, and declared, "In sorrow shalt thou eat of it all the days of thy life." He had apportioned them the good, but withheld the evil. Now He declares that they shall eat of it, that is, they should be acquainted with evil all the days of their life.

The race from that time forward was to be afflicted by Satan's temptations. A life of perpetual toil and anxiety was appointed unto Adam, instead of the happy, cheerful labor he had hitherto enjoyed. They should be subject to disappointment, grief, and pain, and finally come to dissolution. They were made of the dust of the earth, and unto dust should they return.

They were informed that they would have to lose their Eden home. They had yielded to Satan's deception and believed the word of Satan, that God would lie. By their transgression they had opened a way for Satan to gain access to them more readily, and it was not safe for them to remain in the Garden of Eden, lest in their state of sin they gain access to the tree of life and perpetuate a life of sin. They entreated to be permitted to remain, although they acknowledged that they had forfeited all right to blissful Eden. They promised that they would in the future yield to God implicit obedience. They were informed that in their fall from innocence to guilt they gained no strength but great weakness. They had not preserved their integrity while they were in a state of holy, happy innocence, and they would have far less strength to remain true and loyal in a state of conscious guilt. They were filled with keenest anguish and remorse. They now realized that the penalty of sin was death.

Angels were commissioned to immediately guard the way of the tree of life. It was Satan's studied plan that Adam and Eve should disobey God, receive His frown, and then partake of the tree of life, that they might perpetuate a life of sin. But holy angels were sent to debar their way to the tree of life. Around these angels flashed beams of light on every side, which had the appearance of glittering swords.

Chapter 5—The Plan of Salvation

Sorrow filled heaven, as it was realized that man was lost and that world which God had created was to be filled with mortals doomed to misery, sickness, and death, and there was no way of escape for the offender. The whole family of Adam must die. I saw the lovely Jesus and beheld an expression of sympathy and sorrow upon His countenance. Soon I saw Him approach the exceeding bright light which enshrouded the Father. Said my accompanying angel, He is in close converse with His Father. The anxiety of the angels seemed to be intense while Jesus was communing with His Father. Three times He was shut in by the glorious light about the Father, and the third time He came out from the Father, His person could be seen. His countenance was calm, free from all perplexity and doubt, and shone with benevolence and loveliness, such as words cannot express.

He then made known to the angelic host that a way of escape had been made for lost man. He told them that He had been pleading with His Father, and had offered to give His life a ransom, to take the sentence of death upon Himself, that through Him man might find pardon; that through the merits of His blood, and obedience to the law of God, they could have the favor of God and be brought into the beautiful garden and eat of the fruit of the tree of life.

At first the angels could not rejoice, for their Commander concealed nothing from them, but opened before them the plan of salvation. Jesus told them that He would stand between the wrath of His Father and guilty man, that He would bear iniquity and scorn, and but few would receive Him as the Son of God. Nearly all would hate and reject Him. He would leave all His glory in heaven, appear upon earth as a man, humble Himself as a man, become acquainted by His own experience with the various temptations with which man would be beset, that He might know how to succor those who should be tempted; and that finally, after His mission as a teacher would be accomplished, He would be delivered into the hands of men and endure almost every cruelty and suffering that Satan and his angels could inspire wicked men to inflict; that He would die the cruelest of deaths, hung up between the heavens and the earth as a guilty sinner; that He would suffer dreadful hours of agony, which even angels could not look upon, but would veil their faces from the sight. Not merely agony of body would He suffer, but mental agony, that with which bodily suffering could in no wise be compared. The weight of the sins of the whole world would be upon Him. He told them He would die and rise again the third day, and would ascend to His Father to intercede for wayward, guilty man.

The One Possible Way of Salvation

The angels prostrated themselves before Him. They offered their lives. Jesus said to them that He would by His death save many, that the life of an angel could not pay the debt. His life alone could be accepted of His Father as a ransom for man. Jesus also told them that they would have a part to act, to be with Him and at different times strengthen Him; that He would take man's fallen nature, and His strength would not be even equal with theirs; that they would be witnesses of His humiliation and great sufferings; and that as they would witness His sufferings and the hatred of men toward Him, they would be stirred with the deepest emotion, and through their love for Him would wish to rescue and deliver Him from His murderers; but that they must not interfere to prevent anything they should behold; and that they should act a part at His resurrection; that the plan of salvation was devised, and His Father had accepted the plan.

With a holy sadness Jesus comforted and cheered the angels and informed them that hereafter those whom He should redeem would be with Him, and that by His death He should ransom many and destroy him who had the power of death. And His Father would give Him the kingdom and the greatness of the kingdom under the whole heaven, and He would possess it forever and ever. Satan and sinners would be destroyed, nevermore to disturb heaven or the purified new earth. Jesus bade the heavenly host be reconciled to the plan that His Father had accepted and rejoice that through His death fallen man could again be exalted to obtain favor with God and enjoy heaven.

Then joy, inexpressible joy, filled heaven. And the heavenly host sang a song of praise and adoration. They touched their harps and sang a note higher than they had done before, for the great mercy and condescension of God in yielding up His dearly Beloved to die for a race of rebels. Praise and adoration were poured forth for the self-denial and sacrifice of Jesus; that He would consent to leave the bosom of His Father and choose a life of suffering and anguish, and die an ignominious death to give life to others.

Said the angel, "Think ye that the Father yielded up His dearly beloved Son without a struggle? No, no. It was even a struggle with the God of heaven, whether to let guilty man perish, or to give His beloved Son to die for him."

31

Angels were so interested for man's salvation that there could be found among them those who would yield their glory and give their life for perishing man, "But," said my accompanying angel, "that would avail nothing. The transgression was so great that an angel's life would not pay the debt. Nothing but the death and intercessions of His Son would pay the debt and save lost man from hopeless sorrow and misery."

But the work of the angels was assigned them, to ascend and descend with strengthening balm from glory to soothe the Son of God in His sufferings and minister unto Him. Also, their work would be to guard and keep the subjects of grace from the evil angels and the darkness constantly thrown around them by Satan. I saw that it was impossible for God to alter or change His law to save lost, perishing man; therefore He suffered His beloved Son to die for man's transgression.

Satan again rejoiced with his angels that he could, by causing man's fall, pull down the Son of God from His exalted position. He told his angels that when Jesus should take fallen man's nature, he could overpower Him and hinder the accomplishment of the plan of salvation.

I was shown Satan as he once was, a happy, exalted angel. Then I was shown him as he now is. He still bears a kingly form. His features are still noble, for he is an angel fallen. But the expression of his countenance is full of anxiety, care, unhappiness, malice, hate, mischief, deceit, and every evil. That brow which was once so noble, I particularly noticed. His forehead commenced from his eyes to recede. I saw that he had so long bent himself to evil that every good quality was debased, and every evil trait was developed. His eyes were cunning, sly, and showed great penetration. His frame was large, but the flesh hung loosely about his hands and face. As I beheld him, his chin was resting upon his left hand. He appeared to be in deep thought. A smile was upon his countenance, which made me tremble, it was so full of evil and satanic slyness. This smile is the one he wears just before he makes sure of his victim, and as he fastens the victim in his snare, this smile grows horrible.

In humility and inexpressible sadness Adam and Eve left the lovely garden wherein they had been so happy until they disobeyed the command of God. The atmosphere was changed. It was no longer unvarying as before the transgression. God clothed them with coats of skins to protect them from the sense of chilliness and then of heat to which they were exposed.

God's Unchangeable Law

All heaven mourned on account of the disobedience and fall of Adam and Eve, which brought the wrath of God upon the whole human race. They were cut off from communing with God, and were plunged in hopeless misery. The law of God could not be changed to meet man's necessity, for in God's arrangement it was never to lose its force nor give up the smallest part of its claims.

The angels of God were commissioned to visit the fallen pair and inform them that although they could no longer retain possession of their holy estate, their Eden home, because of their transgression of the law of God, yet their case was not altogether hopeless. They were then informed that the Son of God, who had conversed with them in Eden, had been moved with pity as He viewed their hopeless condition, and had volunteered to take upon Himself the punishment due to them, and die for them that man might yet live, through faith in the atonement Christ proposed to make for him. Through Christ a door of hope was opened, that man, notwithstanding his great sin, should not be under the absolute control of Satan. Faith in the merits of the Son of God would so elevate man that he could resist the devices of Satan. Probation would be granted him in which, through a life of repentance and faith in the atonement of the Son of God, he might be redeemed from his transgression of the Father's law, and thus be elevated to a position where his efforts to keep His law could be accepted.

The angels related to them the grief that was felt in heaven as it was announced that they had transgressed the law of God, which had made it expedient for Christ to make the great sacrifice of His own precious life.

When Adam and Eve realized how exalted and sacred was the law of God, the transgression of which made so costly a sacrifice necessary to save them and their posterity from utter ruin, they pleaded to die themselves, or to let them and their posterity endure the penalty of their transgression, rather than that the beloved Son of God should make this great sacrifice. The anguish of Adam was increased. He saw that his sins were of so great magnitude as to involve fearful consequences. And must it be that heaven's honored Commander, who had walked with him and talked with him while in his holy innocence, whom angels honored and worshiped, must be brought down from his exalted position to die because of his transgression?

Adam was informed that an angel's life could not pay the debt. The law of Jehovah, the foundation of His government in heaven and upon earth, was as sacred as God Himself; and for this reason the life of an angel could not be accepted of God as a sacrifice for its transgression. His law is of more importance in His sight than the holy angels around His throne. The Father could not abolish or change one precept of His law to meet man in his fallen condition. But the Son of God, who had in unison with the Father created man, could make an atonement for man acceptable to God, by giving His life a sacrifice and bearing the wrath of His Father. Angels informed Adam that, as his transgression had brought death and wretchedness, life and immortality would be brought to light through the sacrifice of Jesus Christ.

A View of the Future

To Adam were revealed future important events, from his expulsion from Eden to the Flood, and onward to the first advent of Christ upon the earth; His love for Adam and his posterity would lead the Son of God to condescend to take human nature, and thus elevate, through His own humiliation, all who would believe on Him. Such a sacrifice was of sufficient value to save the whole world; but only a few would avail themselves of the salvation brought to them through such a wonderful sacrifice. The many would not comply with the conditions required of them that they might be partakers of His great salvation. They would prefer sin and transgression of the law of God rather than repentance and obedience, relying by faith upon the merits of the sacrifice offered. This sacrifice was of such infinite value as to make a man who should avail himself of it more precious than fine gold, even a man than the golden wedge of Ophir.

Adam was carried down through successive generations and saw the increase of crime, of guilt and defilement, because man would yield to his naturally strong inclinations to transgress the holy law of God. He was shown the curse of God resting more and more heavily upon the human race, upon the cattle, and upon the earth, because of man's continued transgression. He was shown that iniquity and violence would steadily increase; yet amid all the tide of human misery and woe, there would ever be a few who would preserve the knowledge of God and would remain unsullied amid the prevailing moral degeneracy. Adam was made to comprehend what sin is—the transgression of the law. He was shown that moral, mental, and physical degeneracy would result to the race, from transgression, until the world would be filled with human misery of every type.

The days of man were shortened by his own course of sin in transgressing the righteous law of God. The race was finally so greatly depreciated that they appeared inferior and almost valueless. They were generally incompetent to appreciate the mystery of Calvary, the grand and elevated facts of the atonement, and the plan of salvation, because of the indulgence of the carnal mind. Yet, notwithstanding the weakness, and enfeebled mental, moral, and physical powers of the human race, Christ, true to the purpose for which He left heaven, continues His interest in the feeble, depreciated, degenerate specimens of humanity, and invites them to hide their weakness and great deficiencies in Him. If they will come unto Him, He will supply all their needs.

The Sacrificial Offering

When Adam, according to God's special directions, made an offering for sin, it was to him a most painful ceremony. His hand must be raised to take life, which God alone could give, and make an offering for sin. It was the first time he had witnessed death. As he looked upon the bleeding victim, writhing in the agonies of death, he was to look forward by faith to the Son of God, whom the victim prefigured, who was to die man's sacrifice.

This ceremonial offering, ordained of God, was to be a perpetual reminder to Adam of his guilt, and also a penitential acknowledgment of his sin. This act of taking life gave Adam a deeper and more perfect sense of his transgression, which nothing less than the death of God's dear Son could expiate. He marveled at the infinite goodness and matchless love which would give such a ransom to save the guilty. As Adam was slaying the innocent victim, it seemed to him that he was shedding the blood of the Son of God by his own hand. He knew that if he had remained steadfast to God, and true to His holy law, there would have been no death of beast nor of man. Yet in the sacrificial offerings, pointing to the great and perfect offering of God's dear Son, there appeared a star of hope to illuminate the dark and terrible future, and relieve it of its utter hopelessness and ruin.

In the beginning the head of each family was considered ruler and priest of his own household. Afterward, as the race multiplied upon the earth, men of divine appointment performed this solemn worship of sacrifice for the people. The blood of beasts was to be associated in the minds of sinners with the blood of the Son of God. The death of the victim was to evidence to all that the penalty of sin was death. By the act of sacrifice the sinner acknowledged his guilt and manifested his faith, looking forward to the great and perfect sacrifice of the Son of God, which the offering of beasts prefigured. Without the atonement of the Son of God there could be no communication of blessing or salvation from God to man. God was jealous for the honor of His law. The transgression of that law caused a fearful separation between God and man. To Adam in his innocency was granted communion, direct, free, and happy, with his Maker. After his transgression God would communicate to man through Christ and angels.

Chapter 6—Cain and Abel and Their Offerings

This chapter is based on Genesis 4:1-15.

Cain and Abel, the sons of Adam, were very unlike in character. Abel feared God. Cain cherished rebellious feelings and murmured against God because of the curse pronounced upon Adam and because the ground was cursed for his sin. These brothers had been instructed in regard to the provision made for the salvation of the human race. They were required to carry out a system of humble obedience, showing their reverence for God and their faith and dependence upon the promised Redeemer, by slaying the firstlings of the flock and solemnly presenting them with the blood as a burnt offering to God. This sacrifice would lead them to continually keep in mind their sin and the Redeemer to come, who was to be the great sacrifice for man.

Cain brought his offering unto the Lord with murmuring and infidelity in his heart in regard to the promised Sacrifice. He was unwilling to strictly follow the plan of obedience and procure a lamb and offer it with the fruit of the ground. He merely took of the ground and disregarded the requirement of God. God had made known to Adam that without shedding of blood there could be no remission of sin. Cain was not particular to bring even the best of the fruits. Abel advised his brother not to come before the Lord without the blood of sacrifice. Cain, being the eldest, would not listen to his brother. He despised his counsel, and with doubt and murmuring in regard to the necessity of the ceremonial offerings, he presented his offering. But God did not accept it.

Abel brought of the firstlings of his flock and of the fat, as God had commanded; and in full faith of the Messiah to come, and with humble reverence, he presented the offering. God had respect unto his offering. A light flashes from heaven and consumes the offering of Abel. Cain sees no manifestation that his is accepted. He is angry with the Lord and with his brother. God condescends to send an angel to Cain to converse with him.

The angel inquires of him the reason of his anger, and informs him that if he does well and follows the directions God has given, He will accept him and respect his offering. But if he will not humbly submit to God's arrangements, and believe and obey Him, He cannot accept his offering. The angel tells Cain that it was no injustice on the part of God, or partiality shown to Abel, but that it was on account of his own sin and disobedience of God's express command that He could not respect his offering—and if he would do well he would be accepted of God, and his brother should listen to him, and he should take the lead, because he was the eldest.

But even after being thus faithfully instructed, Cain did not repent. Instead of censuring and abhorring himself for his unbelief, he still complains of the injustice and partiality of God. And in his jealousy and hatred he contends with Abel and reproaches him. Abel meekly points out his brother's error and shows him that the wrong is in himself. But Cain hates his brother from the moment that God manifests to him the tokens of His acceptance. His brother Abel seeks to appease his wrath by contending for the compassion of God in saving the lives of their parents when He might have brought upon them immediate death. He tells Cain that God loves them, or He would not have given His Son, innocent and holy, to suffer the wrath which man, by his disobedience, deserves to suffer.

The Beginnings of Death

While Abel justifies the plan of God, Cain becomes enraged, and his anger increases and burns against Abel until in his rage he slays him. God inquires of Cain for his brother, and Cain utters a guilty falsehood: "I know not: am I my brother's keeper?" God informs Cain that He knew in regard to his sin—that He was acquainted with his every act, and even the thoughts of his heart, and says to him, "Thy brother's blood crieth unto me from the ground. And now art thou cursed from the earth, which hath opened her mouth to receive thy brother's blood from thy hand; when thou tillest the ground, it shall not henceforth yield unto thee her strength; a fugitive and a vagabond shalt thou be in the earth."

The curse upon the ground at first had been felt but lightly; but now a double curse rested upon it. Cain and Abel represent the two classes, the righteous and the wicked, the believers and unbelievers, which should exist from the fall of man to the second coming of Christ. Cain's slaying his brother Abel represents the wicked who will be envious of the righteous and will hate them because they are better than themselves. They will be jealous of the righteous and will persecute and put them to death because their right-doing condemns their sinful course.

Adam's life was one of sorrow, humility, and continual repentance. As he taught his children and grandchildren the fear of the Lord, he was often bitterly reproached for his sin which resulted in so much misery upon his posterity. When he left the beautiful Eden, the thought that he must die thrilled him with horror. He looked upon death as a dreadful calamity. He was first made acquainted with the dreadful reality of death in the human family by his own son Cain slaying his brother Abel. Filled with the bitterest remorse for his own transgression, and deprived of his son Abel, and looking upon Cain as his murderer, and knowing the curse God pronounced upon him, bowed down Adam's heart with grief. Most bitterly did he reproach himself for his first great transgression. He entreated pardon from God through the promised Sacrifice. Deeply had he felt the wrath of God for his crime committed in Paradise. He witnessed the general corruption which afterward finally provoked God to destroy the inhabitants of the earth by a flood. The sentence of death pronounced upon him by his Maker, which at first appeared so terrible to him, after he had lived some hundreds of years, looked just and merciful in God, to bring to an end a miserable life.

As Adam witnessed the first signs of decaying nature in the falling leaf and in the drooping flowers, he mourned more deeply than men now mourn over their dead. The drooping flowers were not so deep a cause of grief, because more tender and delicate; but the tall, noble, sturdy trees to cast off their leaves, to decay, presented before him the general dissolution of beautiful nature, which God had created for the special benefit of man.

To his children and to their children, to the ninth generation, he delineated the perfections of his Eden home, and also his fall and its dreadful results, and the load of grief brought upon him on account of the rupture in his family which ended in the death of Abel. He related to them the sufferings God had brought him through to teach him the necessity of strictly adhering to His law. He declared to them that sin would be punished in whatever form it existed. He entreated them to obey God, who would deal mercifully with them if they should love and fear Him.

Angels held communication with Adam after his fall, and informed him of the plan of salvation, and that the human race was not beyond redemption. Although fearful separation had taken place between God and man, yet provision had been made through the offering of His beloved Son by which man might be saved. But their only hope was through a life of humble repentance and faith in the provision made. All those who could thus accept Christ as their only Saviour, should be again brought into favor with God through the merits of His Son.

Chapter 7—Seth and Enoch

This chapter is based on Genesis 4:25, 26; 5:3-8, 18-24; Jude 14, 15.

Seth was a worthy character, and was to take the place of Abel in right doing. Yet he was a son of Adam, like sinful Cain, and inherited from the nature of Adam no more natural goodness than did Cain. He was born in sin, but by the grace of God, in receiving the faithful instructions of his father Adam, he honored God in doing His will. He separated himself from the corrupt descendants of Cain and labored, as Abel would have done had he lived, to turn the minds of sinful men to revere and obey God.

Enoch was a holy man. He served God with singleness of heart. He realized the corruptions of the human family and separated himself from the descendants of Cain and reproved them for their great wickedness. There were those upon the earth who acknowledged God, who feared and worshiped Him. Yet righteous Enoch was so distressed with the increasing wickedness of the ungodly, that he would not daily associate with them, fearing that he should be affected by their infidelity and that his thoughts might not ever regard God with that holy reverence which was due His exalted character. His soul was vexed as he daily witnessed their trampling upon the authority of God. He chose to be separate from them, and spent much of his time in solitude, which he devoted to reflection and prayer. He waited before God and prayed to know His will more perfectly, that he might perform it. God communed with Enoch through His angels and gave him divine instruction. He made known to him that He would not always bear with man in his rebellion—that His purpose was to destroy the sinful race by bringing a flood of waters upon the earth.

The pure and lovely Garden of Eden, from which our first parents were driven, remained until God purposed to destroy the earth by a flood. God had planted that garden and specially blessed it, and in His wonderful providence He withdrew it from the earth, and will return it to the earth again more gloriously adorned than before it was removed from the earth. God purposed to preserve a specimen of His perfect work of creation free from the curse wherewith He had cursed the earth.

The Lord opened more fully to Enoch the plan of salvation, and by the Spirit of prophecy carried him down through the generations which should live after the Flood, and showed him the great events connected with the second coming of Christ and the end of the world. (Jude 1:14.)

Enoch was troubled in regard to the dead. It seemed to him that the righteous and the wicked would go to the dust together, and that would be their end. He could not clearly see the life of the just beyond the grave. In prophetic vision he was instructed in regard to the Son of God, who was to die man's sacrifice, and was shown the coming of Christ in the clouds of heaven, attended by the angelic host, to give life to the righteous dead and ransom them from their graves. He also saw the corrupt state of the world at the time when Christ should appear the second time—that there would be a boastful, presumptuous, self-willed generation arrayed in rebellion against the law of God and denying the only Lord God and our Lord Jesus Christ, and trampling upon His blood and despising His atonement. He saw the righteous crowned with glory and honor while the wicked were separated from the presence of the Lord and consumed with fire.

Enoch faithfully rehearsed to the people all that God had revealed to him by the Spirit of prophecy. Some believed his words and turned from their wickedness to fear and worship God.

Enoch Translated

Enoch continued to grow more heavenly while communing with God. His face was radiant with a holy light which would remain upon his countenance while instructing those who would hear his words of wisdom. His heavenly and dignified appearance struck the people with awe. The Lord loved Enoch because he steadfastly followed Him and abhorred iniquity and earnestly sought heavenly knowledge, that he might do His will perfectly. He yearned to unite himself still more closely to God, whom he feared, reverenced, and adored. God would not permit Enoch to die as other men, but sent His angels to take him to heaven without seeing death. In the presence of the righteous and the wicked, Enoch was removed from them. Those who loved him thought that God might have left him in some of his places of retirement, but after seeking him diligently, and being unable to find him, reported that he was not, for God took him.

The Lord here teaches a lesson of the greatest importance by the translation of Enoch, a descendant of fallen Adam, that all would be rewarded, who by faith would rely upon the promised Sacrifice and faithfully obey His commandments. Two classes are here again represented which were to exist until the second coming of Christ—the righteous and the wicked, the rebellious and the loyal. God will remember the righteous, who fear Him. On account of His dear Son He will respect and honor them and give them everlasting life. But the wicked, who trample upon His authority, He will cut off and destroy from the earth, and they will be as though they had not been.

After Adam's fall from a state of perfect happiness to a state of misery and sin, there was danger of man's becoming discouraged and inquiring, "What profit is it that we have kept His ordinance, and that we have walked mournfully before the Lord" (Malachi 3:14), since a heavy curse is resting upon the human race, and death is the portion of us all? But the instructions which God gave to Adam, and which were repeated by Seth and fully exemplified by Enoch, cleared away the darkness and gloom, and gave hope to man, that as through Adam came death, through Jesus, the promised Redeemer, would come life and immortality.

In the case of Enoch the desponding faithful were taught that, although living among a corrupt and sinful people, who were in open and daring rebellion against God, their Creator, yet if they would obey Him and have faith in the promised Redeemer, they could work righteousness like the faithful Enoch, be accepted of God, and finally exalted to His heavenly throne.

Enoch, separating himself from the world, and spending much of his time in prayer and in communion with God, represents God's loyal people in the last days, who will be separate from the world. Unrighteousness will prevail to a dreadful extent upon the earth. Men will give themselves up to follow every imagination of their corrupt hearts and carry out their deceptive philosophy and rebel against the authority of high heaven.

God's people will separate themselves from the unrighteous practices of those around them and will seek for purity of thought and holy conformity to His will until His divine image will be reflected in them. Like Enoch, they will be fitting for translation to heaven. While they endeavor to instruct and warn the world, they will not conform to the spirit and customs of unbelievers but will condemn them by their holy conversation and godly example. Enoch's translation to heaven just before the destruction of the world by a flood represents the translation of all the living righteous from the earth previous to its destruction by fire. The saints will be glorified in the presence of those who have hated them for their loyal obedience to God's righteous commandments.

Chapter 8—The Flood

This chapter is based on Genesis 6; 7; 8 and 9:8-17.

The descendants of Seth were called the sons of God; the descendants of Cain, the sons of men. As the sons of God mingled with the sons of men, they became corrupt and, by intermarriage with them, lost, through the influence of their wives, their peculiar, holy character, and united with the sons of Cain in their idolatry. Many cast aside the fear of God and trampled upon His commandments. But there were a few that did righteousness, who feared and honored their Creator. Noah and his family were among the righteous few.

The wickedness of man was so great, and increased to such a fearful extent, that God repented that He had made man upon the earth, for He saw that the wickedness of man was great, and that every imagination of the thoughts of his heart was only evil continually.

More than one hundred years before the Flood the Lord sent an angel to faithful Noah to make known to him that He would no longer have mercy upon the corrupt race. But He would not have them ignorant of His design. He would instruct Noah and make him a faithful preacher to warn the world of its coming destruction, that the inhabitants of the earth might be left without excuse. Noah was to preach to the people, and also to prepare an ark as God should direct him for the saving of himself and family. He was not only to preach, but his example in building the ark was to convince all that he believed what he preached.

Noah and his family were not alone in fearing and obeying God. But Noah was the most pious and holy of any upon the earth, and was the one whose life God preserved to carry out His will in building the ark and warning the world of its coming doom. Methuselah, the grandfather of Noah, lived until the very year of the Flood; and there were others who believed the preaching of Noah, and aided him in building the ark, who died before the flood of waters came upon the earth. Noah, by his preaching and example in building the ark, condemned the world.

God gave all who chose an opportunity to repent and turn to Him. But they believed not the preaching of Noah. They mocked at his warnings and ridiculed the building of that immense vessel on dry land. Noah's efforts to reform his fellow men did not succeed. But for more than one hundred years he persevered in his efforts to turn men to repentance and to God. Every blow struck upon the ark was preaching to the people. Noah directed, he preached, he worked, while the people looked on in amazement and regarded him as a fanatic.

Building the Ark

God gave Noah the exact dimensions of the ark and explicit directions in regard to the construction of it in every particular. In many respects it was not made like a vessel but prepared like a house, the foundation like a boat which would float upon water. There were no windows in the sides of the ark. It was three stories high, and the light they received was from a window in the top. The door was in the side. The different apartments prepared for the reception of different animals were so made that the window in the top gave light to all. The ark was made of the cypress or gopher wood, which would know nothing of decay for hundreds of years. It was a building of great durability, which no wisdom of man could invent. God was the designer, and Noah His master builder.

After Noah had done all in his power to make every part of the work correct, it was impossible that it could of itself withstand the violence of the storm which God in His fierce anger was to bring upon the earth. The work of completing the building was a slow process. Every piece of timber was closely fitted, and every seam covered with pitch. All that men could do was done to make the work perfect; yet, after all, God alone could preserve the building upon the angry, heaving billows, by His miraculous power.

A multitude at first apparently received the warning of Noah, yet did not fully turn to God with true repentance. There was some time given them before the Flood was to come, in which they were to be placed upon probation—to be proved and tried. They failed to endure the trial. The prevailing degeneracy overcame them, and they finally joined others who were corrupt in deriding and scoffing at faithful Noah. They would not leave off their sins but continued in polygamy and in the indulgence of their corrupt passions.

The period of their probation was drawing near its close. The unbelieving, scoffing inhabitants of the world were to have a special sign of God's divine power. Noah had faithfully followed the instructions God had given to him. The ark was finished exactly as God had directed. He had laid in store immense quantities of food for man and beast. And after this was accomplished, God commanded the faithful Noah, "Come thou and all thy house into the ark; for thee have I seen righteous before Me."

The Animals Enter the Ark

Angels were sent to collect from the forest and field the beasts which God had created. Angels went before these animals, and they followed, two and two, male and female, and clean beasts by sevens. These beasts, from the most ferocious, down to the most gentle and harmless, peacefully and solemnly marched into the ark. The sky seemed clouded with birds of every description. They came flying to the ark, two and two, male and female, and the clean birds by sevens. The world looked on with wonder—some with fear, but they had become so hardened by rebellion that this most signal manifestation of God's power had but a momentary influence upon them. For seven days these animals were coming into the ark, and Noah was arranging them in the places prepared for them.

And as the doomed race beheld the sun shining in its glory and the earth clad in almost its Eden beauty, they drove away their rising fears by boisterous merriment, and by their deeds of violence seemed to be encouraging upon themselves the visitation of the already awakened wrath of God.

Everything was now ready for the closing of the ark, which could not have been done by Noah from within. An angel is seen by the scoffing multitude descending from heaven, clothed with brightness like the lightning. He closes that massive outer door, and then takes his course upward to heaven again.

Seven days were the family of Noah in the ark before the rain began to descend upon the earth. In this time they were arranging for their long stay while the waters should be upon the earth. And these were days of blasphemous merriment by the unbelieving multitude. They thought, because the prophecy of Noah was not fulfilled immediately after he entered the ark, that he was deceived and that it was impossible that the world could be destroyed by a flood. Previous to this there had been no rain upon the earth. A mist had risen from the waters, which God caused to descend at night like dew, reviving vegetation and causing it to flourish.

Notwithstanding the solemn exhibition they had witnessed of God's power—of the unnatural occurrence of the beasts' leaving the forests and fields, and going into the ark, and the angel of God clothed with brightness and terrible in majesty descending from heaven and closing the door; yet they hardened their hearts and continued to revel and sport over the signal manifestations of divine power.

The Storm Breaks

But upon the eighth day the heavens gathered blackness. The muttering thunders and vivid lightning flashes began to terrify man and beast. The rain descended from the clouds above them. This was something they had never witnessed, and their hearts began to faint with fear. The beasts were roving about in the wildest terror, and their discordant voices seemed to moan out their own destiny and the fate of man. The storm increased in violence until water seemed to come from heaven like mighty cataracts. The boundaries of rivers broke away, and the waters rushed to the valleys. The foundations of the great deep also were broken up. Jets of water would burst up from the earth with indescribable force, throwing massive rocks hundreds of feet into the air, and then they would bury themselves deep in the earth.

The people first beheld the destruction of the works of their hands. Their splendid buildings, their beautifully arranged gardens and groves, where they had placed their idols, were destroyed by lightning from heaven. Their ruins were scattered everywhere. They had erected altars in groves, and consecrated them to their idols, whereon they offered human sacrifices. These which God detested were torn down in His wrath before them, and they were made to tremble before the power of the living God, the Maker of the heavens and the earth, and they were made to know that it was their abominations and horrible, idolatrous sacrifices which had called for their destruction.

The violence of the storm increased, and there were mingled with the warring of the elements, the wailings of the people who had despised the authority of God. Trees, buildings, rocks, and earth were hurled in every direction. The terror of man and beast was beyond description. And even Satan himself, who was compelled to be amid the warring elements, feared for his own existence. He had delighted to control so powerful a race, and wished them to live to practice their abominations, and increase their rebellion against the God of heaven. He uttered imprecations against God, charging Him with injustice and cruelty. Many of the people, like Satan, blasphemed God, and if they could have carried out their rebellion, would have torn Him from His throne of justice.

While many were blaspheming and cursing their Creator, others were frantic with fear, stretching their hands toward the ark, pleading for admittance. But this was impossible. God had closed the door, the only entrance, and shut Noah in and the ungodly out. He alone could open the door. Their fear and repentance came too late. They were compelled to know that there was a living God who was mightier than man, whom they had defied and blasphemed. They called upon Him earnestly, but His ear was not open to their cry. Some in their desperation sought to break into the ark, but that firm-made structure resisted all their efforts. Some clung to the ark until borne away with the furious surging of the waters, or their hold was broken off by rocks and trees that were hurled in every direction.

Those who had slighted the warning of Noah and ridiculed that faithful preacher of righteousness repented too late of their unbelief. The ark was severely rocked and tossed about. The beasts within expressed, by their varied noises, the wildest terror; yet amid all the warring of the elements, the surging of the waters, and the hurling about of trees and rocks, the ark rode safely. Angels that excel in strength guided the ark and preserved it from harm. Every moment during that frightful storm of forty days and forty nights the preservation of the ark was a miracle of almighty power.

The animals exposed to the tempest rushed toward man, choosing the society of human beings, as though expecting help of them. Some of the people bound their children and themselves upon powerful beasts, knowing that they would be tenacious for life, and would climb to the highest points to escape the rising water. The storm did not abate its fury—the waters increased faster than at first. Some fastened themselves to lofty trees upon the highest points of land, but these trees were torn up by the roots and carried with violence through the air and appeared as though angrily hurled, with stones and earth, into the swelling, boiling billows. Upon the loftiest heights human beings and beasts strove to hold their position until all were hurled together into the foaming waters, which nearly reached the highest points of land. The loftiest heights were at length reached, and man and beast alike perished by the waters of the Flood.

Anxiously did Noah and his family watch the decrease of the waters. He desired to go forth upon the earth again. He sent out a raven which flew back and forth to and from the ark. He did not receive the information he desired, and he sent forth a dove, which, finding no rest, returned to the ark again. After seven days the dove was sent forth again, and when the olive leaf was seen in its mouth, there was great rejoicing by this family of eight, which had so long been shut up in the ark.

Again an angel descended and opened the door of the ark. Noah could remove the top, but he could not open the door which God had shut. God spoke to Noah through the angel who opened the door, and bade the family of Noah go forth out of the ark and bring forth with them every living thing.

Noah's Sacrifice and God's Promise

Noah did not forget God, who had so graciously preserved them, but immediately erected an altar and took of every clean beast, and of every clean fowl, and offered burnt offerings on the altar, showing his faith in Christ the great sacrifice, and manifesting his gratitude to God for their wonderful preservation. The offering of Noah came up before God like a sweet savor. He accepted the offering and blessed Noah and his family. Here a lesson is taught all who should live upon the earth, that for every manifestation of God's mercy and love toward them the first act of all should be to render to Him grateful thanks and humble worship.

And lest man should be terrified with gathering clouds and falling rains, and should be in continual dread, fearing another flood, God graciously encourages the family of Noah by a promise. "And I will establish My covenant with you; neither shall all flesh be cut off any more by the waters of a flood; neither shall there any more be a flood to destroy the earth. And God said, This is the token of the covenant which I make between Me and you and every living creature that is with you, for perpetual generations: I do set My bow in the cloud, and it shall be for a token of a covenant between Me and the earth. And it shall come to pass, when I bring a cloud over the earth, that the bow shall be seen in the cloud.... And the bow shall be in the cloud; and I will look upon it, that I may remember the everlasting covenant between God and every living creature of all flesh that is upon the earth."

What a condescension on the part of God! What compassion for erring man, to place the beautiful, variegated rainbow in the clouds, a token of the covenant of the great God with man! This rainbow was to evidence the fact to all generations that God destroyed the inhabitants of the earth by a flood, because of their great wickedness. It was His design that as the children of aftergenerations should see the bow in the cloud and should inquire the reason of this glorious arch that spanned the heavens, their parents could explain to them the destruction of the old world by a flood, because the people gave themselves up to all manner of wickedness, and that the hands of the Most High had bent the bow and placed it in the clouds as a token that He would never again bring a flood of waters on the earth.

This symbol in the clouds is to confirm the belief of all, and establish their confidence in God, for it is a token of divine mercy and goodness to man; that although God had been provoked to destroy the earth by the Flood, yet His mercy still encompasseth the earth. God says when He looketh upon the bow in the cloud He will remember. He would not have us understand that He would ever forget, but He speaks to man in his own language, that man may better understand Him.

Chapter 9—The Tower of Babel

This chapter is based on Genesis 11:1-9.

Some of the descendants of Noah soon began to apostatize. A portion followed the example of Noah and obeyed God's commandments; others were unbelieving and rebellious, and even these did not believe alike in regard to the Flood. Some disbelieved in the existence of God, and in their own minds accounted for the Flood from natural causes. Others believed that God existed and that He destroyed the antediluvian race by a flood; and their feelings, like Cain's, rose in rebellion against God because He destroyed the people from the earth and cursed the earth the third time by a flood.

Those who were enemies of God felt daily reproved by the righteous conversation and godly lives of those who loved, obeyed, and exalted God. The unbelieving consulted among themselves and agreed to separate from the faithful, whose righteous lives were a continual restraint upon their wicked course. They journeyed a distance from them and selected a large plain wherein to dwell. They built them a city, and then conceived the idea of building a large tower to reach unto the clouds, that they might dwell together in the city and tower, and be no more scattered.

They reasoned that they would secure themselves in case of another flood, for they would build their tower to a much greater height than the waters prevailed in the time of the Flood, and all the world would honor them, and they would be as gods and rule over the people. This tower was calculated to exalt its builders, and was designed to turn the attention of others who should live upon the earth from God to join with them in their idolatry. Before the work of building was accomplished, people dwelt in the tower. Rooms were splendidly furnished, decorated, and devoted to their idols. Those who did not believe in God imagined if their tower could reach unto the clouds, they would be able to discover reasons for the Flood.

They exalted themselves against God. But He would not permit them to complete their work. They had built their tower to a lofty height when the Lord sent two angels to confound them in their work. Men had been appointed for the purpose of receiving word from the workmen at the top of the tower, calling for material for their work, which the first would communicate to the second, and he to the third, until the word reached those on the ground. As the word was passing from one to another in its descent, the angels confounded their language, and when the word reached the workmen upon the ground, material was called for which had not been required. And after the laborious process of getting the material to the workmen at the top of the tower, it was not that which they wished for. Disappointed and enraged, they reproached those whom they supposed were at fault.

After this there was no harmony in their work. Angry with one another, and unable to account for the misunderstanding and strange words among them, they left the work and separated from each other and scattered abroad in tile earth. Up to this time men had spoken but one language. Lightning from heaven, as a token of God's wrath, broke off the top of their tower, casting it to the ground. Thus God would show to rebellious man that He is supreme.

Chapter 10—Abraham and the Promised Seed

The Lord selected Abraham to carry out His will. He was directed to leave his idolatrous nation and separate from his kindred. The Lord had revealed Himself to Abraham in his youth and given him understanding and preserved him from idolatry. He designed to make him an example of faith and true devotion for His people who should afterward live upon the earth. His character was marked for integrity, generosity, and hospitality. He commanded respect as a mighty prince among the people. His reverence and love for God, and his strict obedience in performing His will, gained for him the respect of his servants and neighbors. His godly example and righteous course, united with his faithful instructions to his servants and all his household, led them to fear, love, and reverence the God of Abraham. The Lord appeared to Abraham and promised him that his seed should be like the stars of heaven for number. He also made known to him, through the figure of the horror of great darkness which came upon him, the long, servile bondage of his descendants in Egypt.

In the beginning God gave to Adam one wife, thus showing his order. He never designed that man should have a plurality of wives. Lamech was the first who departed in this respect from God's wise arrangement. He had two wives, which created discord in his family. The envy and jealousy of both made Lamech unhappy. When men began to multiply upon the face of the earth, and daughters were born unto them, they took them wives of all which they chose. This was one of the great sins of the inhabitants of the old world, which brought the wrath of God upon them. This custom was practiced after the Flood, and became so common that even righteous men fell into the practice and had a plurality of wives. Yet it was no less sin because they became corrupted and departed in this thing from God's order.

The Lord said of Noah and his family, who were saved in the ark, "For thee have I seen righteous before Me in this generation." Genesis 7:1. Noah had but one wife, and their united family discipline was blessed of God. Because Noah's sons were righteous they were preserved in the ark with their righteous father. God has not sanctioned polygamy in a single instance. It is contrary to His will. He knew that the happiness of man would be destroyed by it. Abraham's peace was greatly marred by his unhappy marriage with Hagar.

Wavering at God's Promises

After Abraham's separation from Lot the Lord said to him, "Lift up now thine eyes, and look from the place where thou art northward, and southward, and eastward, and westward: for all the land which thou seest, to thee will I give it, and to thy seed for ever. And I will make thy seed as the dust of the earth: so that if a man can number the dust of the earth, then shall thy seed also be numbered." "The word of the Lord came unto Abram in a vision, saying, Fear not, Abram: I am thy shield, and thy exceeding great reward.... And Abram said, Behold, to me Thou hast given no seed: and, lo, one born in my house is mine heir."

As Abraham had no son, he at first thought that his trusty servant, Eliezer, should become his son by adoption, and his heir. But God informed Abraham that his servant should not be his son and heir, but that he should really have a son. "And He brought him forth abroad, and said, Look now toward heaven, and tell the stars, if thou be able to number them: and He said unto him, So shall thy seed be."

If Abraham and Sarah had waited in confiding faith for the fulfillment of the promise that they should have a son, much unhappiness would have been avoided. They believed that it would be just as God had promised, but could not believe that Sarah in her old age would have a son. Sarah suggested a plan whereby she thought the promise of God could be fulfilled. She entreated Abraham to take Hagar as his wife. In this they both lacked faith and a perfect trust in the power of God. By hearkening to the voice of Sarah and taking Hagar as his wife Abraham failed to endure the test of his faith in God's unlimited power, and brought upon himself and upon Sarah much unhappiness. The Lord intended to prove the firm faith and reliance of Abraham upon the promises He had made him.

Hagar's Haughtiness

Hagar was proud and boastful, and carried herself haughtily before Sarah. She flattered herself that she was to be the mother of a great nation God had promised to make of Abraham. And Abraham was compelled to listen to complaints from Sarah in regard to the conduct of Hagar, charging Abraham with wrong in the matter. Abraham is grieved and tells Sarah that Hagar is her servant, and that she can have the control of her, but refuses to send her away, for she is to be the mother of his child, through whom he thinks the promise is to be fulfilled. He informs Sarah that he should not have taken Hagar for his wife if it had not been her special request.

Abraham was also compelled to listen to Hagar's complaints of abuse from Sarah. Abraham is in perplexity. If he seeks to redress the wrongs of Hagar he increases the jealousy and unhappiness of Sarah, his first and much-loved wife. Hagar flees from the face of Sarah. An angel of God meets her and comforts her and also reproves her for her haughty conduct, in bidding her return to her mistress and submit herself under her hands.

After the birth of Ishmael the Lord manifested Himself again to Abraham and said unto him, "I will establish My covenant between Me and thee and thy seed after thee in their generations for an everlasting covenant." Again the Lord repeated by His angel His promise to give Sarah a son, and that she should be a mother of many nations. Abraham did not yet understand the promise of God. His mind immediately rested upon Ishmael, as though through him would come the many nations promised, and he exclaimed, in his affection for his son, "O that Ishmael might live before Thee!"

Again the promise is more definitely repeated to Abraham: "Sarah thy wife shall bear thee a son indeed; and thou shalt call his name Isaac: and I will establish My covenant with him for an everlasting covenant, and with his seed after him." Angels are sent the second time to Abraham on their way to destroy Sodom, and they repeat the promise more distinctly that Sarah shall have a son.

The Promised Son

After the birth of Isaac the great joy manifested by Abraham and Sarah caused Hagar to be very jealous. Ishmael had been instructed by his mother that he was to be especially blessed of God, as the son of Abraham, and to be heir to that which was promised to him. Ishmael partook of his mother's feelings and was angry because of the joy manifested at the birth of Isaac. He despised Isaac, because he thought he was preferred before him. Sarah saw the disposition manifested by Ishmael against her son Isaac, and she was greatly moved. She related to Abraham the disrespectful conduct of Ishmael to her and to her son Isaac, and said to him, "Cast out this bondwoman and her son; for the son of this bondwoman shall not be heir with my son, even with Isaac."

Abraham was greatly distressed. Ishmael was his son, beloved by him. How could he send him away? He prayed to God in his perplexity, for he knew not what course to take. The Lord informed Abraham, through His angels, to listen to the voice of Sarah his wife, and that he should not let his affections for his son or for Hagar prevent his compliance with her wishes. For this was the only course he could pursue to restore harmony and happiness again to his family. Abraham had the consoling promise from the angel, that Ishmael, although separated from his father's house, should not die nor be forsaken of God, that he should be preserved because he was the son of Abraham. God also promised to make of Ishmael a great nation.

Abraham was of a noble, benevolent disposition, which was manifested in his pleading so earnestly for the people of Sodom. His strong spirit suffered much. He was bowed with grief, and his paternal feelings were deeply moved as he sent away Hagar and his son Ishmael to wander as strangers in a strange land.

If God had sanctioned polygamy, He would not have thus directed Abraham to send away Hagar and her son. He would teach all a lesson in this, that the rights and happiness of the marriage relation are to be ever respected and guarded, even at a great sacrifice. Sarah was the first and only true wife of Abraham. She was entitled to rights, as a wife and mother, which no other could have in the family. She reverenced her husband, calling him lord, but she was jealous lest his affections should be divided with Hagar. God did not rebuke Sarah for the course she pursued. Abraham was reproved by the angels for distrusting God's power, which had led him to take Hagar as his wife and to think that through her the promise would be fulfilled.

The Supreme Test of Faith

Again the Lord saw fit to test the faith of Abraham by a most fearful trial. If he had endured the first test and had patiently waited for the promise to be fulfilled in Sarah, and had not taken Hagar as his wife, he would not have been subjected to the closest test that was ever required of man. The Lord bade Abraham, "Take now thy son, thine only son Isaac, whom thou lovest, and get thee into the land of Moriah; and offer him there for a burnt offering upon one of the mountains which I will tell thee of."

Abraham did not disbelieve God and hesitate, but early in the morning he took two of his servants and Isaac, his son, and the wood for the burnt offering, and went unto the place of which God had told him. He did not reveal the true nature of his journey to Sarah, knowing that her affection for Isaac would lead her to distrust God and withhold her son. Abraham did not suffer paternal feelings to control him and lead him to rebel against God. The command of God was calculated to stir the depths of his soul. "Take now thy son." Then, as though to probe the heart a little deeper, He added, "Thine only son Isaac, whom thou lovest"; that is, the only son of promise, "and offer him ... for a burnt offering."

Three days this father traveled with his son, having sufficient time to reason and doubt God if he was disposed to doubt. But he did not distrust God. He did not now reason that the promise would be fulfilled through Ishmael, for God plainly told him that through Isaac should the promise be fulfilled.

Abraham believed that Isaac was the son of promise. He also believed that God meant just what He said when He bade him to go offer him as a burnt offering. He staggered not at the promise of God but believed that God, who had in His providence given Sarah a son in her old age, and who had required him to take that son's life, could also give life again and bring up Isaac from the dead.

Abraham left the servants by the way and proposed to go alone with his son to worship some distance from them. He would not permit his servants to accompany them, lest their love for Isaac might lead them to prevent him from carrying out what God had commanded him to do. He took the wood from the hands of his servants and laid it upon the shoulders of his son. He also took the fire and the knife. He was prepared to execute the dreadful mission given him of God. Father and son walked on together.

"And Isaac spake unto Abraham his father, and said, My father: and he said, Here am I, my son. And he said, Behold the fire and the wood: but where is the lamb for a burnt offering? And Abraham said, My son, God will provide Himself a lamb for a burnt offering: so they went both of them together." Firmly walked on that stern, loving, suffering father by the side of his son. As they came to the place which God had pointed out to Abraham, he built there an altar and laid the wood in order, ready for the sacrifice, and then informed Isaac of the command of God to offer him as a burnt offering. He repeated to him the promise that God several times had made to him, that through Isaac he should become a great nation, and that in performing the command of God in slaying him, God would fulfill His promise, for He was able to raise him from the dead.

The Angel's Message

Isaac believed in God. He had been taught implicit obedience to his father, and he loved and reverenced the God of his father. He could have resisted his father if he had chosen to do so. But after affectionately embracing his father, he submitted to be bound and laid upon the wood. And as his father's hand was raised to slay his son, an angel of God, who had marked all the faithfulness of Abraham on the way to Moriah, called to him out of heaven, and said, "Abraham, Abraham: and he said, Here am I. And he said, Lay not thine hand upon the lad, neither do thou anything unto him: for now I know that thou fearest God, seeing thou hast not withheld thy son, thine only son from Me.

"And Abraham lifted up his eyes, and looked, and behold behind him a ram caught in a thicket by his horns: and Abraham went and took the ram, and offered him up for a burnt offering in the stead of his son."

Abraham had now fully and nobly borne the test, and by his faithfulness redeemed his lack of perfect trust in God, which lack led him to take Hagar as his wife. After the exhibition of Abraham's faith and confidence, God renewed His promise to him. "And the angel of the Lord called unto Abraham out of heaven the second time, and said, By myself I have sworn, saith the Lord, for because thou hast done this thing, and hast not withheld thy son, thine only son: that in blessing I will bless thee, and in multiplying I will multiply thy seed as the stars of the heaven, and as the sand which is upon the sea shore; and thy seed shall possess the gate of his enemies; and in thy seed shall all the nations of the earth be blessed; because thou hast obeyed My voice."

Chapter 11—The Marriage of Isaac

This chapter is based on Genesis 24.

The Canaanites were idolaters, and the Lord had commanded that His people should not intermarry with them, lest they should be led into idolatry. Abraham was old, and he expected soon to die. Isaac was yet unmarried. Abraham was afraid of the corrupting influence surrounding Isaac, and was anxious to have a wife selected for him who would not lead him from God. He committed this matter to his faithful, experienced servant, who ruled over all that he had.

Abraham required his servant to make a solemn oath before the Lord that he would not take a wife for Isaac of the Canaanites, but that he would go unto Abraham's kindred, who believed in the true God, and select a wife for Isaac. He charged him to beware and not take Isaac to the country from which he came, for they were nearly all affected with idolatry. If he could not find a wife for Isaac who would leave her kindred and come where he was, then he should be clear of the oath which he had made.

This important matter was not left with Isaac, for him to select for himself, independent of his father. Abraham told his servant that God would send His angel before him to direct him in his choice. The servant to whom this mission was entrusted started on his long journey. As he entered the city where Abraham's kindred dwelt, he prayed earnestly to God to direct him in his choice of a wife for Isaac. He asked that certain evidence might be given him, that he should not err in the matter. He rested by a well, which was a place of the greatest gathering. Here he particularly noticed the engaging manners and courteous conduct of Rebekah, and all the evidence he had asked of God he received that Rebekah was the one whom God had been pleased to select to become Isaac's wife. She invited the servant to her father's house. He then related to Rebekah's father and her brother the evidence he had received from the Lord that Rebekah should become the wife of his master's son Isaac.

Abraham's servant then said to them, "And now if ye will deal kindly and truly with my master, tell me: and if not, tell me; that I may turn to the right hand, or to the left." The father and brother answered, "The thing proceedeth from the Lord: we cannot speak unto thee bad or good. Behold, Rebekah is before thee; take her, and go, and let her be thy master's son's wife, as the Lord hath spoken. And it came to pass, that, when Abraham's servant heard their words, he worshiped the Lord, bowing himself to the earth."

After all had been arranged, the consent of the father and brother had been obtained, then Rebekah was consulted, whether she would go with the servant of Abraham a great distance from her father's family, to become the wife of Isaac. She believed from the circumstances that had taken place that God's hand had selected her to be Isaac's wife, "and she said, I will go."

Marriage contracts were then generally made by the parents; yet no compulsion was used to make them marry those they could not love. But the children had confidence in the judgment of their parents, and followed their counsel, and bestowed their affections upon those whom their God-fearing, experienced parents chose for them. It was considered a crime to follow a course contrary to this.

An Example of Filial Obedience

Isaac had been trained in the fear of God to a life of obedience. And when he was forty years old he submitted to have the God-fearing, experienced servant of his father choose for him. He believed that God would direct in regard to his obtaining a wife.

Isaac's case is left on record as an example for children to imitate in after generations, especially those who profess to fear God.

The course which Abraham pursued in the education of Isaac, that caused him to love a life of noble obedience, is recorded for the benefit of parents, and should lead them to command their households after them. They should instruct their children to yield to, and respect, their authority. And they should feel that a responsibility rests upon them to guide the affections of their children, that they may be placed upon persons who their judgment would teach them would be suitable companions for their sons and their daughters.

Chapter 12—Jacob and Esau

This chapter is based on Genesis 25:19-34 and 27:1-32.

God knows the end from the beginning. He knew, before the birth of Jacob and Esau, just what characters they would both develop. He knew that Esau would not have a heart to obey Him. He answered the troubled prayer of Rebekah and informed her that she would have two children, and the elder should serve the younger. He presented the future history of her two sons before her, that they would be two nations, the one greater than the other, and the elder should serve the younger. The first-born was entitled to peculiar advantages and special privileges, which belonged to no other members of the family.

Isaac loved Esau better than Jacob, because Esau provided him venison. He was pleased with his bold, courageous spirit manifested in hunting wild beasts. Jacob was the favorite son of his mother, because his disposition was mild and better calculated to make his mother happy. Jacob had learned from his mother what God had taught her, that the elder should serve the younger, and his youthful reasoning led him to conclude that this promise could not be fulfilled while Esau had the privileges which were conferred on the first-born. And when Esau came in from the field, faint with hunger, Jacob improved the opportunity to turn Esau's necessity to his own advantage, and proposed to feed him with pottage if he would renounce all claim to his birthright, and Esau sold his birthright to Jacob.

Esau took two idolatrous wives, which was a great grief to Isaac and Rebekah. Notwithstanding this, Isaac loved Esau better than Jacob. And when he thought that he was about to die he requested Esau to prepare him meat, that he might bless him before he died. Esau did not tell his father that he had sold his birthright to Jacob and confirmed it with an oath. Rebekah heard the words of Isaac, and she remembered the words of the Lord, "The elder shall serve the younger," and she knew that Esau had lightly regarded his birthright and sold it to Jacob. She persuaded Jacob to deceive his father and by fraud receive the blessing of his father, which she thought could not be obtained in any other way. Jacob was at first unwilling to practice this deception, but finally consented to his mother's plans.

Rebekah was acquainted with Isaac's partiality for Esau, and was satisfied that reasoning would not change his purpose. Instead of trusting in God, the Disposer of events, she manifested her lack of faith by persuading Jacob to deceive his father. Jacob's course in this was not approbated by God. Rebekah and Jacob should have waited for God to bring about His own purposes in His own way, and in His own time, instead of trying to bring about the foretold events by the aid of deception.

If Esau had received the blessing of his father, which was bestowed upon the first-born, his prosperity could have come from God alone; and He would have blessed him with prosperity, or brought upon him adversity, according to his course of action. If he should love and reverence God, like righteous Abel, he would be accepted and blessed of God. If, like wicked Cain, he had no respect for God nor for His commandments, but followed his own corrupt course, he would not receive a blessing from God but would be rejected of God, as was Cain. If Jacob's course should be righteous, if he should love and fear God, he would be blessed of God, and the prospering hand of God would be with him, even if he did not obtain the blessings and privileges generally bestowed upon the first-born.

Jacob's Years of Exile

Rebekah repented in bitterness for the wrong counsel which she gave to Jacob, for it was the means of separating him from her forever. He was compelled to flee for his life from the wrath of Esau, and his mother never saw his face again. Isaac lived many years after he gave Jacob the blessing, and was convinced, by the course of Esau and Jacob, that the blessing rightly belonged to Jacob.

Jacob was not happy in his marriage relation, although his wives were sisters. He formed the marriage contract with Laban for his daughter Rachel, whom he loved. After he had served seven years for Rachel, Laban deceived him and gave him Leah. When Jacob realized the deception that had been practiced upon him, and that Leah had acted her part in deceiving him, he could not love Leah. Laban wished to retain the faithful services of Jacob a greater length of time, therefore deceived him by giving him Leah, instead of Rachel. Jacob reproved Laban for thus trifling with his affections, in giving him Leah, whom he had not loved. Laban entreated Jacob not to put away Leah, for this was considered a great disgrace, not only to the wife, but to the whole family. Jacob was placed in a most trying position, but he decided to still retain Leah, and also marry her sister. Leah was loved in a much less degree than Rachel.

Laban was selfish in his dealings with Jacob. He thought only of advantaging himself by the faithful labors of Jacob. He would have left the artful Laban long before, but he was afraid of encountering Esau. He heard the complaint of Laban's sons, saying, "Jacob hath taken away all that was our father's; and of that which was our father's hath he gotten all this glory. And Jacob beheld the countenance of Laban, and, behold, it was not toward him as before."

Jacob was distressed. He knew not which way to turn. He carried his case to God and interceded for direction from Him. The Lord mercifully answered his distressed prayer. "And the Lord said unto Jacob, Return unto the land of thy fathers, and to thy kindred; and I will be with thee.

"And Jacob sent and called Rachel and Leah to the field unto his flock, and said unto them, I see your father's countenance, that it is not toward me as before; but the God of my father hath been with me. And ye know that with all my power I have served your father. And your father hath deceived me, and changed my wages ten times; but God suffered him not to hurt me." Jacob related to them the dream given him of God, to leave Laban and go unto his kindred. Rachel and Leah expressed their dissatisfaction of their father's proceedings. As Jacob rehearsed his wrongs to them and proposed to leave Laban, Rachel and Leah said to Jacob, "Is there yet any portion or inheritance for us in our father's house? Are we not counted of him strangers? for he hath sold us, and hath quite devoured also our money. For all the riches which God hath taken from our father, that is ours, and our children's; now then, whatsoever God hath said unto thee, do."

The Return to Canaan

In the absence of Laban, Jacob took his family and all that he had, and left Laban. After he had pursued his journey three days, Laban learned that he had left him, and he was very angry. And he pursued after him, determined to bring him back by force. But the Lord had pity upon Jacob, and as Laban was about to overtake him, gave him a dream not to speak good or bad to Jacob. That is, he should not force him to return, or urge him by flattering inducements.

When Laban met Jacob he inquired why he had stolen away unawares and carried away his daughters as captives taken with the sword. Laban told him, "It is in the power of my hand to do you hurt: but the God of your father spake unto me yesternight, saying, Take thou heed that thou speak not to Jacob either good or bad." Jacob then rehearsed to Laban the ungenerous course he had pursued toward him, that he had only studied his own advantage. He appealed to Laban as to the uprightness of his conduct while with him, and said, "That which was torn of beasts I brought not unto thee; I bare the loss of it; of my hand didst thou require it, whether stolen by day, or stolen by night. Thus I was; in the day the drought consumed me, and the frost by night; and my sleep departed from mine eyes."

Jacob said, "Thus have I been twenty years in thy house; I served thee fourteen years for thy two daughters, and six years for thy cattle: and thou hast changed my wages ten times. Except the God of my father, the God of Abraham, and the fear of Isaac, had been with me, surely thou hadst sent me away now empty. God hath seen mine affliction and the labour of my hands, and rebuked thee yesternight."

Laban then assured Jacob that he had an interest for his daughters and their children, that he could not harm them. He proposed to make a covenant between them. And Laban said, "Now therefore come thou, let us make a covenant, I and thou; and let it be for a witness between me and thee. And Jacob took a stone, and set it up for a pillar. And Jacob said unto his brethren, Gather stones; and they took stones, and made an heap: and they did eat there upon the heap."

And Laban said, "The Lord watch between me and thee, when we are absent one from another. If thou shalt afflict my daughters, or if thou shalt take other wives besides my daughters; no man is with us; see, God is witness betwixt me and thee."

Jacob made a solemn covenant before the Lord that he would not take other wives. "And Laban said to Jacob, Behold this heap, and behold this pillar, which I have cast betwixt me and thee; this heap be witness, and this pillar be witness, that I will not pass over this heap to thee, and that thou shalt not pass over this heap and this pillar unto me, for harm. The God of Abraham, and the God of Nahor, the God of their father, judge betwixt us. And Jacob swear by the fear of his father Isaac."

As Jacob went on his way, the angels of God met him. And when he saw them, he said, "This is God's host." He saw the angels of God in a dream, encamping around about him. Jacob sent a humble, conciliatory message to his brother Esau. "And the messengers returned to Jacob, saying, We came to thy brother

Esau, and also he cometh to meet thee, and four hundred men with him. Then Jacob was greatly afraid and distressed: and he divided the people that was with him, and the flocks, and herds, and the camels, into two bands; and said, If Esau come to the one company, and smite it, then the other company which is left shall escape.

"And Jacob said, O God of my father Abraham, and God of my father Isaac, the Lord which saidst unto me, Return unto thy country, and to thy kindred, and I will deal well with thee: I am not worthy of the least of all the mercies, and of all the truth, which Thou hast shewed unto Thy servant; for with my staff I passed over this Jordan; and now I am become two bands. Deliver me, I pray Thee, from the hand of my brother, from the hand of Esau: for I fear him, lest he will come and smite me, and the mother with the children. And Thou saidst, I will surely do thee good, and make thy seed as the sand of the sea, which cannot be numbered for multitude."

Chapter 13—Jacob and the Angel

This chapter is based on Genesis 32:24-33:11.

Jacob's wrong in receiving his brother's blessing by fraud was again brought forcibly before him, and he was afraid that God would permit Esau to take his life. In his distress he prayed to God all night. An angel was represented to me as standing before Jacob, presenting his wrong before him in its true character. As the angel turns to leave him, Jacob lays hold of him, and will not let him go. He makes supplications with tears. He pleads that he has deeply repented of his sins and the wrongs against his brother, which had been the means of separating him from his father's house for twenty years. He ventures to plead the promises of God and the tokens of His favor to him from time to time in his absence from his father's house.

All night Jacob wrestled with the angel, making supplication for a blessing. The angel seemed to be resisting his prayer, by continually calling his sins to his remembrance, at the same time endeavoring to break away from him. Jacob was determined to hold the angel, not by physical strength, but by the power of living faith. In his distress Jacob referred to the repentance of his soul, the deep humility he had felt for his wrongs. The angel regarded his prayer with seeming indifference, continually making efforts to release himself from the grasp of Jacob. He might have exercised his supernatural power and forced himself from Jacob's grasp, but he did not choose to do this.

But when he saw that he prevailed not against Jacob, to convince him of his supernatural power, he touched his thigh, which was immediately out of joint. But Jacob would not give up his earnest efforts for bodily pain. His object was to obtain a blessing, and pain of body was not sufficient to divert his mind from his object. His determination was stronger in the last moments of the conflict than at the beginning. His faith grew more earnest and persevering until the very last, even till the breaking of the day. He would not let go his hold of the angel until he blessed him. "And he said, Let me go, for the day breaketh. And he said, I will not let thee go, except thou bless me." The angel then inquired, "What is thy name? And he said, Jacob. And he said, Thy name shall be called no more Jacob, but Israel: for as a prince hast thou power with God and with men, and hast prevailed."

Prevailing Faith

Jacob's persevering faith prevailed. He held fast the angel until he obtained the blessing he desired, and the assurance of the pardon of his sins. His name was then changed from Jacob, the supplanter, to Israel, which signifies a prince of God. "And Jacob asked him, and said, Tell me, I pray thee, thy name. And he said, Wherefore is it that thou dost ask after my name? And he blessed him there. And Jacob called the name of the place Peniel: for I have seen God face to face, and my life is preserved." It was Christ that was with Jacob through that night, with whom he wrestled, and whom he perseveringly held until He blessed him.

The Lord heard the supplications of Jacob, and changed the purposes of Esau's heart. He did not sanction any wrong course which Jacob pursued. His life had been one of doubt, perplexity, and remorse because of his sin, until his earnest wrestling with the angel, and the evidence he there obtained that God had pardoned his sins.

"Yea, he had power over the angel, and prevailed. He wept, and made supplication unto Him: He found him in Bethel, and there He spake with us; even the Lord God of hosts; the Lord is his memorial." Hosea 12:4, 5.

Esau was marching against Jacob with an army, for the purpose of killing his brother. But while Jacob was wrestling with the angel that night, another angel was sent to move upon the heart of Esau in his sleeping hours. In his dream he saw Jacob in exile from his father's house for twenty years, because he was afraid of his life. And he marked his sorrow to find his mother dead. He saw in his dream Jacob's humility and angels of God around about him. He dreamed that when they met he had no mind to harm him. When Esau awoke he related his dream to his four hundred men and told them that they must not injure Jacob, for the God of his father was with him. And when they should meet Jacob, not one of them should do him harm.

"And Jacob lifted up his eyes, and looked, and, behold, Esau came, and with him four hundred men.... And he passed over before them, and bowed himself to the ground seven times, until he came near to his brother. And Esau ran to meet him, and embraced him, and fell on his neck, and kissed him; and they wept." Jacob entreated Esau to accept a peace offering, which Esau declined, but Jacob urged him: "Take, I pray thee, my blessing that is brought to thee; because God hath dealt graciously with me, and because I have enough. And he urged him, and he took it."

An Object Lesson

Jacob and Esau represent two classes: Jacob, the righteous, and Esau, the wicked. Jacob's distress when he learned that Esau was marching against him with four hundred men, represents the trouble of the righteous as the decree goes forth to put them to death, just before the coming of the Lord. As the wicked gather about them, they will be filled with anguish, for, like Jacob, they can see no escape for their lives. The angel placed himself before Jacob, and he took hold of the angel and held him and wrestled with him all night. So also will the righteous, in their time of trouble and anguish, wrestle in prayer with God, as Jacob wrestled with the angel. Jacob in his distress prayed all night for deliverance from the hand of Esau. The righteous in their mental anguish will cry to God day and night for deliverance from the hand of the wicked who surround them.

Jacob confessed his unworthiness: "I am not worthy of the least of all the mercies, and of all the truth, which Thou hast shewed unto Thy servant." The righteous in their distress will have a deep sense of their unworthiness and with many tears will acknowledge their utter unworthiness and, like Jacob, will plead the promises of God through Christ, made to just such dependent, helpless, repenting sinners.

Jacob took firm hold of the angel in his distress and would not let Him go. As he made supplication with tears, the angel reminded him of his past wrongs and endeavored to escape from Jacob, to test and prove him. So will the righteous, in the day of their anguish, be tested, proved, and tried, to manifest their strength of faith, their perseverance and unshaken confidence in the power of God to deliver them.

Jacob would not be turned away. He knew that God was merciful, and he appealed to His mercy. He pointed back to his past sorrow for, and repentance of, his wrongs, and urged his petition for deliverance from the hand of Esau. Thus his importuning continued all night. As he reviewed his past wrongs he was driven almost to despair. But he knew that he must have help from God, or perish. He held the angel fast and urged his petition with agonizing, earnest cries, until he prevailed.

Thus will it be with the righteous. As they review the events of their past lives, their hopes will almost sink. But as they realize that it is a case of life or death they will earnestly cry unto God, and appeal to Him in regard to their past sorrow for, and humble repentance of, their many sins, and then will refer to

His promise, "Let him take hold of My strength, that he may make peace with Me; and he shall make peace with Me." Isaiah 27:5. Thus will their earnest petitions be offered to God day and night. God would not have heard the prayer of Jacob and mercifully saved his life if he had not previously repented of his wrongs in obtaining the blessing by fraud.

The righteous, like Jacob, will manifest unyielding faith and earnest determination, which will take no denial. They will feel their unworthiness but will have no concealed wrongs to reveal. If they had sins, unconfessed and unrepented of, to appear then before them, while tortured with fear and anguish, with a lively sense of all their unworthiness, they would be overwhelmed. Despair would cut off their earnest faith, and they could not have confidence to plead with God thus earnestly for deliverance, and their precious moments would be spent in confessing hidden sins and bewailing their hopeless condition.

The period of probation is the time granted to all to prepare for the day of God. If any neglect the preparation and heed not the faithful warnings given, they will be without excuse. Jacob's earnest, persevering wrestling with the angel should be an example for Christians: Jacob prevailed because he was persevering and determined.

All who desire the blessing of God, as did Jacob, and will lay hold of the promises, as he did, and be as earnest and persevering as he was, will succeed as he succeeded. There is so little exercise of true faith and so little of the weight of truth resting upon many professed believers because they are indolent in spiritual things. They are unwilling to make exertions, to deny self, to agonize before God, to pray long and earnestly for the blessing, and therefore they do not obtain it. That faith which will live through the time of trouble must be daily in exercise now. Those who do not make strong efforts now to exercise persevering faith, will be wholly unprepared to exercise that faith which will enable them to stand in the day of trouble.

Chapter 14—The Children of Israel

This chapter is based on Genesis 37; 39; 41-48; Exodus 1-4.

Joseph listened to his father's instructions and feared the Lord. He was more obedient to his father's righteous teachings than any of his brethren. He treasured his instructions and, with integrity of heart, loved to obey God. He was grieved at the wrong conduct of some of his brethren and meekly entreated them to pursue a righteous course and leave off their wicked acts. This only embittered them against him. His hatred of sin was such that he could not endure to see his brethren sinning against God. He laid the matter before his father, hoping that his authority might reform them. This exposure of their wrongs enraged his brethren against him. They had observed their father's strong love for Joseph, and were envious of him. Their envy grew into hatred, and finally to murder.

The angel of God instructed Joseph in dreams which he had innocently related to his brethren: "For, behold, we were binding sheaves in the field, and, lo, my sheaf arose, and also stood upright; and, behold, your sheaves stood round about, and made obeisance to my sheaf. And his brethren said to him, Shalt thou indeed reign over us? or shalt thou indeed have dominion over us? And they hated him yet the more for his dreams, and for his words.

"And he dreamed yet another dream, and told it his brethren, and said, Behold, I have dreamed a dream more; and, behold, the sun and the moon and the eleven stars made obeisance to me. And he told it to his father, and to his brethren: and his father rebuked him, and said unto him, What is this dream that thou hast dreamed? Shall I and thy mother and thy brethren indeed come to bow down ourselves to thee to the earth? And his brethren envied him; but his father observed the saying."

Joseph in Egypt

Joseph's brethren purposed to kill him, but were finally content to sell him as a slave, to prevent his becoming greater than themselves. They thought they had placed him where they would be no more troubled with his dreams, and where there would not be a possibility of their fulfillment. But the very course which they pursued God overruled to bring about that which they designed never should take place—that he should have dominion over them.

God did not leave Joseph to go into Egypt alone. Angels prepared the way for his reception. Potiphar, an officer of Pharaoh, captain of the guard, bought him of the Ishmaelites. And the Lord was with Joseph, and He prospered him and gave him favor with his master, so that all he possessed he entrusted to Joseph's care. "And he left all that he had in Joseph's hand; and he knew not ought he had, save the bread which he did eat." It was considered an abomination for a Hebrew to prepare food for an Egyptian.

When Joseph was tempted to deviate from the path of right, to transgress the law of God and prove untrue to his master, he firmly resisted and gave evidence of the elevating power of the fear of God in his answer to his master's wife. After speaking of the great confidence of his master in him, by entrusting all that he had with him, he exclaimed, "How then can I do this great wickedness and sin against God?" He would not be persuaded to deviate from the path of righteousness and trample upon God's law by any inducements or threats.

And when he was accused, and a base crime was falsely laid to his charge, he did not sink in despair. In the consciousness of innocence and right he still trusted God. And God, who had hitherto supported him, did not forsake him. He was bound with fetters and kept in a gloomy prison. Yet God turned even this misfortune into a blessing. He gave him favor with the keeper of the prison, and to Joseph was soon committed the charge of all the prisoners.

Here is an example to all generations who should live upon the earth. Although they may be exposed to temptations, yet they should ever realize that there is a defense at hand, and it will be their own fault if they are not preserved. God will be a present help, and His Spirit a shield. Although surrounded with the severest temptations, there is a source of strength to which they can apply and resist them.

How fierce was the assault upon Joseph's morals. It came from one of influence, the most likely to lead astray. Yet how promptly and firmly was it resisted. He suffered for his virtue and integrity, for she who would lead him astray revenged herself upon the virtue she could not subvert, and by her influence caused him to be cast into prison, by charging him with a foul wrong. Here Joseph suffered because he would not yield his integrity. He had placed his reputation and interest in the hands of God. And although he was suffered to be afflicted for a time, to prepare him to fill an important position, yet God safely guarded that reputation that was blackened by a wicked accuser, and afterward, in His own good time, caused it to shine. God made even the prison the way to his elevation. Virtue will in time bring its own reward. The shield which covered Joseph's heart was the fear of God, which caused him to be faithful and just to his master and true to God.

Although Joseph was exalted as a ruler over all the land, yet he did not forget God. He knew that he was a stranger in a strange land, separated from his father and his brethren, which often caused him sadness, but he firmly believed that God's hand had overruled his course, to place him in an important position. And, depending on God continually, he performed all the duties of his office, as ruler over the land of Egypt, with faithfulness.

Joseph walked with God. He would not be persuaded to deviate from the path of righteousness and transgress God's law, by any inducement or threats. His self-control and patience in adversity and his unwavering fidelity are left on record for the benefit of all who should afterward live on the earth. When Joseph's brethren acknowledged their sin before him, he freely forgave them and showed by his acts of benevolence and love that he harbored no resentful feelings for their former cruel conduct toward him.

Days of Prosperity

The children of Israel were not slaves. They had never sold their cattle, their lands, and themselves to Pharaoh for food, as many of the Egyptians had done. They had been granted a portion of land wherein to dwell, with their flocks and cattle, on account of the service Joseph had been to the kingdom. Pharaoh appreciated his wisdom in the management of all things connected with the kingdom, especially in the preparations for the long years of famine which came upon the land of Egypt. He felt that the whole kingdom was indebted for their prosperity to the wise management of Joseph; and, as a token of his gratitude, he said to Joseph, "The land of Egypt is before thee; in the best of the land make thy father and brethren to dwell; in the land of Goshen let them dwell: and if thou knowest any men of activity among them, then make them rulers over my cattle."

"And Joseph placed his father and his brethren, and gave them a possession in the land of Egypt, in the best of the land, in the land of Rameses, as Pharaoh had commanded. And Joseph nourished his father, and his brethren, and all his father's household, with bread, according to their families."

No tax was required of Joseph's father and brethren by the king of Egypt, and Joseph was allowed the privilege of supplying them liberally with food. The king said to his rulers, Are we not indebted to the God of Joseph, and to him, for this liberal supply of food? Was it not because of his wisdom that we laid in so abundantly? While other lands are perishing, we have enough! His management has greatly enriched the kingdom.

"And Joseph died, and all his brethren, and all that generation. And the children of Israel were fruitful, and increased abundantly, and multiplied, and waxed exceeding mighty; and the land was filled with them. Now there rose up a new king over Egypt, which knew not Joseph. And he said unto his people, Behold, the people of the children of Israel are more and mightier than we: Come on, let us deal wisely with them; lest they multiply, and it come to pass, that, when there falleth out any war, they join also unto our enemies, and fight against us, and so get them up out of the land."

The Oppression

This new king of Egypt learned that the children of Israel were of great service to the kingdom. Many of them were able and understanding workmen, and he was not willing to lose their labor. This new king ranked the children of Israel with that class of slaves who had sold their flocks, their herds, their lands, and themselves to the kingdom. "Therefore they did set over them taskmasters to afflict them with their burdens. And they built for Pharaoh treasure-cities, Pithom and Raamses.

"But the more they afflicted them, the more they multiplied and grew. And they were grieved because of the children of Israel. And the Egyptians made the children of Israel to serve with rigour: and they made their lives bitter with hard bondage, in mortar, and in brick, and in all manner of service in the field: all their service, wherein they made them serve, was with rigour."

They compelled their women to work in the fields, as though they were slaves. Yet their numbers did not decrease. As the king and his rulers saw that they continually increased, they consulted together to compel them to accomplish a certain amount every day. They thought to subdue them with hard labor, and were angry because they could not decrease their numbers and crush out their independent spirit.

And because they failed to accomplish their purpose, they hardened their hearts to go still further. The king commanded that the male children should be killed as soon as they were born. Satan was the mover in these matters. He knew that a deliverer was to be raised up among the Hebrews to rescue them from oppression. He thought that if he could move the king to destroy the male children, the purpose of God would be defeated. The women feared God and did not do as the king of Egypt commanded them, but saved the male children alive.

The women dared not murder the Hebrew children, and because they obeyed not the command of the king, the Lord prospered them. As the king of Egypt was informed that his command had not been obeyed, he was very angry. He then made his command more urgent and extensive. He charged all his people to keep a strict watch, saying, "Every son that is born in Egypt ye shall cast into the river, and every daughter ye shall save alive."

Moses

When this cruel decree was in full force, Moses was born. His mother hid him as long as she could with any safety, and then prepared a little vessel of bulrushes, making it secure with pitch, that no water might enter the little ark, and placed it at the edge of the water, while his sister should be lingering around the water with apparent indifference. She was anxiously watching to see what would become of her little brother. Angels were also watching, that no harm should come to the helpless infant, which had been placed there by an affectionate mother and committed to the care of God by her earnest prayers mingled with tears.

And these angels directed the footsteps of Pharaoh's daughter to the river, near the very spot where lay the innocent little stranger. Her attention was attracted to the little strange vessel, and she sent one of her waiting maids to fetch it to her. And when she had removed the cover of this singularly constructed little vessel, she saw a lovely babe, "and, behold, the babe wept. And she had compassion on him." She knew that a tender Hebrew mother had taken this singular means to preserve the life of her much-loved babe, and she decided at once that it should be her son. The sister of Moses immediately came forward and inquired, "Shall I go and call to thee a nurse of the Hebrew women, that she may nurse the child for thee? And Pharaoh's daughter said to her, Go."

Joyfully sped the sister to her mother and related to her the happy news and conducted her with all haste to Pharaoh's daughter, where the child was committed to the mother to nurse, and she was liberally paid for the bringing up of her own son. Thankfully did this mother enter upon her now safe and happy task. She believed that God had preserved his life. Faithfully did she improve the precious opportunity of educating her son in reference to a life of usefulness. She was more particular in his instruction than in that of her other children; for she felt confident that he was preserved for some great work. By her faithful teachings she instilled into his young mind the fear of God and love for truthfulness and justice.

She did not rest here in her efforts but earnestly prayed to God for her son that he might be preserved from every corrupting influence. She taught him to bow and pray to God, the living God, for He alone could hear him and help him in any emergency. She sought to impress his mind with the sinfulness of idolatry. She knew that he was to be soon separated from her influence and given up to his adopted royal mother, to be surrounded with influences calculated to make him disbelieve in the existence of the Maker of the heavens and of the earth.

The instructions he received from his parents were such as to fortify his mind and shield him from being lifted up and corrupted with sin and becoming proud amid the splendor and extravagance of court life. He had a clear mind and an understanding heart, and never lost the pious impressions he received in his youth. His mother kept him as long as she could, but she was obliged to separate from him when he was about twelve years old, and he then became the son of Pharaoh's daughter.

Here Satan was defeated. By moving Pharaoh to destroy the male children, he thought to turn aside the purposes of God and destroy the one whom God would raise up to deliver His people. But that very decree, appointing the Hebrew children to death, was the means God overruled to place Moses in the royal family, where he had advantages to become a learned man and eminently qualified to lead his people from Egypt.

Pharaoh expected to exalt his adopted grandson to the throne. He educated him to stand at the head of the armies of Egypt and lead them to battle. Moses was a great favorite with Pharaoh's host and was honored because he conducted warfare with superior skill and wisdom. "And Moses was learned in all the wisdom of the Egyptians, and was mighty in words and in deeds." The Egyptians regarded Moses as a remarkable character.

Special Preparation for Leadership

Angels instructed Moses that God had chosen him to deliver the children of Israel. The rulers among the children of Israel were also taught by angels that the time for their deliverance was nigh, and that Moses was the man whom God would use to accomplish this work. Moses thought that the children of Israel would be delivered by warfare, and that he would stand at the head of the Hebrew host, to conduct the warfare against the Egyptian armies and deliver his brethren from the yoke of oppression. Having this in view, Moses guarded his affections, that they might not be strongly placed upon his adopted mother or upon Pharaoh, lest it should be more difficult for him to remain free to do the will of God.

The Lord preserved Moses from being injured by the corrupting influences around him. The principles of truth, received in his youth from God-fearing parents, were never forgotten by him. And when he most needed to be shielded from the corrupting influences attending a life at court, then the lessons of his youth bore fruit. The fear of God was before him. And so strong was his love for his brethren, and so great was his respect for the Hebrew faith, that he would not conceal his parentage for the honor of being an heir of the royal family.

When Moses was forty years old, "he went out unto his brethren, and looked on their burdens; and he spied an Egyptian smiting an Hebrew, one of his brethren. And he looked this way and that way, and when he saw that there was no man, he slew the Egyptian, and hid him in the sand. And when he went out the second day, behold, two men of the Hebrews strove together: and he said to him that did the wrong, Wherefore smitest thou thy fellow? And he said, Who made thee a prince and a judge over us? intendest thou to kill me, as thou killedst the Egyptian? And Moses feared, and said, Surely this thing is known. Now when Pharaoh heard this thing he sought to slay Moses. But Moses fled from the face of Pharaoh, and dwelt in the land of Midian." The Lord directed his course, and he found a home with Jethro, a man that worshiped God. He was a shepherd, also priest of Midian. His daughters tended his flocks. But Jethro's flocks were soon placed under the care of Moses, who married Jethro's daughter and remained in Midian forty years.

Moses was too fast in slaying the Egyptian. He supposed that the people of Israel understood that God's special providence had raised him up to deliver them. But God did not design to deliver the children of Israel by warfare, as Moses thought, but by His own mighty power, that the glory might be ascribed to Him alone. God overruled the act of Moses in slaying the Egyptian to bring about His purpose. He had in His providence brought Moses into the royal family of Egypt, where he had received a thorough education; and yet he was not prepared for God to entrust to him the great work He had raised him up to accomplish. Moses could not immediately leave the king's court and the indulgences granted him as the king's grandson to perform the special work of God. He must have time to obtain an experience and be educated in the school of adversity and poverty. While he was living in retirement, the Lord sent His angels to especially instruct him in regard to the future. Here he learned more fully the great lesson of self-control and humility. He kept the flocks of Jethro, and while he was performing his humble duties as a shepherd, God was preparing him to become a spiritual shepherd of His sheep, even of His people Israel.

As Moses led the flock to the desert and came to the mountain of God, even to Horeb, "the angel of the Lord appeared unto him in a flame of fire out of the midst of a bush." "And the Lord said, I have surely seen the affliction of My people which are in Egypt, and have heard their cry by reason of their taskmasters; for I know their sorrows; and I am come down to deliver them out of the hand of the Egyptians, and to bring them up out of that land unto a good land and a large, unto a land flowing with milk and honey.... Now therefore, behold, the cry of the children of Israel is come up unto Me: and I have also seen the oppression wherewith the Egyptians oppress them. Come now therefore, and I will send thee unto Pharaoh, that thou mayest bring forth My people the children of Israel out of Egypt."

The time had fully come when God would have Moses exchange the shepherd's staff for the rod of God, which He would make powerful in accomplishing signs and wonders, in delivering His people from oppression, and in preserving them when pursued by their enemies.

Moses consented to perform the mission. He first visited his father-in-law and obtained his consent for himself and his family to return into Egypt. He did not dare to tell Jethro his message to Pharaoh, lest he should be unwilling to let his wife and children accompany him on such a dangerous mission. The Lord strengthened him and removed his fears by saying to him, "Return into Egypt: for all the men are dead which sought thy life."

Chapter 15—God's Power Revealed

This chapter is based on Exodus 5:1-12:28.

Many years had the children of Israel been in servitude to the Egyptians. Only a few families went down into Egypt, but they had become a large multitude. And being surrounded with idolatry, many of them had lost the knowledge of the true God and had forgotten His law. And they united with the Egyptians in their worship of the sun, moon, and stars, also of beasts and images, the work of men's hands.

Everything around the children of Israel was calculated to make them forget the living God. Yet there were those among the Hebrews who preserved the knowledge of the true God, the Maker of the heavens and of the earth. They were grieved to see their children daily witnessing, and even engaging in, the abominations of the idolatrous people around them, and bowing down to Egyptian deities, made of wood and stone, and offering sacrifice to these senseless objects. The faithful were grieved, and in their distress they cried unto the Lord for deliverance from the Egyptian yoke, that He would bring them out of Egypt, where they might be rid of idolatry and the corrupting influences which surrounded them.

But many of the Hebrews were content to remain in bondage rather than to go to a new country and meet with the difficulties attending such a journey. Therefore the Lord did not deliver them by the first display of His signs and wonders before Pharaoh. He overruled events to more fully develop the tyrannical spirit of Pharaoh, and that He might manifest His great power to the Egyptians, and also before His people, to make them anxious to leave Egypt and choose the service of God.

Although many of the Israelites had become corrupted by idolatry, yet the faithful stood firm. They had not concealed their faith, but openly acknowledged before the Egyptians that they served the only true and living God. They rehearsed the evidences of God's existence and power from creation down. The Egyptians had an opportunity of becoming acquainted with the faith of the Hebrews and their God. They had tried to subvert the faithful worshipers of the true God, and were annoyed because they had not succeeded, either by threats, the promise of rewards, or by cruel treatment.

The last two kings who had occupied the throne of Egypt had been tyrannical and had cruelly entreated the Hebrews. The elders of Israel had endeavored to encourage the sinking faith of the Israelites, by referring to the promise made to Abraham, and the prophetic words of Joseph just before he died, foretelling their deliverance from Egypt. Some would listen and believe. Others looked at their own sad condition, and would not hope.

Israel Influenced by their Environment

The Egyptians had learned the expectations of the children of Israel and derided their hopes of deliverance and spoke scornfully of the power of their God. They pointed them to their own situation as a people, as merely a nation of slaves, and tauntingly said to them, If your God is so just and merciful, and possesses power above the Egyptian gods, why does He not make you a free people? Why not manifest His greatness and power, and exalt you?

The Egyptians then called the attention of the Israelites to their own people, who worshiped gods of their own choosing, which the Israelites termed false gods. They exultingly said that their gods had prospered them, and had given them food and raiment and great riches, and that their gods had also given the Israelites into their hands to serve them, and that they had power to oppress them and destroy their lives, so that they should be no people. They derided the idea that the Hebrews would ever be delivered from slavery.

Pharaoh boasted that he would like to see their God deliver them from his hands. These words destroyed the hopes of many of the children of Israel. It appeared to them very much as the king and his counselors had said. They knew that they were treated as slaves, and that they must endure just that degree of oppression their taskmasters and rulers might put upon them. Their male children had been hunted and slain. Their own lives were a burden, and they were believing in, and worshiping, the God of heaven.

Then they contrasted their condition with that of the Egyptians. They did not believe at all in a living God who had power to save or to destroy. Some of them worshiped idols, images of wood and stone, while others chose to worship the sun, moon, and stars; yet they were prospered and wealthy. And some of the Hebrews thought that if God was above all gods He would not thus leave them as slaves to an idolatrous nation.

The faithful servants of God understood that it was because of their unfaithfulness to God as a people, and their disposition to intermarry with other nations, and thus being led into idolatry, that the Lord suffered them to go into Egypt. And they firmly declared to their brethren that God would soon bring them up from Egypt and break their oppressive yoke.

The time had come when God would answer the prayers of His oppressed people, and would bring them from Egypt with such mighty displays of His power that the Egyptians would be compelled to acknowledge that the God of the Hebrews, whom they had despised, was above all gods. He would now punish them for their idolatry and for their proud boasting of the mercies bestowed upon them by their senseless gods. God would glorify His own name, that other nations might hear of His power and tremble at His mighty acts, and that His people, by witnessing His miraculous works, should fully turn from their idolatry to render to Him pure worship.

In the deliverance of Israel from Egypt, God plainly showed His distinguished mercy to His people before all the Egyptians. God saw fit to execute His judgments upon Pharaoh, that he might know by sad experience, since he would not otherwise be convinced, that His power was superior to all others. That His name might be declared throughout all the earth, He would give exemplary and demonstrative proof to all nations of His divine power and justice. It was the design of God that these exhibitions of power should strengthen the faith of His people, and that their posterity should steadfastly worship Him alone who had wrought such merciful wonders in their behalf.

Moses declared to Pharaoh, after he required the people to make brick without straw, that God, whom he pretended not to know, would compel him to yield to His claims and acknowledge His authority as supreme Ruler.

The Plagues

The miracle of the rod's becoming a serpent and the river's being turned to blood did not move the hard heart of Pharaoh, only to increase his hatred of the Israelites. The work of the magicians led him to believe that these miracles were performed by magic, but he had abundant evidence that this was not the case when the plague of frogs was removed. God could have caused them to disappear and return to dust in a moment, but He did not do this, lest, after they should be removed, the king and the Egyptians should say that it was the result of magic, like the work of the magicians. They died, and then they gathered them together into heaps. Their bodies they could see before them, and they corrupted the atmosphere. Here the king and all Egypt had evidences which their vain philosophy could not dispose of, that this work was not magic but a judgment from the God of heaven.

The magicians could not produce the lice. The Lord would not suffer them to make it even appear to their own sight, or to that of the Egyptians, that they could produce the plague of the lice. He would remove all excuse of unbelief from Pharaoh. He compelled even the magicians themselves to say, "This is the finger of God."

Next came the plague of the swarms of flies. They were not such flies as harmlessly annoy us in some seasons of the year, but the flies brought upon Egypt were large and venomous. Their sting was very painful upon man and beast. God separated His people from the Egyptians and suffered no flies to appear throughout their coasts.

The Lord then sent the plague of the murrain upon their cattle, and at the same time preserved the cattle of the Hebrews, that not one of them died. Next came the plague of the boil upon man and beast, and the magicians could not protect themselves from it. The Lord then sent upon Egypt the plague of the hail mingled with fire, with lightnings and thunder. The time of each plague was given before it came, that it might not be said to have happened by chance. The Lord demonstrated to the Egyptians that the whole earth was under the command of the God of the Hebrews—that thunder, hail, and storm obey His voice. Pharaoh, the proud king who once inquired, "Who is the Lord, that I should obey His voice?" humbled himself and said, "I have sinned ... : the Lord is righteous, and I and my people are wicked." He begged of Moses to be his intercessor with God, that the terrific thunder and lightning might cease.

The Lord next sent the dreadful plague of the locusts. The king chose to receive the plagues rather than to submit to God. Without remorse he saw his whole kingdom under the miracle of these dreadful judgments. The Lord then sent darkness upon Egypt. The people were not merely deprived of light, but the atmosphere was very oppressive, so that breathing was difficult; yet the Hebrews had a pure atmosphere and light in their dwellings.

One more dreadful plague God brought upon Egypt, more severe than any before it. It was the king and the idolatrous priests who opposed to the last the request of Moses. The people desired that the Hebrews should be permitted to leave Egypt. Moses related to Pharaoh and to the people of Egypt, also to the Israelites, the nature and effect of the last plague. On that night, so terrible to the Egyptians and so glorious to the people of God, was the solemn ordinance of the passover instituted.

It was very hard for the Egyptian king and a proud and idolatrous people to yield to the requirements of the God of heaven. Very slow was the king of Egypt to yield. While under most grievous affliction he would yield a little; but when the affliction was removed, he would take back all he had granted. Thus, plague after plague was brought upon Egypt, and he yielded no more than he was compelled to by the dreadful visitations of God's wrath. The king even persisted in his rebellion after Egypt had been ruined.

Moses and Aaron related to Pharaoh the nature and effect of each plague which should follow his refusal to let Israel go. Every time he saw these plagues come exactly as he was told they would come; yet he would not yield. First, he would only grant them permission to sacrifice to God in the land of Egypt; then, after Egypt had suffered by God's wrath, he granted that the men alone should go. After Egypt had been nearly destroyed by the plague of the locusts, then he granted that their children and their wives might go also, but would not let their cattle go. Moses then told the king that the angel of God would slay their first-born.

Every plague had come a little closer and more severe, and this was to be more dreadful than any before it. But the proud king was exceedingly angry, and humbled not himself. And when the Egyptians saw the great preparations being made among the Israelites for that dreadful night, they ridiculed the token of blood upon their doorposts.

Chapter 16—Israel's Escape From Bondage

This chapter is based on Exodus 12:29-15:19.

The children of Israel had followed the directions given them of God; and while the angel of death was passing from house to house among the Egyptians, they were all ready for their journey and waiting for the rebellious king and his great men to bid them go.

"And it came to pass, that at midnight the Lord smote all the firstborn in the land of Egypt, from the firstborn of Pharaoh that sat on his throne unto the firstborn of the captive that was in the dungeon; and all the firstborn of cattle. And Pharaoh rose up in the night, he, and all his servants, and all the Egyptians; and there was a great cry in Egypt; for there was not a house where there was not one dead. And he called for Moses and Aaron by night, and said, Rise up, and get you forth from among my people, both ye and the children of Israel; and go, serve the Lord, as ye have said. Also take your flocks and your herds, as ye have said, and be gone; and bless me also. And the Egyptians were urgent upon the people, that they might send them out of the land in haste; for they said, We be all dead men.

"And the people took their dough before it was leavened, their kneading troughs being bound up in their clothes upon their shoulders. And the children of Israel did according to the word of Moses; and they borrowed of the Egyptians jewels of silver, and jewels of gold, and raiment: and the Lord gave the people favor in the sight of the Egyptians, so that they lent unto them such things as they required. And they spoiled the Egyptians."

The Lord revealed this to Abraham about four hundred years before it was fulfilled: "And He said unto Abram, Know of a surety that thy seed shall be a stranger in a land that is not theirs, and shall serve them; and they shall afflict them four hundred years; and also that nation, whom they shall serve, will I judge; and afterward shall they come out with great substance." Genesis 15:13, 14.

"And a mixed multitude went up also with them; and flocks, and herds, even very much cattle." The children of Israel went out of Egypt with their possessions, which did not belong to Pharaoh, for they had never sold them to him. Jacob and his sons took their flocks and cattle with them into Egypt. The children of Israel had become exceedingly numerous, and their flocks and herds had greatly increased. God had judged the Egyptians by sending the plagues upon them, and made them hasten His people out of Egypt with all that they possessed.

"And it came to pass, when Pharaoh had let the people go, that God led them not through the way of the land of the Philistines, although that was near; for God said, Lest peradventure the people repent when they see war, and they return to Egypt: but God led the people about, through the way of the wilderness of the Red Sea. And the children of Israel went up harnessed out of the land of Egypt. And Moses took the bones of Joseph up with him: for he had straitly sworn the children of Israel, saying, God will surely visit you; and ye shall carry up my bones away hence with you.

The Pillar of Fire

"And they took their journey from Succoth, and encamped in Etham, in the edge of the wilderness. And the Lord went before them by day in a pillar of a cloud, to lead them the way; and by night in a pillar of fire, to give them light; to go by day and night: He took not away the pillar of the cloud by day, nor the pillar of fire by night, from before the people."

The Lord knew that the Philistines would oppose their passing through their land. They would say of them, They have stolen away from their masters in Egypt, and would make war with them. Thus God, by bringing them by way of the sea, revealed Himself a compassionate God as well as a God of judgment. The Lord informed Moses that Pharaoh would pursue them, and He directed him just where to encamp before the sea. He told Moses that He would be honored before Pharaoh and all his host.

After the Hebrews had been gone from Egypt some days, the Egyptians told Pharaoh that they had fled and would never return to serve him again. And they mourned because they had permitted them to leave Egypt. It was a very great loss for them to be deprived of their services, and they regretted that they had consented to let them go. Notwithstanding all they had suffered from the judgments of God, they were so hardened by their continual rebellion that they decided to pursue the children of Israel and bring them back by force unto Egypt. The king took a very large army and six hundred chariots, and pursued after them, and overtook them while encamped by the sea.

"And when Pharaoh drew nigh, the children of Israel lifted up their eyes, and, behold, the Egyptians marched after them; and they were sore afraid: and the children of Israel cried out unto the Lord. And they said unto Moses, Because there were no graves in Egypt, hast thou taken us away to die in the wilderness? wherefore hast thou dealt thus with us, to carry us forth out of Egypt? Is not this the word that we did tell thee in Egypt, saying, Let us alone, that we may serve the Egyptians? For it had been better for us to serve the Egyptians, than that we should die in the wilderness. And Moses said unto the people, Fear ye not, stand still, and see the salvation of the Lord, which He will shew to you today: for the Egyptians whom ye have seen today, ye shall see them again no more for ever. The Lord shall fight for you, and ye shall hold your peace."

How soon the Israelites distrusted God! They had witnessed all His judgments upon Egypt to compel the king to let Israel go, but when their confidence in God was tested, they murmured, notwithstanding they had seen such evidences of His power in their wonderful deliverance. Instead of trusting in God in their necessity, they murmured at faithful Moses, reminding him of their words of unbelief which they uttered in Egypt. They accused him of being the cause of all their distress. He encouraged them to trust in God and withhold their expressions of unbelief, and they should see what the Lord would do for them. Moses earnestly cried to the Lord to deliver His chosen people.

Deliverance at the Red Sea

"And the Lord said unto Moses, Wherefore criest thou unto Me? Speak unto the children of Israel, that they go forward: but lift thou up thy rod, and stretch out thine hand over the sea, and divide it: and the children of Israel shall go on dry ground through the midst of the sea." God would have Moses understand that He would work for His people—that their necessity would be His opportunity. When they should go as far as they could, he must bid them still go forward; that he should use the rod God had given him to divide the waters.

"And I, behold, I will harden the hearts of the Egyptians, and they shall follow them: and I will get Me honour upon Pharaoh, and upon all his host, upon his chariots, and upon his horsemen. And the Egyptians shall know that I am the Lord, when I have gotten Me honour upon Pharaoh, upon his chariots, and upon his horsemen. And the angel of God, which went before the camp of Israel, removed and went behind them; and the pillar of the cloud went from before their face, and stood behind them: and it came between the camp of the Egyptians and the camp of Israel; and it was a cloud of darkness to them, but it gave light by night to these: so that the one came not near the other all the night."

The Egyptians could not see the Hebrews, for the cloud of thick darkness was before them, which cloud was all light to the Israelites. Thus did God display His power to prove His people, whether they would trust in Him after giving them such tokens of His care and love for them, and to rebuke their unbelief and murmuring. "And Moses stretched out his hand over the sea; and the Lord caused the sea to go back by a strong east wind all that night, and made the sea dry land, and the waters were divided. And the children of Israel went into the midst of the sea upon the dry ground: and the waters were a wall unto them on their right hand, and on their left." The waters rose up and stood, like congealed walls, on either side while Israel walked in the midst of the sea on dry ground.

The Egyptian host was triumphing through that night that the children of Israel were again in their power. They thought there was no possibility of their escape; for before them stretched the Red Sea, and their large armies were close behind them. In the morning, as they came up to the sea, lo, there was a dry path, the waters were divided, and stood like a wall upon either side, and the children of Israel were halfway through the sea, walking on dry land. They waited awhile to decide what course they had better pursue. They were disappointed and enraged that, as the Hebrews were almost in their power, and they were sure of them, an unexpected way was opened for them in the sea. They decided to follow them.

"And the Egyptians pursued, and went in after them, to the midst of the sea, even all Pharaoh's horses, his chariots, and his horsemen. And it came to pass, that in the morning watch the Lord looked unto the host of the Egyptians through the pillar of fire and of the cloud, and troubled the host of the Egyptians, and took off their chariot wheels, that they drave them heavily: so that the Egyptians said, Let us flee from the face of Israel; for the Lord fighteth for them against the Egyptians."

The Egyptians dared to venture in the path God had prepared for His people, and angels of God went through their host and removed their chariot wheels. They were plagued. Their progress was very slow, and they began to be troubled. They remembered the judgments that the God of the Hebrews had brought upon them in Egypt to compel them to let Israel go, and they thought that God might deliver them all into the hands of the Israelites. They decided that God was fighting for the Israelites, and they were terribly afraid and were turning about to flee from them, when "the Lord said unto Moses, Stretch out thine hand over the sea, that the waters may come again upon the Egyptians, upon their chariots, and upon their horsemen.

"And Moses stretched forth his hand over the sea, and the sea returned to his strength when the morning appeared; and the Egyptians fled against it; and the Lord overthrew the Egyptians in the midst of the sea. And the waters returned, and covered the chariots, and the horsemen, and all the host of Pharaoh that came into the sea after them; there remained not so much as one of them. But the children of Israel walked upon dry land in the midst of the sea; and the waters were a wall unto them on their right hand, and on their left. Thus the Lord saved Israel that day out of the hand of the Egyptians; and Israel saw the Egyptians dead upon the sea shore. And Israel saw that great work which the Lord did upon the Egyptians: and the people feared the Lord, and believed the Lord, and His servant Moses."

As the Hebrews witnessed the marvelous work of God in the destruction of the Egyptians, they united in an inspired song of lofty eloquence and grateful praise.

Chapter 17—Israel's Journeyings

This chapter is based on Genesis 32 and 33.

The children of Israel traveled in the wilderness and for three days could find no good water to drink. They were suffering with thirst, "and the people murmured against Moses, saying, What shall we drink? And he cried unto the Lord; and the Lord shewed him a tree, which when he had cast into the waters, the waters were made sweet: there He made for them a statute and an ordinance, and there He proved them, and said, If thou wilt diligently hearken to the voice of the Lord thy God, and wilt do that which is right in His sight, and wilt give ear to His commandments, and keep all His statutes, I will put none of these diseases upon thee, which I have brought upon the Egyptians; for I am the Lord that healeth thee."

The children of Israel seemed to possess an evil heart of unbelief. They were unwilling to endure hardships in the wilderness. When they met with difficulties in the way, they would regard them as impossibilities. Their confidence in God would fail, and they could see nothing before them but death. "And the whole congregation of the children of Israel murmured against Moses and Aaron in the wilderness: and the children of Israel said unto them, Would to God we had died by the hand of the Lord in the land of Egypt, when we sat by the flesh pots, and when we did eat bread to the full, for ye have brought us forth into this wilderness, to kill this whole assembly with hunger."

They had not really suffered the pangs of hunger. They had food for the present, but they feared for the future. They could not see how the host of Israel was to subsist, in their long travels through the wilderness, upon the simple food they then had, and in their unbelief they saw their children famishing. The Lord was willing that they should be brought short in their food, and that they should meet with difficulties, that their hearts should turn to Him who had hitherto helped them, that they might believe in Him. He was ready to be to them a present help. If, in their want, they would call upon Him, He would manifest to them tokens of His love and continual care.

But they seemed to be unwilling to trust the Lord any further than they could witness before their eyes the continual evidences of His power. If they had possessed true faith and a firm confidence in God, inconveniences and obstacles, or even real suffering, would have been cheerfully borne, after the Lord had wrought in such a wonderful manner for their deliverance from servitude. Moreover, the Lord promised them if they would obey His commandments, no disease should rest upon them, for He said, "I am the Lord that healeth thee."

After this sure promise from God it was criminal unbelief in them to anticipate that they and their children might die with hunger. They had suffered greatly in Egypt by being overtaxed in labor. Their children had been put to death, and in answer to their prayers of anguish, God had mercifully delivered them. He promised to be their God, to take them to Himself as a people and to lead them to a large and good land.

But they were ready to faint at any suffering they should have to endure in the way to that land. They had endured much in the service of the Egyptians, but now could not endure suffering in the service of God. They were ready to give up to gloomy doubts and sink in discouragement when they were tried. They murmured against God's devoted servant Moses and charged him with all their trials, and expressed a wicked wish that they had remained in Egypt, where they could sit by the flesh pots and eat bread to the full.

A Lesson for Our Day

The unbelief and murmurings of the children of Israel illustrate the people of God now upon the earth. Many look back to them, and marvel at their unbelief and continual murmurings, after the Lord had done so much for them, in giving them repeated evidences of His love and care for them. They think that they should not have proved ungrateful. But some who thus think, murmur and repine at things of less consequence. They do not know themselves. God frequently proves them, and tries their faith in small things; and they do not endure the trial any better than did ancient Israel.

Many have their present wants supplied; yet they will not trust the Lord for the future. They manifest unbelief and sink into despondency and gloom at anticipated want. Some are in continual trouble lest they shall come to want and their children suffer. When difficulties arise or when they are brought into strait places—when their faith and their love to God are tested—they shrink from the trial and murmur at the process by which God has chosen to purify them. Their love does not prove pure and perfect, to bear all things.

The faith of the people of the God of heaven should be strong, active, and enduring—the substance of things hoped for. Then the language of such will be, "Bless the Lord, O my soul: and all that is within me, bless His holy name," for He hath dealt bountifully with me.

Self-denial is considered by some to be real suffering. Depraved appetites are indulged. And a restraint upon the unhealthy appetites would lead even many professed Christians to now start back, as though actual starvation would be the consequence of a plain diet. And, like the children of Israel, they would prefer slavery, diseased bodies, and even death, rather than to be deprived of the flesh pots. Bread and water is all that is promised to the remnant in the time of trouble.

The Manna

"And when the dew that lay was gone up, behold, upon the face of the wilderness there lay a small round thing, as small as the hoar frost on the ground. And when the children of Israel saw it, they said one to another, It is manna: for they wist not what it was. And Moses said unto them, This is the bread which the Lord hath given you to eat. This is the thing which the Lord hath commanded, Gather of it every man, according to his eating, an omer for every man, according to the number of your persons; take ye every man for them which are in his tents.

"And the children of Israel did so, and gathered, some more, some less. And when they did mete it with an omer, he that gathered much had nothing over, and he that gathered little had no lack; they gathered every man according to his eating. And Moses said, Let no man leave of it till the morning. Notwithstanding they hearkened not to Moses; but some of them left of it until the morning, and it bred worms, and stank: and Moses was wroth with them. And they gathered it every morning, every man according to his eating: and when the sun waxed hot, it melted.

"And it came to pass, that on the sixth day they gathered twice as much bread, two omers for one man: and all the rulers of the congregation came and told Moses. And he said unto them, This is that which the Lord hath said, Tomorrow is the rest of the holy Sabbath unto the Lord: bake that which ye will bake today, and seethe that ye will seethe; and that which remaineth over, lay up for you to be kept until the morning. And they laid it up till the morning as Moses bade: and it did not stink, neither was there any worm therein. And Moses said, Eat that today; for today is a Sabbath unto the Lord: today ye shall not find it in the field. Six days ye shall gather it; but on the seventh day, which is the Sabbath, in it there shall be none."

The Lord is no less particular now in regard to His Sabbath than when He gave the foregoing special directions to the children of Israel. He required them to bake that which they would bake, and seethe (that is, boil) that which they would seethe, on the sixth day, preparatory to the rest of the Sabbath.

God manifested His great care and love for His people in sending them bread from heaven. "Man did eat angels' food"; that is, food provided for them by the angels. The threefold miracle of the manna—a double quantity on the sixth day, and none on the seventh, and its keeping fresh through the Sabbath, while on other days it would become unfit for use— was designed to impress them with the sacredness of the Sabbath.

After they were abundantly supplied with food, they were ashamed of their unbelief and murmurings, and promised to trust the Lord for the future, but they soon forgot their promise and failed at the first trial of their faith.

Water From the Rock

They journeyed from the wilderness of Sin, and pitched in Rephidim, and there was no water for the people to drink. "Wherefore the people did chide with Moses, and said, Give us water that we may drink. And Moses said unto them, Why chide ye with me? wherefore do ye tempt the Lord? And the people thirsted there for water; and the people murmured against Moses, and said, Wherefore is this that thou hast brought us up out of Egypt, to kill us and our children and our cattle with thirst? And Moses cried unto the Lord, saying, What shall I do unto this people? they be almost ready to stone me.

"And the Lord said unto Moses, Go on before the people, and take with thee of the elders of Israel; and thy rod, wherewith thou smotest the river, take in thine hand, and go. Behold, I will stand before thee there upon the rock in Horeb, and thou shalt smite the rock, and there shall come water out of it, that the people may drink. And Moses did so in the sight of the elders of Israel. And he called the name of the place Massah, and Meribah, because of the chiding of the children of Israel, and because they tempted the Lord, saying, Is the Lord among us, or not?"

God directed the children of Israel to encamp in that place, where there was no water, to prove them, to see if they would look to Him in their distress, or murmur as they had previously done. In view of what God had done for them in their wonderful deliverance, they should have believed in Him in their distress. They should have known that He would not permit them to perish with thirst, whom He had promised to take unto Himself as His people. But instead of entreating the Lord in humility to provide for their necessity, they murmured against Moses, and demanded of him water.

God had been continually manifesting His power in a wonderful manner before them, to make them understand that all the benefits they received came from Him; that He could give them, or remove them, according to His own will. At times they had a full sense of this, and humbled themselves greatly before the Lord; but when thirsty or when hungry, they charged it all upon Moses, as though they had left Egypt to please him. Moses was grieved with their cruel murmurings. He inquired of the Lord what he should do, for the people were ready to stone him. The Lord bade him go smite the rock with the rod of God. The cloud of His glory rested directly before the rock. "He clave the rocks in the wilderness, and gave them drink as out of the great depths. He brought streams also out of the rock, and caused waters to run down like rivers." Psalm 78:15, 16.

Moses smote the rock, but it was Christ who stood by him and caused the water to flow from the flinty rock. The people tempted the Lord in their thirst, and said, If God has brought us out here, why does He not give us water, as well as bread. That if showed criminal unbelief and made Moses afraid that God would punish them for their wicked murmurings. The Lord tested the faith of His people, but they did not endure the trial. They murmured for food and for water, and complained of Moses. Because of their unbelief, God suffered their enemies to make war with them, that He might manifest to His people from whence cometh their strength.

Delivered From Amalek

"Then came Amalek, and fought with Israel in Rephidim. And Moses said unto Joshua, Choose us out men, and go out, fight with Amalek: tomorrow I will stand on the top of the hill with the rod of God in mine hand. So Joshua did as Moses had said to him, and fought with Amalek: and Moses, Aaron, and Hur went up to the top of the hill. And it came to pass, when Moses held up his hand, that Israel prevailed: and when he let down his hand, Amalek prevailed. But Moses' hands were heavy; and they took a stone, and put it under him, and he sat thereon; and Aaron and Hur stayed up his hands, the one on the one side, and the other on the other side; and his hands were steady until the going down of the sun."

Moses held up his hands toward heaven, with the rod of God in his right hand, entreating help from God. Then Israel prevailed and drove back their enemies. When Moses let down his hands, it was seen that Israel soon lost all they had gained, and were being overcome by their enemies. Moses again held up his hands toward heaven, and Israel prevailed, and the enemy was driven back.

This act of Moses, reaching up his hands toward God, was to teach Israel that while they made God their trust and laid hold upon His strength and exalted His throne, He would fight for them and subdue their enemies. But when they should let go their hold upon His strength and should trust to their own power, they would be even weaker than their enemies, who had not the knowledge of God, and their enemies would prevail over them. Then "Joshua discomfited Amalek and his people with the edge of the sword.

"And the Lord said unto Moses, Write this for a memorial in a book, and rehearse it in the ears of Joshua: for I will utterly put out the remembrance of Amalek from under heaven. And Moses built an altar, and called the name of it Jehovah-nissi: for he said, Because the Lord hath sworn that the Lord will have war with Amalek from generation to generation." If the children of Israel had not murmured against the Lord, He would not have suffered their enemies to make war with them.

Jethro's Visit

Before Moses left Egypt he had sent back his wife and children to his father-in-law. And after Jethro heard of the wonderful deliverance of the Israelites from Egypt, he visited Moses in the wilderness, and brought his wife and children to him. "And Moses went out to meet his father in law, and did obeisance, and kissed him; and they asked each other of their welfare; and they came into the tent. And Moses told his father in law all that the Lord had done unto Pharaoh and to the Egyptians for Israel's sake, and all the travail that had come upon them by the way, and how the Lord delivered them.

"And Jethro rejoiced for all the goodness which the Lord had done to Israel, whom he had delivered out of the hand of the Egyptians. And Jethro said, Blessed be the Lord, who hath delivered you out of the hand of the Egyptians, and out of the hand of Pharaoh, who hath delivered the people from under the hand of the Egyptians. Now I know that the Lord is greater than all gods: for in the thing wherein they dealt proudly He was above them. And Jethro, Moses' father in law, took a burnt offering and sacrifices for God: and Aaron came, and all the elders of Israel, to eat bread with Moses' father in law before God."

Jethro's discerning eye soon saw that the burdens upon Moses were very great, as the people brought all their matters of difficulty to him, and he instructed them in regard to the statutes and law of God. He said to Moses, "Hearken now unto my voice, I will give thee counsel, and God shall be with thee: Be thou for the people to God-ward, that thou mayest bring the causes unto God: and thou shalt teach them ordinances and laws, and shalt shew them the way wherein they must walk, and the work that they must do. Moreover thou shalt provide out of all the people able men, such as fear God, men of truth, hating covetousness; and place such over them, to be rulers of thousands, and rulers of hundreds, rulers of fifties, and rulers of tens: and let them judge the people at all seasons: and it shall be, that every great matter they shall bring unto thee, but every small matter they shall judge: so shall it be easier for thyself, and they shall bear the burden with thee. If thou shalt do this thing, and God command thee so, then thou shalt be able to endure, and all this people shall also go to their place in peace.

"So Moses hearkened to the voice of his father in law, and did all that he had said. And Moses chose able men out of all Israel, and made them heads over the people, rulers of thousands, rulers of hundreds, rulers of fifties, and rulers of tens. And they judged the people at all seasons: the hard cases they brought unto Moses, but every small matter they judged themselves. And Moses let his father in law depart; and he went his way into his own land."

Moses was not above being instructed by his father-in-law. God had exalted him greatly and wrought wonders by his hand. Yet Moses did not reason that God had chosen him to instruct others, and had accomplished wonderful things by his hand, and he therefore needed not to be instructed. He gladly listened to the suggestions of his father-in-law, and adopted his plan as a wise arrangement.

Chapter 18—The Law of God

This chapter is based on Exodus 19 and 20.

After the children of Israel left Rephidim, they came to the "desert of Sinai, and had pitched in the wilderness; and there Israel camped before the mount. And Moses went up unto God, and the Lord called unto him out of the mountain, saying, Thus shalt thou say to the house of Jacob, and tell the children of Israel; Ye have seen what I did unto the Egyptians, and how I bare you on eagles' wings, and brought you unto Myself. Now therefore, if ye will obey My voice indeed, and keep My covenant, then ye shall be a peculiar treasure unto Me above all people: for all the earth is Mine: and ye shall be unto Me a kingdom of priests, and an holy nation. These are the words which thou shalt speak unto the children of Israel. And Moses came and called for the elders of the people, and laid before their faces all these words which the Lord commanded him. And all the people answered together, and said, All that the Lord hath spoken we will do. And Moses returned the words of the people unto the Lord."

The people here entered into a solemn covenant with God and accepted Him as their ruler, by which they became the peculiar subjects of His divine authority. "And the Lord said unto Moses, Lo, I come unto thee in a thick cloud, that the people may hear when I speak with thee, and believe thee for ever." When the Hebrews had met with difficulties in the way, they were disposed to murmur against Moses and Aaron, and accuse them of leading the host of Israel from Egypt to destroy them. God would honor Moses before them, that they might be led to confide in his instructions, and know that He had put His Spirit upon him.

Preparation to Approach God

The Lord then gave Moses express directions in regard to preparing the people for Him to approach nigh to them, that they might hear His law spoken, not by angels, but by Himself. "And the Lord said unto Moses, Go unto the people, and sanctify them today and tomorrow, and let them wash their clothes, and be ready against the third day: for the third day the Lord will come down in the sight of all the people upon Mount Sinai."

The people were required to refrain from worldly labor and care, and to possess devotional thoughts. God required them also to wash their clothes. He is no less particular now than He was then. He is a God of order, and requires His people now upon the earth to observe habits of strict cleanliness. And those who worship God with unclean garments and persons do not come before Him in an acceptable manner. He is not pleased with their lack of reverence for Him, and He will not accept the service of filthy worshipers, for they insult their Maker. The Creator of the heavens and of the earth considered cleanliness of so much importance that He said, "And let them wash their clothes."

"And thou shalt set bounds unto the people round about, saying, Take heed to yourselves, that ye go not up into the mount, or touch the border of it: whosoever toucheth the mount shall be surely put to death: there shall not an hand touch it, but he shall surely be stoned, or shot through; whether it be beast or man, it shall not live: when the trumpet soundeth long, they shall come up to the mount." This command was designed to impress the minds of this rebellious people with a profound veneration for God, the author and authority of their laws.

God's Manifestation in Awful Grandeur

"And it came to pass on the third day in the morning, that there were thunders and lightnings, and a thick cloud upon the mount, and the voice of the trumpet exceeding loud; so that all the people that was in the camp trembled." The angelic host that attended the divine Majesty summoned the people by a sound resembling that of a trumpet, which waxed louder and louder until the whole earth trembled.

"And Moses brought forth the people out of the camp to meet with God; and they stood at the nether part of the mount. And Mount Sinai was altogether on a smoke, because the Lord descended upon it in fire: and the smoke thereof ascended as the smoke of a furnace, and the whole mount quaked greatly." The divine Majesty descended in a cloud with a glorious retinue of angels, who appeared as flames of fire.

"And when the voice of the trumpet sounded long, and waxed louder and louder, Moses spake, and God answered him by a voice. And the Lord came down upon Mount Sinai, on the top of the mount: and the Lord called Moses up to the top of the mount; and Moses went up. And the Lord said unto Moses, Go down, charge the people, lest they break through unto the Lord to gaze, and many of them perish. And let the priests also, which come near to the Lord, sanctify themselves, lest the Lord break forth upon them."

Thus the Lord, in awful grandeur, spoke His law from Sinai, that the people might believe. He then accompanied the giving of His law with sublime exhibitions of His authority, that they might know that He is the only true and living God. Moses was not permitted to enter within the cloud of glory, but only draw nigh and enter the thick darkness which surrounded it. And he stood between the people and the Lord.

God's Law Proclaimed

After the Lord had given them such evidences of His power, He told them who He was: "I am the Lord thy God, which have brought thee out of the land of Egypt, out of the house of bondage." The same God who exalted His power among the Egyptians now spoke His law:

"Thou shalt have no other gods before Me.

"Thou shalt not make unto thee any graven image, or any likeness of any thing that is in heaven above, or that is in the earth beneath, or that is in the water under the earth: thou shalt not bow down thyself to them, nor serve them: for I the Lord thy God am a jealous God, visiting the iniquity of the fathers upon the children unto the third and fourth generation of them that hate Me; and shewing mercy unto thousands of them that love Me, and keep My commandments.

"Thou shalt not take the name of the Lord thy God in vain; for the Lord will not hold him guiltless that taketh His name in vain.

"Remember the Sabbath day, to keep it holy. Six days shalt thou labour, and do all thy work: but the seventh day is the Sabbath of the Lord thy God: in it thou shalt not do any work, thou, nor thy son, nor thy daughter, thy manservant, nor thy maidservant, nor thy cattle, nor thy stranger that is within thy gates: for in six days the Lord made heaven and earth, the sea, and all that in them is, and rested the seventh day: wherefore the Lord blessed the Sabbath day, and hallowed it.

"Honour thy father and thy mother; that thy days may be long upon the land which the Lord thy God giveth thee.

"Thou shalt not kill.

"Thou shalt not commit adultery.

"Thou shalt not steal.

"Thou shalt not bear false witness against thy neighbour.

"Thou shalt not covet thy neighbour's house, thou shalt not covet thy neighbour's wife, nor his manservant, nor his maidservant, nor his ox, nor his ass, nor anything that is thy neighbour's."

The first and second commandments spoken by Jehovah are precepts against idolatry; for idolatry, if practiced, would lead men to great lengths in sin and rebellion, and result in the offering of human sacrifices. God would guard against the least approach to such abominations. The first four commandments were given to show men their duty to God. The fourth is the connecting link between the great God and man. The Sabbath, especially, was given for the benefit of man and for the honor of God. The last six precepts show the duty of man to his fellow man.

The Sabbath was to be a sign between God and His people forever. In this manner was it to be a sign—all who should observe the Sabbath, signified by such observance that they were worshipers of the living God, the creator of the heavens and the earth. The Sabbath was to be a sign between God and His people as long as He should have a people upon the earth to serve Him.

"And all the people saw the thunderings, and the lightnings, and the noise of the trumpet, and the mountain smoking: and when the people saw it, they removed, and stood afar off. And they said unto Moses, Speak thou with us, and we will hear: but let not God speak with us, lest we die. And Moses said unto the people, Fear not: for God is come to prove you, and that His fear may be before your faces, that ye sin not.

"And the people stood afar off, and Moses drew near unto the thick darkness where God was. And the Lord said unto Moses, Thus thou shalt say unto the children of Israel, Ye have seen that I have talked with you from heaven." The majestic presence of God at Sinai, and the commotions in the earth occasioned by His presence, the fearful thunderings and lightnings which accompanied this visitation of God, so impressed the minds of the people with fear and reverence to His sacred majesty that they instinctively drew back from the awful presence of God, lest they should not be able to endure His terrible glory.

The Peril of Idolatry

Again, God would guard the children of Israel from idolatry. He said unto them, "Ye shall not make with Me gods of silver, neither shall ye make unto you gods of gold." They were in danger of imitating the example of the Egyptians, and making to themselves images to represent God.

The Lord said to Moses, "Behold, I send an Angel before thee, to keep thee in the way, and to bring thee into the place which I have prepared. Beware of Him, and obey His voice, provoke Him not; for He will not pardon your transgressions: for My name is in Him. But if thou shalt indeed obey His voice, and do all that I speak; then I will be an enemy unto thine enemies, and an adversary unto thine adversaries; for Mine Angel shall go before thee, and bring thee in unto the Amorites, and the Hittites, and the Perizzites, and the Canaanites, the Hivites, and the Jebusites: and I will cut them off." The angel who went before Israel was the Lord Jesus Christ. "Thou shalt not bow down to their gods, nor serve them, nor do after their works: but thou shalt utterly overthrow them, and quite break down their images. And ye shall serve the Lord your God, and He shall bless thy bread, and thy water; and I will take sickness away from the midst of thee." Exodus 23:24, 25.

God would have His people understand that He alone should be the object of their worship; and when they should overcome the idolatrous nations around them, they should not preserve any of the images of their worship, but utterly destroy them. Many of these heathen deities were very costly, and of beautiful workmanship, which might tempt those who had witnessed idol worship, so common in Egypt, to even regard these senseless objects with some degree of reverence. The Lord would have His people know that it was because of the idolatry of these nations, which had led them to every degree of wickedness, that He would use the Israelites as His instruments to punish them and destroy their gods.

"I will send My fear before thee, and will destroy all the people to whom thou shalt come, and I will make all thine enemies turn their backs unto thee. And I will send hornets before thee, which shall drive out the Hivite, the Canaanite, and the Hittite, from before thee. I will not drive them out from before thee in one year; lest the land become desolate, and the beast of the field multiply against thee. By little and little I will drive them out from before thee, until thou be increased, and inherit the land. And I will set thy bounds from the Red Sea even unto the sea of the Philistines, and from the desert unto the river: for I will deliver the inhabitants of the land into your hand: and thou shalt drive them out before thee. Thou shalt make no covenant with them, nor with their gods. They shall not dwell in thy land, lest they make thee sin against Me: for if thou serve their gods, it will surely be a snare unto thee." Exodus 23:27-33. These promises of God to His people were on condition of their obedience. If they would serve the Lord fully, He would do great things for them.

After Moses had received the judgments from the Lord, and had written them for the people, also the promises, on condition of obedience, the Lord said unto him, "Come up unto the Lord, thou, and Aaron, Nadab, and Abihu, and seventy of the elders of Israel; and worship ye afar off. And Moses alone shall come near the Lord: but they shall not come nigh; neither shall the people go up with him. And Moses came and told the people all the words of the Lord, and all the judgments: and all the people answered with one voice, and said, All the words which the Lord hath said will we do." Exodus 24:1-3.

Moses had written, not the Ten Commandments, but the judgments which God would have them observe, and the promises on condition that they would obey Him. He read this to the people, and they pledged themselves to obey all the words which the Lord had said. Moses then wrote their solemn pledge in a book and offered sacrifice unto God for the people. "And he took the book of the covenant, and read in the audience of the people: and they said, All that the Lord hath said will we do, and be obedient. And Moses took the blood, and sprinkled it on the people, and said, Behold the blood of the covenant which the Lord hath made with you concerning all these words." The people repeated their solemn pledge to the Lord to do all that He had said, and to be obedient. (Exodus 24:7, 8.)

God's Eternal Law

The law of God existed before man was created. The angels were governed by it. Satan fell because he transgressed the principles of God's government. After Adam and Eve were created, God made known to them His law. It was not then written, but was rehearsed to them by Jehovah.

The Sabbath of the fourth commandment was instituted in Eden. After God had made the world and created man upon the earth, He made the Sabbath for man. After Adam's sin and fall nothing was taken from the law of God. The principles of the Ten Commandments existed before the fall and were of a character suited to the condition of a holy order of beings. After the fall the principles of those precepts were not changed, but additional precepts were given to meet man in his fallen state.

A system was then established requiring the sacrificing of beasts, to keep before fallen man that which the serpent made Eve disbelieve, that the penalty of disobedience is death. The transgression of God's law made it necessary for Christ to die a sacrifice, and thus make a way possible for man to escape the penalty, and yet the honor of God's law be preserved. The system of sacrifices was to teach man humility, in view of his fallen condition, and lead him to repentance and to trust in God alone, through the promised Redeemer, for pardon for past transgression of His law. If the law of God had not been transgressed, there never would have been death, and there would have been no need of additional precepts to suit man's fallen condition.

Adam taught his descendants the law of God, which law was handed down to the faithful through successive generations. The continual transgression of God's law called for a flood of waters upon the earth. The law was preserved by Noah and his family, who for right-doing were saved in the ark by a miracle of God. Noah taught his descendants the Ten Commandments. The Lord preserved a people for Himself from Adam down, in whose hearts was His law. He says of Abraham, He "obeyed My voice, and kept My charge, My commandments, My statutes, and My laws." Genesis 26:5.

The Lord appeared unto Abraham, and said unto him:

"I am the Almighty God; walk before Me, and be thou perfect. And I will make My covenant between Me and thee, and will multiply thee exceedingly." Genesis 17:1, 2. "And I will establish My covenant between Me and thee and thy seed after thee in their generations, for an everlasting covenant, to be a God unto thee, and to thy seed after thee." Genesis 17:7.

He then required of Abraham and his seed, circumcision, which was a circle cut in the flesh, as a token that God had cut them out and separated them from all nations as His peculiar treasure. By this sign they solemnly pledged themselves that they would not intermarry with other nations, for by so doing they would lose their reverence for God and His holy law, and would become like the idolatrous nations around them.

By the act of circumcision they solemnly agreed to fulfill on their part the conditions of the covenant made with Abraham, to be separate from all nations and to be perfect. If the descendants of Abraham had kept separate from other nations, they would not have been seduced into idolatry. By keeping separate from other nations, a great temptation to engage in their sinful practices and rebel against God would be removed from them. They lost in a great measure their peculiar, holy character by mingling with the nations around them. To punish them, the Lord brought a famine upon their land, which compelled them to go down into Egypt to preserve their lives. But God did not forsake them while they were in Egypt, because of His covenant with Abraham. He suffered them to be oppressed by the Egyptians, that they might turn to Him in their distress, choose His righteous and merciful government, and obey His requirements.

There were but a few families that first went down into Egypt. These increased to a great multitude. Some were careful to instruct their children in the law of God, but many of the Israelites had witnessed so much idolatry that they had confused ideas of God's law. Those who feared God cried to Him in anguish of spirit to break their yoke of grievous bondage and bring them from the land of their captivity, that they might be free to serve Him. God heard their cries and raised up Moses as His instrument to accomplish the deliverance of His people. After they had left Egypt, and the waters of the Red Sea had been divided before them, the Lord proved them to see if they would trust in Him who had taken them, a nation from another nation, by signs, temptations, and wonders. But they failed to endure the trial. They murmured against God because of difficulties in the way and wished to return again to Egypt.

Written in Tables of Stone

To leave them without excuse, the Lord Himself condescended to come down upon Sinai, enshrouded in glory and surrounded by His angels, and in a most sublime and awful manner made known His law of Ten Commandments. He did not trust them to be taught by anyone, not even His angels, but spoke His law with an audible voice in the hearing of all the people. He did not, even then, trust them to the short memory of a people who were prone to forget His requirements, but wrote them with His own holy finger upon tables of stone. He would remove from them all possibility of mingling with His holy precepts any tradition, or of confusing His requirements with the practices of men.

He then came still closer to His people, who were so readily led astray, and would not leave them with merely the ten precepts of the Decalogue. He commanded Moses to write, as He should bid him, judgments and laws, giving minute directions in regard to what He required them to perform, and thereby guarded the ten precepts which He had engraved upon the tables of stone. These specific directions and requirements were given to draw erring man to the obedience of the moral law, which he is so prone to transgress.

If man had kept the law of God, as given to Adam after his fall, preserved in the ark by Noah, and observed by Abraham, there would have been no necessity for the ordinance of circumcision. And if the descendants of Abraham had kept the covenant, of which circumcision was a token or pledge, they would never have gone into idolatry or been suffered to go down into Egypt, and there would have been no necessity of God's proclaiming His law from Sinai and engraving it upon tables of stone and guarding it by definite directions in the judgments and statutes of Moses.

The Judgments and Statutes

Moses wrote these judgments and statutes from the mouth of God while he was with Him in the mount. If the people of God had obeyed the principles of the Ten Commandments, there would have been no need of the specific directions given to Moses, which he wrote in a book, relative to their duty to God and to one another. The definite directions which the Lord gave to Moses in regard to the duty of His people to one another, and to the stranger, are the principles of the Ten Commandments simplified and given in a definite manner, that they need not err.

The Lord instructed Moses definitely in regard to the ceremonial sacrifices which were to cease at the death of Christ. The system of sacrifices foreshadowed the offering of Christ as a Lamb without blemish.

The Lord first established the system of sacrificial offerings with Adam after his fall, which he taught to his descendants. This system was corrupted before the Flood, and by those who separated themselves from the faithful followers of God and engaged in the building of the tower of Babel. They sacrificed to gods of their own [making] instead of the God of heaven. They offered sacrifices not because they had faith in the Redeemer to come but because they thought they should please their gods by offering a great many beasts upon polluted idol altars. Their superstition led them to great extravagances. They taught the people that the more valuable the sacrifice the greater pleasure would it give their idol gods, and the greater would be the prosperity and riches of their nation. Hence, human beings were often sacrificed to these senseless idols. Those nations had laws and regulations to control the actions of the people, which were cruel in the extreme. Their laws were made by those whose hearts were not softened by grace; and while they would pass over the most debasing crimes, a small offense would call forth the most cruel punishment from those in authority.

Moses had this in view when he said to Israel, "Behold, I have taught you statutes and judgments, even as the Lord my God commanded me, that ye should do so in the land whither ye go to possess it. Keep therefore and do them; for this is your wisdom and your understanding in the sight of the nations, which shall hear all these statutes, and say, Surely this great nation is a wise and understanding people. For what nation is there so great, who hath God so nigh unto them, as the Lord our God is in all things that we call upon Him for? And what nation is there so great, that hath statutes and judgments so righteous as all this law, which I set before you this day?" Deuteronomy 4:5-8.

Chapter 19—The Sanctuary

This chapter is based on Exodus 25 to 40.

The tabernacle was made according to the commandment of God. The Lord raised up men and qualified them with more than natural abilities to perform the most ingenious work. Neither Moses nor those workmen were left to plan the form and workmanship of the building. God Himself devised the plan and gave it to Moses, with particular directions as to its size and form and the materials to be used, and specified every article of furniture which was to be in it. He presented before Moses a miniature model of the heavenly sanctuary and commanded him to make all things according to the pattern shown him in the mount. Moses wrote all the directions in a book and read them to the most influential people.

Then the Lord required the people to bring a free-will offering, to make Him a sanctuary, that He might dwell among them. "And all the congregation of the children of Israel departed from the presence of Moses. And they came, every one whose heart stirred him up, and every one whom his spirit made willing, and they brought the Lord's offering to the work of the tabernacle of the congregation, and for all His service, and for the holy garments. And they came, both men and women, as many as were willing hearted, and brought bracelets, and earrings, and rings, and tablets, all jewels of gold: and every man that offered offered an offering of gold unto the Lord."

Great and expensive preparations were necessary. Precious and costly materials must be collected. But the Lord accepted only the free-will offerings. Devotion to the work of God and sacrifice from the heart were first required in preparing a place for God. And while the building of the sanctuary was going on, and the people were bringing their offerings unto Moses, and he was presenting them to the workmen, all the wise men who wrought in the work examined the gifts and decided that the people had brought enough, and even more than they could use. And Moses proclaimed throughout the camp, saying, "Let neither man nor woman make any more work for the offering of the sanctuary. So the people were restrained from bringing."

Recorded for Later Generations

The repeated murmurings of the Israelites, and the visitations of God's wrath because of their transgressions, are recorded in sacred history for the benefit of God's people who should afterward live upon the earth, but more especially to prove a warning to those who should live near the close of time. Also their acts of devotion, their energy and liberality in bringing their free-will offerings to Moses are recorded for the benefit of the people of God. Their example in preparing material for the tabernacle so cheerfully is an example for all who truly love the worship of God. Those who prize the blessing of God's sacred presence, when preparing a building that He may meet with them, should manifest greater interest and zeal in the sacred work in proportion as they value their heavenly blessings higher than their earthly comforts. They should realize that they are preparing a house for God.

It is of some consequence that a building prepared expressly for God to meet with His people, should be arranged with care—made comfortable, neat, and convenient, for it is to be dedicated to God and presented to Him, and He is to be entreated to abide in that house and make it sacred by His holy presence. Enough should be willingly given to the Lord to liberally accomplish the work, and then the workmen be able to say, Bring no more offerings.

According to the Pattern

After the building of the tabernacle was completed, Moses examined all the work, and compared it with the pattern, and directions he had received of God, and he saw that every part of it agreed with the pattern; and he blessed the people.

God gave a pattern of the ark to Moses, with special directions how to make it. The ark was made to contain the tables of stone, on which God engraved, with His own finger, the Ten Commandments. It was in form like a chest, and was overlaid and inlaid with pure gold. It was ornamented with crowns of gold round about the top. The cover of this sacred chest was the mercy seat, made of solid gold. On each end of the mercy seat was fixed a cherub of pure, solid gold. Their faces were turned toward each other and were looking reverentially downward toward the mercy seat, which represented all the heavenly angels looking with interest and reverence upon the law of God deposited in the ark in the heavenly sanctuary. These cherubs had wings. One wing of each angel was stretched forth on high, while the other wing of each angel covered his form. The ark of the earthly sanctuary was the pattern of the true ark in heaven.

There, beside the heavenly ark, stand living angels, at either end of the ark, each with one wing overshadowing the mercy seat, and stretching forth on high, while the other wings are folded over their forms in token of reverence and humility.

In the earthly ark Moses was required to place the tables of stone. These were called the tables of the testimony; and the ark was called the ark of the testimony, because they contained God's testimony in the Ten Commandments.

Two Apartments

The tabernacle was composed of two apartments, separated by a curtain, or vail. All the furniture of the tabernacle was made of solid gold, or plated with gold. The curtains of the tabernacle were of a variety of colors, most beautifully arranged, and in these curtains were wrought, with threads of gold and silver, cherubim, which were to represent the angelic host, who are connected with the work of the heavenly sanctuary and who are ministering angels to the saints upon the earth.

Within the second vail was placed the ark of the testimony, and the beautiful and rich curtain was drawn before the sacred ark. This curtain did not reach to the top of the building. The glory of God, which was above the mercy seat, could be seen from both apartments, but in a much less degree from the first apartment.

Directly before the ark, but separated by the curtain, was the golden altar of incense. The fire upon this altar was kindled by the Lord Himself, and was sacredly cherished by feeding it with holy incense, which filled the sanctuary with its fragrant cloud day and night. Its fragrance extended for miles around the tabernacle. When the priest offered the incense before the Lord he looked to the mercy seat. Although he could not see it he knew it was there, and as the incense arose like a cloud, the glory of the Lord descended upon the mercy seat and filled the most holy place and was visible in the holy place, and the glory often so filled both apartments that the priest was unable to officiate and was obliged to stand at the door of the tabernacle.

The priest in the holy place, directing his prayer by faith to the mercy seat, which he could not see, represents the people of God directing their prayers to Christ before the mercy seat in the heavenly sanctuary. They cannot behold their Mediator with the natural eye, but with the eye of faith they see Christ before the mercy seat and direct their prayers to Him, and with assurance claim the benefits of His mediation.

These sacred apartments had no windows to admit light. The candlestick was made of purest gold and was kept burning night and day, and gave light to both apartments. The light of the lamps upon the candlestick reflected upon the boards plated with gold, at the sides of the building, and upon the sacred furniture and upon the curtains of beautiful colors with cherubim wrought with threads of gold and silver, which appearance was glorious beyond description. No language can describe the beauty and loveliness and sacred glory which these apartments presented. The gold in the sanctuary reflected the colors of the curtains, which appeared like the different colors of the rainbow.

Only once a year could the high priest enter into the most holy place, after the most careful and solemn preparation. No mortal eye but that of the high priest could look upon the sacred grandeur of that apartment, because it was the especial dwelling place of God's visible glory. The high priest always entered it with trembling, while the people waited his return with solemn silence. Their earnest desires were to God for His blessing. Before the mercy seat God conversed with the high priest. If he remained an unusual time in the most holy, the people were often terrified, fearing that because of their sins or some sin of the priest, the glory of the Lord had slain him. But when the sound of the tinkling of the bells upon his garments was heard, they were greatly relieved. He then came forth and blessed the people.

After the work of the tabernacle was finished, "a cloud covered the tent of the congregation, and the glory of the Lord filled the tabernacle. And Moses was not able to enter into the tent of the congregation, because the cloud abode thereon, and the glory of the Lord filled the tabernacle." For "the cloud of the Lord was upon the tabernacle by day, and fire was on it by night, in the sight of all the house of Israel, throughout all their journeys."

The tabernacle was constructed so as to be taken to pieces and borne with them in all their journeyings.

The Guiding Cloud

The Lord directed the Israelites in all their travels through the wilderness. When it was for the good of the people and the glory of God that they should pitch their tents in a certain place and there abide, God signified His will to them by the pillar of cloud resting low directly over the tabernacle. And there it remained until God would have them journey again. Then the cloud of glory was lifted up high above the tabernacle, and then they journeyed again.

In all their journeyings they observed perfect order. Every tribe bore a standard, with the sign of their father's house on it, and every tribe was commanded to pitch by their own standard. And when they traveled the different tribes marched in order, every tribe under their own standard. When they rested from their journeyings, the tabernacle was erected, and then the different tribes pitched their tents in order, in just such a position as God commanded, around the tabernacle, at a distance from it.

When the people journeyed, the ark of the covenant was borne before them. "And the cloud of the Lord was upon them by day, when they went out of the camp. And it came to pass, when the ark set forward, that Moses said, Rise up, Lord, and let Thine enemies be scattered; and let them that hate Thee flee before Thee. And when it rested, he said, Return, O Lord, unto the many thousands of Israel."

Chapter 20—The Spies and Their Report

This chapter is based on Numbers 13, 14.

The Lord commanded Moses to send men to search the land of Canaan, which He would give unto the children of Israel. A ruler of each tribe was to be selected for this purpose. They went and, after forty days, returned from their search, and came before Moses and Aaron and all the congregation of Israel, and showed them the fruit of the land. All agreed that it was a good land, and they exhibited the rich fruit which they had brought as evidence. One cluster of grapes was so large that two men carried it between them on a staff. They also brought of the figs and the pomegranates, which grew there in abundance.

After they had spoken of the fertility of the land, all but two spoke very discouragingly of their being able to possess it. They said that the people were very strong that dwelt in the land, and the cities were surrounded with great and high walls; and, more than all this, they saw the children of the giant Anak there. They then described how the people were situated around Canaan, and the impossibility of their ever being able to possess it.

As the people listened to this report they gave vent to their disappointment with bitter reproaches and wailing. They did not wait and reflect and reason that God, who had brought them out thus far, would certainly give them the land. But they yielded to discouragement at once. They limited the power of the Holy One and trusted not in God, who had hitherto led them. They reproached Moses and murmuringly said to one another, This, then, is the end of all our hopes. This is the land that we have been traveling from Egypt to obtain.

Caleb and Joshua sought to obtain a hearing, but the people were so excited that they could not command themselves to listen to these two men. After they were calmed a little, Caleb ventured to speak. He said to the people, "Let us go up at once, and possess it; for we are well able to overcome it." But the men that went up with him said, "We are not able to go up against the people; for they are stronger than we." And they continued to repeat their evil report, and declared that all the men were of great stature. "And there we saw the giants, the sons of Anak, which come of the giants: and we were in our own sight as grasshoppers, and so we were in their sight.

Israel Murmurs Again

"And all the congregation lifted up their voice, and cried; and the people wept that night. And all the children of Israel murmured against Moses and against Aaron: and the whole congregation said unto them, Would God that we had died in the land of Egypt! or would God we had died in this wilderness! And wherefore hath the Lord brought us unto this land, to fall by the sword, that our wives and our children should be a prey? were it not better for us to return into Egypt? And they said one to another, Let us make a captain, and let us return into Egypt. Then Moses and Aaron fell on their faces before all the assembly of the congregation of the children of Israel."

The Israelites not only gave vent to their complaints against Moses but accused God Himself of dealing deceitfully with them by promising them a land which they were unable to possess. Their rebellious spirit here rose so high that, forgetful of the strong arm of Omnipotence which had brought them out of the land of Egypt and had thus far conducted them by a series of miracles, they resolved to choose a commander to lead them back to Egypt, where they had been slaves and had suffered so many hardships. They actually appointed them a captain, thus discarding Moses, their patient, suffering leader; and they murmured bitterly against God.

Moses and Aaron fell upon their faces before the Lord in the presence of all the assembly of the congregation, to implore the mercy of God in favor of a rebellious people. But their distress and grief were too great for utterance. They remained upon their faces in utter silence. Caleb and Joshua rent their clothes as an expression of the greatest sorrow. "And they spake unto all the company of the children of Israel, saying, The land, which we passed through to search it, is an exceeding good land. If the Lord delight in us, then He will bring us into this land, and give it us; a land which floweth with milk and honey. Only rebel not ye against the Lord, neither fear ye the people of the land; for they are bread for us: their defence is departed from them, and the Lord is with us: fear them not."

"Their defence is departed from them." That is, the Canaanites had filled up the measure of their iniquity, and the divine protection was withdrawn from them, and they felt perfectly secure and were unprepared for battle; and, by the covenant of God, the land is ensured to us. Instead of these words having the designed effect upon the people, they increased their determined rebellion. They became in a rage and cried out with a loud and angry cry that Caleb and

Joshua should be stoned, which would have been done had not the Lord interposed by a most signal display of His terrible glory in the tabernacle of the congregation before all the children of Israel.

Moses' Prevailing Plea

Moses went into the tabernacle to converse with God. "And the Lord said unto Moses, How long will this people provoke Me? and how long will it be ere they believe Me, for all the signs which I have shewed among them? I will smite them with the pestilence, and disinherit them, and will make of thee a greater nation and mightier than they. And Moses said unto the Lord, Then the Egyptians shall hear it, (for Thou broughtest up this people in Thy might from among them;) and they will tell it to the inhabitants of this land: for they have heard that Thou Lord art among this people, that Thou Lord art seen face to face, and that Thy cloud standeth over them, and that Thou goest before them, by day time in a pillar of a cloud, and in a pillar of fire by night. Now if Thou shalt kill all this people as one man, then the nations which have heard the fame of Thee will speak, saying, Because the Lord was not able to bring this people unto the land which He sware unto them, therefore He hath slain them in the wilderness."

Moses again refuses to have Israel destroyed and himself made a mightier nation than was Israel. This favored servant of God manifests his love for Israel and shows his zeal for the glory of his Maker and the honor of his people: As Thou hast forgiven this people from Egypt even until now, Thou hast been long-suffering and merciful hitherto toward this ungrateful people; however unworthy they may be, Thy mercy is the same. He pleads, Wilt Thou not, therefore, spare them this once, and add this one more instance of divine patience to the many Thou hast already given?

"And the Lord said, I have pardoned according to thy word: but as truly as I live, all the earth shall be filled with the glory of the Lord. Because all those men which have seen My glory, and My miracles, which I did in Egypt and in the wilderness, and have tempted Me now these ten times, and have not hearkened to My voice; surely they shall not see the land which I sware unto their fathers, neither shall any of them that provoked Me see it: but My servant Caleb, because he had another spirit with him, and hath followed Me fully, him will I bring into the land whereinto he went; and his seed shall possess it."

Back to the Wilderness

The Lord bade the Hebrews return and go into the wilderness by the way of the Red Sea. They were very near the good land, but, by their wicked rebellion, they forfeited the protection of God. Had they received the report of Caleb and Joshua, and gone immediately up, God would have given them the land of Canaan. But they were unbelieving and showed such an insolent spirit against God that they brought upon themselves the denunciation that they should never enter the Promised Land. It was in pity and mercy that God sent them back by the Red Sea, for the Amalekites and Canaanites, while they were delaying and murmuring, heard of the spies and prepared themselves to make war with the children of Israel.

"And the Lord spake unto Moses and unto Aaron, saying, How long shall I bear with this evil congregation, which murmur against Me? I have heard the murmurings of the children of Israel, which they murmur against Me." The Lord told Moses and Aaron to say to the people that He would do to them as they had spoken. They had said, "Would God we had died in the land of Egypt! or would God we had died in this wilderness!" Now God would take them at their word. He told His servants to say to them that they should fall in the wilderness, from twenty years old and upward, because of their rebellion and murmurings against the Lord. Only Caleb and Joshua should go unto the land of Canaan. "But your little ones, which ye said should be a prey, them will I bring in, and they shall know the land which ye have despised."

The Lord declared that the children of the Hebrews should wander in the wilderness forty years, reckoning from the time they left Egypt, because of the rebellion of their parents, until the parents should all die. Thus should they bear and suffer the consequence of their iniquity forty years, according to the number of days they were searching the land, a day for a year. "And ye shall know My breach of promise." They should fully realize that it was the punishment for their idolatry and rebellious murmurings which had obliged the Lord to change His purpose concerning them. Caleb and Joshua were promised a reward in preference to all the host of Israel, because the latter had forfeited all claim to God's favor and protection.

Chapter 21—The Sin of Moses

This chapter is based on Numbers 20.

Again the congregation of Israel was brought into the wilderness, to the very place where God proved them soon after leaving Egypt. The Lord brought them water out of the rock, which had continued to flow until just before they came again to the rock, when the Lord caused that living stream to cease, to prove His people again, to see if they would endure the trial of their faith or would again murmur against Him.

When the Hebrews were thirsty and could find no water, they became impatient and did not remember the power of God which had, nearly forty years before, brought them water out of the rock. Instead of trusting God, they complained of Moses and Aaron, and said to them, "Would God that we had died when our brethren died before the Lord!" That is, they wished that they had been of that number who had been destroyed by the plague in the rebellion of Korah, Dathan, and Abiram.

They angrily inquired, "Why have ye brought up the congregation of the Lord into this wilderness, that we and our cattle should die there? And wherefore have ye made us to come up out of Egypt, to bring us in unto this evil place? it is no place of seed, or of figs, or of vines, or of pomegranates; neither is there any water to drink.

"And Moses and Aaron went from the presence of the assembly unto the door of the tabernacle of the congregation, and they fell upon their faces: and the glory of the Lord appeared unto them. And the Lord spake unto Moses, saying, Take the rod, and gather thou the assembly together, thou, and Aaron thy brother, and speak ye unto the rock before their eyes; and it shall give forth his water, and thou shalt bring forth to them water out of the rock: so thou shalt give the congregation and their beasts to drink. And Moses took the rod from before the Lord, as He commanded him.

Moses Yields to Impatience

"And Moses and Aaron gathered the congregation together before the rock; and he said unto them, Hear now, ye rebels; must we fetch you water out of this rock? And Moses lifted up his hand, and with his rod he smote the rock twice:

and the water came out abundantly, and the congregation drank, and their beasts also. And the Lord spake unto Moses and Aaron, Because ye believed Me not, to sanctify Me in the eyes of the children of Israel, therefore ye shall not bring this congregation into the land which I have given them."

Here Moses sinned. He became wearied with the continual murmurings of the people against him, and at the commandment of the Lord, took the rod, and, instead of speaking to the rock, as God commanded him, he smote it with the rod twice, after saying, "Must we fetch you water out of this rock?" He here spoke unadvisedly with his lips. He did not say, God will now show you another evidence of His power and bring you water out of this rock. He did not ascribe the power and glory to God for causing water to again flow from the flinty rock, and therefore did not magnify Him before the people. For this failure on the part of Moses, God would not permit him to lead the people to the Promised Land.

This necessity for the manifestation of God's power made the occasion one of great solemnity, and Moses and Aaron should have improved it to make a favorable impression upon the people. But Moses was stirred, and in impatience and anger with the people, because of their murmurings, he said, "Hear now, ye rebels, must we fetch you water out of this rock?" In thus speaking he virtually admitted to murmuring Israel that they were correct in charging him with leading them from Egypt. God had forgiven the people greater transgressions than this error on the part of Moses, but He could not regard a sin in a leader of His people as in those who were led. He could not excuse the sin of Moses and permit him to enter the Promised Land.

The Lord here gave His people unmistakable proof that He who had wrought such a wonderful deliverance for them in bringing them from Egyptian bondage, was the mighty Angel, and not Moses, who was going before them in all their travels, and of whom He had said, "Behold, I send an Angel before thee, to keep thee in the way, and to bring thee into the place which I have prepared. Beware of Him, and obey His voice, provoke Him not; for He will not pardon your transgressions: for My name is in Him." Exodus 23:20, 21.

Moses took glory to himself which belonged to God, and made it necessary for God to do that in his case which should forever satisfy rebellious Israel that it was not Moses who had led them from Egypt, but God Himself. The Lord had committed to Moses the burden of leading His people, while the mighty Angel went before them in all their journeyings and directed all their travels. Because they were so ready to forget that God was leading them by His Angel, and to ascribe to man that which God's power alone could perform, He had proved them and tested them, to see whether they would obey Him. At every trial they failed. Instead of believing in, and acknowledging, God, who had strewed their path with evidences of His power and signal tokens of His care and love, they distrusted Him and ascribed their leaving Egypt to Moses, charging him as the cause of all their disasters. Moses had borne with their stubbornness with remarkable forbearance. At one time they threatened to stone him.

The Heavy Penalty

The Lord would remove this impression forever from their minds, by forbidding Moses to enter the Promised Land. The Lord had highly exalted Moses. He had revealed to him His great glory. He had taken him into a sacred nearness with Himself upon the mount, and had condescended to talk with him as a man speaketh with a friend. He had communicated to Moses, and through him to the people, His will, His statutes, and His laws. His being thus exalted and honored of God made his error of greater magnitude. Moses repented of his sin and humbled himself greatly before God. He related to all Israel his sorrow for his sin. The result of his sin he did not conceal, but told them that for thus failing to ascribe glory to God, he could not lead them to the Promised Land. He then asked them, if this error upon his part was so great as to be thus corrected of God, how God would regard their repeated murmurings in charging him (Moses) with the uncommon visitations of God because of their sins.

For this single instance, Moses had allowed the impression to be entertained that he had brought them water out of the rock, when he should have magnified the name of the Lord among His people. The Lord would now settle the matter with His people, that Moses was merely a man, following the guidance and direction of a mightier than he, even the Son of God. In this He would leave them without doubt. Where much is given, much is required. Moses had been highly favored with special views of God's majesty. The light and glory of God had been imparted to him in rich abundance. His face had reflected upon the people the glory that the Lord had let shine upon him. All will be judged according to the privileges they have had, and the light and benefits bestowed.

The sins of good men, whose general deportment has been worthy of imitation, are peculiarly offensive to God. They cause Satan to triumph, and to taunt the angels of God with the failings of God's chosen instruments, and give the unrighteous occasion to lift themselves up against God. The Lord had Himself led Moses in a special manner, and had revealed to him His glory, as to no other upon the earth. He was naturally impatient, but had taken hold firmly of the grace of God and so humbly implored wisdom from heaven that he was strengthened from God and had overcome his impatience so that he was called of God the meekest man upon the face of the whole earth.

Aaron died at Mount Hor, for the Lord had said that he should not enter the Promised Land, because, with Moses, he had sinned at the time of bringing water from the rock at Meribah. Moses and the sons of Aaron buried him in the mount, that the people might not be tempted to make too great ceremony over his body, and be guilty of the sin of idolatry.

Chapter 22—The Death of Moses

This chapter is based on Deuteronomy 31-34.

Moses was soon to die, and he was commanded to gather the children of Israel together before his death and relate to them all the journeyings of the Hebrew host since their departure from Egypt, and all the great transgressions of their fathers, which brought His judgments upon them, and compelled Him to say that they should not enter the Promised Land. Their fathers had died in the wilderness, according to the word of the Lord. Their children had grown up, and to them the promise was to be fulfilled of possessing the land of Canaan. Many of these were small children when the law was given, and they had no remembrance of the grandeur of the event. Others were born in the wilderness, and lest they should not realize the necessity of their obeying the Ten Commandments and all the laws and judgments given to Moses, he was instructed of God to recapitulate the Ten Commandments, and all the circumstances connected with the giving of the law.

Moses had written in a book all the laws and judgments given him of God, and had faithfully recorded all His instructions given them by the way, and all the miracles which He had performed for them, and all the murmurings of the children of Israel. Moses had also recorded his being overcome in consequence of their murmurings.

Final Instruction to Israel

All the people were assembled before him, and he read the events of their past history out of the book which he had written. He read also the promises of God to them if they would be obedient, and the curses which would come upon them if they were disobedient.

Moses told them that, for their rebellion, the Lord had several times purposed to destroy them, but he had interceded for them so earnestly that God had graciously spared them. He reminded them of the miracles which the Lord did unto Pharaoh and all the land of Egypt. He said to them, "But your eyes have seen all the great acts of the Lord which He did. Therefore shall ye keep all the commandments which I command you this day, that ye may be strong, and go in and possess the land, whither ye go to possess it." Deuteronomy 11:7, 8.

Moses especially warned the children of Israel against being seduced into idolatry. He earnestly charged them to obey the commandments of God. If they would prove obedient and love the Lord and serve Him with their undivided affections, He would give them rain in due season and cause their vegetation to flourish, and increase their cattle. They should also enjoy especial and exalted privileges, and should triumph over their enemies.

Moses instructed the children of Israel in an earnest, impressive manner. He knew that it was his last opportunity to address them. He then finished writing in a book all the laws, judgments, and statutes which God had given him, also the various regulations respecting sacrificial offerings. He placed the book in the hands of men in the sacred office and requested that, for safe keeping, it should be put in the side of the ark, for God's care was continually upon that sacred chest. This book of Moses was to be preserved, that the judges of Israel might refer to it if any case should come up to make it necessary. An erring people often understand God's requirements to suit their own case; therefore the book of Moses was preserved in a most sacred place, for future reference.

Moses closed his last instructions to the people by a most powerful, prophetic address. It was pathetic and eloquent. By inspiration of God he blessed separately the tribes of Israel. In his closing words he dwelt largely upon the majesty of God and the excellency of Israel, which would ever continue if they would obey God and take hold of His strength.

The Decease and Resurrection of Moses

"And Moses went up from the plains of Moab unto the mountain of Nebo, to the top of Pisgah, that is over against Jericho. And the Lord shewed him all the land of Gilead, unto Dan. And all Naphtali, and the land of Ephraim, and Manasseh, and all the land of Judah, unto the utmost sea, and the south, and the plain of the valley of Jericho, the city of palm trees, unto Zoar. And the Lord said unto him, This is the land which I sware unto Abraham, unto Isaac, and unto Jacob, saying, I will give it unto thy seed: I have caused thee to see it with thine eyes, but thou shalt not go over thither. So Moses the servant of the Lord died there in the land of Moab, according to the word of the Lord. And He buried him in a valley in the land of Moab, over against Beth-peor: but no man knoweth of his sepulchre unto this day. And Moses was an hundred and twenty years old when he died: his eye was not dim, nor his natural force abated." Deuteronomy 34:1-7.

It was not the will of God that anyone should go up with Moses to the top of Pisgah. There he stood, upon a high prominence on Pisgah's top, in the presence of God and heavenly angels. After he had viewed Canaan to his satisfaction, he lay down, like a tired warrior, to rest. Sleep came upon him, but it was the sleep of death. Angels took his body and buried it in the valley. The Israelites could never find the place where he was buried. His secret burial was to prevent the people from sinning against the Lord by committing idolatry over his body.

Satan exulted that he had succeeded in causing Moses to sin against God. For this transgression Moses came under the dominion of death. If he had continued faithful, and his life had not been marred with that one transgression, in failing to give God the glory of bringing water from the rock, he would have entered the Promised Land, and would have been translated to heaven without seeing death. Michael, or Christ, with the angels that buried Moses, came down from heaven, after he had remained in the grave a short time, and resurrected him and took him to heaven.

As Christ and the angels approached the grave, Satan and his angels appeared at the grave and were guarding the body of Moses, lest it should be removed. As Christ and His angels drew nigh, Satan resisted their approach, but was compelled, by the glory and power of Christ and His angels, to fall back. Satan claimed the body of Moses, because of his one transgression; but Christ meekly referred him to His Father, saying, "The Lord rebuke thee." Jude 1:9. Christ told Satan that He knew Moses had humbly repented of this one wrong, that no stain rested upon his character, and that his name in the heavenly book of records stood untarnished. Then Christ resurrected the body of Moses, which Satan had claimed.

At the transfiguration of Christ, Moses, and Elijah who had been translated, were sent to talk with Christ in regard to His sufferings, and be the bearers of God's glory to His dear Son. Moses had been greatly honored of God. He had been privileged to talk with God face to face, as a man speaketh with his friend. And God had revealed to him His excellent glory, as He had never done to any other.

Chapter 23—Entering the Promised Land

This chapter is based on Joshua 1; 3-6; 23 and 24.

After the death of Moses, Joshua was to be the leader of Israel, to conduct them to the Promised Land. He had been prime minister to Moses during the greater part of the time the Israelites had wandered in the wilderness. He had seen the wonderful works of God wrought by Moses, and well understood the disposition of the people. He was one of the twelve spies who were sent out to search the Promised Land, and one of the two who gave a faithful account of its richness and who encouraged the people to go up in the strength of God to possess it. He was well qualified for this important office. The Lord promised Joshua to be with him as He had been with Moses, and to make Canaan fall an easy conquest to him, provided he would be faithful to observe all His commandments. He was anxious as to how he should execute his commission in leading the people to the land of Canaan, but this encouragement removed his fears.

Joshua commanded the children of Israel to prepare for a three-day journey, and that all the men of war should go out to battle. "And they answered Joshua, saying, All that thou commandest us, we will do, and whithersoever thou sendest us, we will go. According as we hearkened unto Moses in all things, so will we hearken unto thee: only the Lord thy God be with thee, as He was with Moses. Whosoever he be that doth rebel against thy commandment, and will not hearken unto thy words in all that thou commandest him, he shall be put to death: only be strong and of a good courage."

The passage of the Israelites over Jordan was to be miraculous. "And Joshua said unto the people, Sanctify yourselves: for tomorrow the Lord will do wonders among you. And Joshua spake unto the priests, saying, Take up the ark of the covenant, and pass over before the people. And they took up the ark of the covenant, and went before the people. And the Lord said unto Joshua, This day will I begin to magnify thee in the sight of all Israel, that they may know that, as I was with Moses, so I will be with thee."

Crossing Jordan

The priests were to go before the people and bear the ark containing the law of God. And as their feet were dipped in the brim of Jordan, the waters were cut off from above, and the priests passed on, bearing the ark, which was a symbol of the Divine Presence; and the Hebrew host followed. When the priests were halfway over Jordan, they were commanded to stand in the bed of the river until all the host of Israel had passed over. Here the then existing generation of the Israelites were convinced that the waters of Jordan were subject to the same power that their fathers had seen displayed at the Red Sea forty years before. Many of these had passed through the Red Sea when they were children. Now they pass over Jordan, men of war, fully equipped for battle.

After all the host of Israel had passed over Jordan, Joshua commanded the priests to come up out of the river. As soon as the priests, bearing the ark of the covenant, came up out of the river, and stood on dry land, Jordan rolled on as before and overflowed all his banks. This wonderful miracle performed for the Israelites greatly increased their faith. That this wonderful miracle might never be forgotten, the Lord directed Joshua to command that men of note, one of each tribe, take up stones from the bed of the river, the place where the priests' feet stood while the Hebrew host was passing over, and bear them upon their shoulders, and erect a monument in Gilgal, to keep in remembrance the fact that Israel passed over Jordan on dry land. After the priests had come up from Jordan, God removed His mighty hand, and the waters rushed like a mighty cataract down their own channel.

When all the kings of the Amorites and the kings of the Canaanites heard that the Lord had stayed the waters of Jordan before the children of Israel, their hearts melted with fear. The Israelites had slain two of the kings of Moab, and their miraculous passage over the swollen and impetuous Jordan filled them with the greatest terror. Joshua then circumcised all the people which had been born in the wilderness. After this ceremony they kept the passover in the plains of Jericho. "And the Lord said unto Joshua, This day have I rolled away the reproach of Egypt from off you."

Heathen nations had reproached the Lord and His people because the Hebrews had not possessed the land of Canaan, which they expected to inherit soon after leaving Egypt. Their enemies had triumphed because they had so long wandered in the wilderness, and they proudly lifted themselves up against God, declaring that He was not able to lead them into the land of Canaan. They had now passed over Jordan on dry land, and their enemies could no longer reproach them.

The manna had continued up to this time, but now as the Israelites were about to possess Canaan and eat of the fruit of the land, they had no more need of it, and it ceased.

The Captain of the Lord's Host

As Joshua withdrew from the armies of Israel, to meditate and pray for God's special presence to attend him, he saw a man of lofty stature, clad in warlike garments, with his sword drawn in his hand. Joshua did not recognize him as one of the armies of Israel, and yet he had no appearance of being an enemy. In his zeal he accosted him, and said, "Art thou for us, or for our adversaries? And He said, Nay; but as captain of the host of the Lord am I now come. And Joshua fell on his face to the earth, and did worship, and said unto Him, What saith my Lord unto His servant? And the Captain of the Lord's host said unto Joshua, Loose thy shoe from off thy foot; for the place whereon thou standest is holy. And Joshua did so."

This was no common angel. It was the Lord Jesus Christ, He who had conducted the Hebrews through the wilderness, enshrouded in the pillar of fire by night and the pillar of cloud by day. The place was made sacred by His presence; therefore Joshua was commanded to put off his shoes.

The Lord then instructed Joshua what course to pursue in order to take Jericho. All the men of war should be commanded to compass the city once each day for six days, and on the seventh day they should go around Jericho seven times.

The Taking of Jericho

"And Joshua the son of Nun called the priests, and said unto them, Take up the ark of the covenant, and let seven priests bear seven trumpets of rams' horns before the ark of the Lord. And he said unto the people, Pass on, and compass the city, and let him that is armed pass on before the ark of the Lord. And it came to pass, when Joshua had spoken unto the people, that the seven priests bearing seven trumpets of rams' horns passed on before the Lord, and blew with the trumpets: and the ark of the covenant followed them.

"And the armed men went before the priests that blew with the trumpets, and the rearward came after the ark, the priests going on, and blowing with the trumpets. And Joshua had commanded the people, saying, Ye shall not shout, nor make any noise with your voice, neither shall any word proceed out of your mouth, until the day I bid you shout; then shall ye shout. So the ark of the Lord compassed the city, going about it once: and they came into the camp, and lodged in the camp."

The Hebrew host marched in perfect order. First went a select body of armed men, clad in their warlike dress, not now to exercise their skill in arms, but only to believe and obey the directions given them. Next followed seven priests with trumpets. Then came the ark of God, glittering with gold, a halo of glory hovering over it, borne by priests in their rich and peculiar dress denoting their sacred office. The vast army of Israel followed in perfect order, each tribe under its respective standard. Thus they compassed the city with the ark of God. No sound was heard but the tread of that mighty host, and the solemn voice of the trumpets, echoed by the hills, and resounding through the city of Jericho.

With wonder and alarm the watchmen of that doomed city mark every move, and report to those in authority. They cannot tell what all this display means. Some ridicule the idea of that city's being taken in this manner, while others are awed, as they behold the splendor of the ark and the solemn and dignified appearance of the priests and the host of Israel following, with Joshua at their head. They remember that the Red Sea, forty years before, parted before them, and that a passage had just been prepared for them through the river Jordan. They are too much terrified to sport. They are strict to keep the gates of the city closely shut, and mighty warriors to guard each gate.

For six days the armies of Israel performed their circuit around the city. On the seventh day they compassed Jericho seven times. The people were commanded, as usual, to be silent. The voice of the trumpets alone was to be heard. The people were to observe, and when the trumpeters should make a longer blast than usual, then all were to shout with a loud voice, for God had given them the city. "And it came to pass on the seventh day, that they rose early about the dawning of the day, and compassed the city after the same manner seven times: only on that day they compassed the city seven times. And it came to pass at the seventh time, when the priests blew with the trumpets, Joshua said unto the people, Shout; for the Lord hath given you the city." "So the people shouted when the priests blew with the trumpets: and it came to pass, when the people heard the sound of the trumpet, and the people shouted with a great shout, that the wall fell down flat, so that the people went up into the city, every man straight before him, and they took the city."

God intended to show the Israelites that the conquest of Canaan was not to be ascribed to them. The Captain of the Lord's host overcame Jericho. He and His angels were engaged in the conquest. Christ commanded the armies of heaven to throw down the walls of Jericho and prepare an entrance for Joshua and the armies of Israel. God, in this wonderful miracle, not only strengthened the faith of His people in His power to subdue their enemies, but rebuked their former unbelief.

Jericho had defied the armies of Israel and the God of heaven. And as they beheld the host of Israel marching around their city once each day, they were alarmed; but they looked at their strong defenses, their firm and high walls, and felt sure that they could resist any attack. But when their firm walls suddenly tottered and fell with a stunning crash, like peals of loudest thunder, they were paralyzed with terror and could offer no resistance.

Joshua a Wise, Consecrated Leader

No stain rested upon the holy character of Joshua. He was a wise leader. His life was wholly devoted to God. Before he died he assembled the Hebrew host, and, following the example of Moses, he recapitulated their travels in the wilderness and also the merciful dealings of God with them. He then eloquently addressed them. He related to them that the king of Moab warred against them and called Balaam to curse them; but God "would not hearken unto Balaam, therefore he blessed you still." He then said to them, "And if it seem evil unto you to serve the Lord, choose you this day whom you will serve; whether the gods which your fathers served that were on the other side of the flood, or the gods of the Amorites, in whose land ye dwell: but as for me and my house, we will serve the Lord.

"And the people answered and said, God forbid that we should forsake the Lord, to serve other gods; for the Lord our God, He it is that brought us up and our fathers out of the land of Egypt, from the house of bondage, and which did those great signs in our sight, and preserved us in all the way wherein we went, and among all the people through whom we passed."

The people renewed their covenant with Joshua. They said unto him, "The Lord our God will we serve, and His voice will we obey." Joshua wrote the words of their covenant in the book containing the laws and statutes given to Moses. Joshua was loved and respected by all Israel, and his death was much lamented by them.

Chapter 24—The Ark of God and the Fortunes of Israel

This chapter is based on 1 Samuel 3-6; 2 Samuel 6 and 1 Kings 8.

The ark of God was a sacred chest, made to be the depository of the Ten Commandments, which law was the representative of God Himself. This ark was considered the glory and strength of Israel. The token of the Divine Presence abode upon it day and night. The priests who ministered before it were sacredly consecrated to the holy office. They wore a breastplate bordered with precious stones of different materials, the same as compose the twelve foundations of the city of God. Within the border were the names of the twelve tribes of Israel, graven on precious stones set in gold. This was a very rich and beautiful work, suspended from the shoulders of the priests, covering the breast.

At the right and left of the breastplate were set two larger stones, which shone with great brilliancy. When difficult matters were brought to the judges, which they could not decide, they were referred to the priests, and they inquired of God, who answered them. If He favored, and if He would grant them success, a halo of light and glory especially rested upon the precious stone at the right. If he disapproved, a vapor or cloud seemed to settle upon the precious stone at the left hand. When they inquired of God in regard to going to battle, the precious stone at the right, when circled with light, said, Go, and prosper. The stone at the left, when shadowed with a cloud, said, Thou shalt not go; thou shalt not prosper.

When the high priest entered within the most holy, once a year, and ministered before the ark in the awful presence of God, he inquired, and God often answered him with an audible voice. When the Lord did not answer by a voice, He let the sacred beams of light and glory rest upon the cherubim upon the right of the ark, in approbation, or favor. If their requests were refused, a cloud rested upon the cherubim at the left.

Four heavenly angels always accompanied the ark of God in all its journeyings, to guard it from all danger and to fulfill any mission required of them in connection with the ark. Jesus, the Son of God, followed by heavenly angels, went before the ark as it came to Jordan; and the waters were cut off before His presence. Christ and angels stood by the ark and the priests in the bed of the river until all Israel had passed over Jordan. Christ and angels attended the circuit of the ark around Jericho and finally cast down the massive walls of the city and delivered Jericho into the hands of Israel.

Result of Eli's Neglect

When Eli was high priest he exalted his sons to the priesthood. Eli alone was permitted to enter the most holy once a year. His sons ministered at the door of the tabernacle and officiated in the slaying of the beasts and at the altar of sacrifice. They continually abused this sacred office. They were selfish, covetous, gluttonous, and profligate. God reproved Eli for his criminal neglect of family discipline. Eli reproved his sons but did not restrain them. After they were placed in the sacred office of priesthood, Eli heard of their conduct in defrauding the children of Israel of their offerings, also their bold transgressions of the law of God and their violent conduct, which caused Israel to sin.

The Lord made known to the child Samuel the judgments He would bring upon Eli's house because of his negligence. "And the Lord said to Samuel, Behold, I will do a thing in Israel, at which both the ears of every one that heareth it shall tingle. In that day I will perform against Eli all things which I have spoken concerning his house: when I begin, I will also make an end. For I have told him that I will judge his house for ever for the iniquity which he knoweth; because his sons made themselves vile, and he restrained them not. And therefore I have sworn unto the house of Eli, that the iniquity of Eli's house shall not be purged with sacrifice nor offering for ever."

The transgressions of Eli's sons were so daring, so insulting, to a holy God, that no sacrifice could atone for such willful transgression. These sinful priests profaned the sacrifices which typified the Son of God. And by their blasphemous conduct they were trampling upon the blood of the atonement, from which was derived the virtue of all sacrifices.

Samuel told Eli the words of the Lord; "and he said, It is the Lord: let Him do what seemeth Him good." Eli knew that God had been dishonored, and he felt that he had sinned. He submitted that God was thus punishing his sinful neglect. The word of the Lord to Samuel was made known by Eli to all Israel. In doing this, he thought to correct in a measure his past sinful negligence. The evil pronounced upon Eli was not long delayed.

The Israelites made war with the Philistines and were overcome, and four thousand of them were slain. The Hebrews were afraid. They knew that if other nations should hear of their defeat they would be encouraged to also make war with them. The elders of Israel decided that their defeat was because the ark of God was not with them. They sent to Shiloh for the ark of the covenant. They thought of their passage over Jordan and the easy conquest of Jericho when they bore the ark, and they decided that all that was necessary was to bring the ark to them, and they would triumph over their enemies. They did not realize that their strength was in their obedience to that law contained in the ark, which was a representative of God Himself. The polluted priests, Hophni and Phinehas, were with the sacred ark, transgressing the law of God. These sinners conducted the ark to the camp of Israel. The confidence of the men of war was restored, and they felt confident of success.

The Ark Taken

"And when the ark of the covenant of the Lord came into the camp, all Israel shouted with a great shout, so that the earth rang again. And when the Philistines heard the noise of the shout, they said, What meaneth the noise of this great shout in the camp of the Hebrews? And they understood that the ark of the Lord was come into the camp. And the Philistines were afraid; for they said, God is come into the camp. And they said, Woe unto us! for there hath not been such a thing heretofore. Woe unto us! who shall deliver us out of the hand of these mighty gods? These are the gods that smote the Egyptians with all the plagues in the wilderness. Be strong, and quit yourselves like men, O ye Philistines, that ye be not servants unto the Hebrews, as they have been to you: quit yourselves like men, and fight. And the Philistines fought, and Israel was smitten, and they fled every man into his tent: and there was a very great slaughter; for there fell of Israel thirty thousand footmen. And the ark of God was taken; and the two sons of Eli, Hophni and Phinehas, were slain."

The Philistines thought that this ark was the Israelites' god. They knew not that the living God, who created the heavens and the earth, and gave His law upon Sinai, sent prosperity and adversity according to the obedience or transgression of His law contained in the sacred chest.

There was a very great slaughter in Israel. Eli was sitting by the wayside, watching with a trembling heart to receive news from the army. He was afraid that the ark of God might be taken and polluted by the Philistine host. A messenger from the army ran to Shiloh and informed Eli that his two sons had been slain. He could bear this with a degree of calmness, for he had reason to expect it. But when the messenger added, "And the ark of God is taken," Eli wavered in anguish upon his seat and fell backward and died. He shared the wrath of God which came upon his sons. He was guilty in a great measure of their transgressions, because he had criminally neglected to restrain them. The capture of the ark of God by the Philistines was considered the greatest calamity which could befall Israel. The wife of Phinehas, as she was about to die, named her child Ichabod, saying, "The glory is departed from Israel: because the ark of God was taken."

In the Land of the Philistines

God permitted His ark to be taken by their enemies, to show Israel how vain it was to trust in the ark, the symbol of His presence, while they were profaning the commandments contained in the ark. God would humble them by removing from them that sacred ark, their boasted strength and confidence.

The Philistines were triumphant, because they had, as they thought, the famous God of the Israelites, which had performed such wonders for them and had made them a terror to their enemies. They took the ark of God to Ashdod and set it in a splendid temple, made in honor to their most popular god Dagon, and placed it by the side of their god. In the morning the priests of these gods entered the temple, and they were terrified to find Dagon fallen upon his face to the ground before the ark of the Lord. They raised Dagon and placed him in his former position. They thought he might have fallen accidentally. But the next morning they found him fallen as before, upon his face to the ground, and the head of Dagon and both his hands were cut off.

The angels of God, who ever accompanied the ark, prostrated the senseless idol god and afterward mutilated it, to show that God, the living God, was above all gods, and that before Him every heathen god was as nothing. The heathen possessed great reverence for their god, Dagon; and when they found it ruinously mutilated and lying upon its face before the ark of God, they were sad and considered it a very bad omen to the Philistines. It was interpreted by them that the Philistines and all their gods would yet be subdued and destroyed by the Hebrews, and the Hebrews' God would be greater and more powerful than all gods. They removed the ark of God from their idol temple and placed it by itself.

The ark of God was kept seven months by the Philistines. They had overcome the Israelites and had taken the ark of God, wherein they supposed their power consisted, and thought that they should ever be in safety and have no more fear of the armies of Israel. But in the midst of their joy at their success a wailing was heard all over the land, and the cause was at length credited to the ark of God. It was borne from place to place in terror, and destruction from God followed its course, until the Philistines were greatly perplexed to know what to do with it. Angels, who accompanied it, guarded it from all harm. And the Philistines did not dare to open the chest; for their God Dagon had met with such a fate that they feared to touch it, or to have it near them. They called for the priests and the diviners, and inquired of them what they should do with the ark of God. They advised them to send it back to the people to whom it belonged, and to send with it a costly trespass offering, which if God would be pleased to accept, they would be healed. They should also understand that God's hand was upon them because they had taken His ark, which belonged alone to Israel.

Returned to Israel

Some were not in favor of this. It was too humiliating to carry back the ark, and they urged that no one of the Philistines would dare venture his life to carry the ark of the God of Israel, which had brought such death upon them. Their counselors entreated the people not to harden their hearts, as the Egyptians and Pharaoh had done, and cause still greater afflictions and plagues to come upon them. And as they were all afraid to take the ark of God, they advised them, saying, "Now therefore make a new cart, and take two milch kine, on which there hath come no yoke, and tie the kine to the cart, and bring their calves home from them: and take the ark of the Lord, and lay it upon the cart; and put the jewels of gold, which ye return Him for a trespass offering, in a coffer by the side thereof; and send it away, that it may go. And see, if it goeth up by the way of His own coast to Beth-shemesh, then He hath done us this great evil: but if not, then we shall know that it is not His hand that smote us: it was a chance that happened to us. And the men did so; and took two milch kine, and tied them to the cart, and shut up their calves at home.... And the kine took the straight way to the way of Beth-shemesh, and went along the highway, lowing as they went, and turned not aside to the right hand or to the left."

The Philistines knew that the cows would not be induced to leave their young calves at home unless they should be urged by some unseen power. The cows went direct to Beth-shemesh, lowing for their calves, yet going directly away from them. The lords of the Philistines followed after the ark unto the border of Beth-shemesh. They dared not trust that sacred chest wholly to the cows. They feared that if any evil happened to it, greater calamities would come upon them. They knew not that angels of God accompanied the ark and guided the cows in their course to the place where it belonged.

Presumption Punished

The people of Beth-shemesh were reaping in the field, and when they saw the ark of God upon the cart, drawn by the cows, they were greatly rejoiced. They knew that it was the work of God. The cows drew the cart containing the ark to a large stone, and stood still of themselves. The Levites took down the ark of the Lord and the offering of the Philistines, and they offered the cart and the cows which had borne the sacred ark, and the offering of the Philistines, unto God as a burnt sacrifice. The lords of the Philistines returned to Ekron, and the plague was stayed.

The men of Beth-shemesh were curious to know what great power could be in that ark, which caused it to accomplish such marvelous things. They looked upon the ark alone as being so powerful, and were not accrediting the power to God. None but men sacredly appointed for the purpose could look upon the ark, divested of its coverings, without being slain, for it was as though looking upon God Himself. And as the people gratified their curiosity and opened the ark to gaze into its sacred recesses, which the heathen idolaters had not dared to do, the angels attending the ark slew above fifty thousand of the people.

And the people of Beth-shemesh were afraid of the ark, and they said, "Who is able to stand before this holy Lord God? and to whom shall He go up from us? And they sent messengers to the inhabitants of Kirjath-jearim, saying, The Philistines have brought again the ark of the Lord; come ye down, and fetch it up to you." The people of Kirjath-jearim brought the ark of the Lord to the house of Abinadab and sanctified his son to keep it. For twenty years the Hebrews were in the power of the Philistines, and they were greatly humbled and repented of their sins, and Samuel interceded for them, and God was again merciful to them. And the Philistines made war with them, and the Lord again wrought in a miraculous manner for Israel, and they overcame their enemies.

The ark remained in the house of Abinadab until David was made king. He gathered together all the chosen men of Israel, thirty thousand, and went to bring up the ark of God. They set the ark upon a new cart and brought it out of the house of Abinadab. Uzzah and Ahu, sons of Abinadab, drove the cart. David and all the house of Israel played before the Lord on all manner of musical instruments. "And when they came to Nachon's threshingfloor, Uzzah put forth his hand to the ark of God, and took hold of it; for the oxen shook it. And the anger of the Lord was kindled against Uzzah; and God smote him there for his error; and there he died by the ark of God." Uzzah was angry with the oxen, because they stumbled. He showed a manifest distrust of God, as though He who had brought the ark from the land of the Philistines could not take care of it. Angels who attended the ark struck down Uzzah for presuming impatiently to put his hand upon the ark of God.

"And David was afraid of the Lord that day, and said, How shall the ark of the Lord come to me? So David would not remove the ark of the Lord unto him into the city of David: but David carried it aside into the house of Obed-edom, the Gittite." David knew that he was a sinful man, and he was afraid that, like Uzzah, he should in some way be presumptuous and call forth the wrath of God upon himself. "And the ark of the Lord continued in the house of Obed-edom the Gittite three months: and the Lord blessed Obed-edom, and all his household."

God would teach His people that, while His ark was a terror and death to those who transgressed His commandments contained in it, it was also a blessing and strength to those who were obedient to His commandments. When David heard that the house of Obed-edom was greatly blessed, and that all that he had prospered, because of the ark of God, he was very anxious to bring it to his own city. But before David ventured to move the sacred ark, he sanctified himself to God and also commanded that all the men highest in authority in the kingdom should keep themselves from all worldly business, and everything which would distract their minds from sacred devotion. Thus should they sanctify themselves for the purpose of conducting the sacred ark to the city of David. "So David went and brought up the ark of God from the house of Obed-edom into the city of David with gladness....

"And they brought in the ark of the Lord, and set it in His place, in the midst of the tabernacle that David had pitched for it: and David offered burnt offerings and peace offerings before the Lord."

In Solomon's Temple

After Solomon had finished building the temple he assembled the elders of Israel and the most influential men among the people, to bring up the ark of the covenant of the Lord out of the city of David. These men consecrated themselves to God and, with great solemnity and reverence, accompanied the priests who bore the ark. "And they brought up the ark of the Lord, and the tabernacle of the congregation, and all the holy vessels that were in the tabernacle, even those did the priests and Levites bring up. And king Solomon, and all the congregation of Israel, that were assembled unto him, were with him before the ark, sacrificing sheep and oxen, that could not be told nor numbered for multitude."

Solomon followed the example of his father David. Every six paces he sacrificed. With singing and with music and great ceremony, "the priests brought in the ark of the covenant of the Lord unto His place, into the oracle of the house, to the most holy place, even under the wings of the cherubims. For the cherubims spread forth their two wings over the place of the ark, and the cherubims covered the ark and the staves thereof above."

A most splendid sanctuary had been made, according to the pattern showed to Moses in the mount and afterward presented by the Lord to David. The earthly sanctuary was made like the heavenly. In addition to the cherubim on the top of the ark, Solomon made two other angels of larger size, standing at each end of the ark, representing the heavenly angels always guarding the law of God. It is impossible to describe the beauty and splendor of this tabernacle. There, as in the tabernacle, the sacred ark was borne in solemn, reverential order, and set in its place beneath the wings of the two stately cherubim that stood upon the floor.

The sacred choir united their voices with all kinds of musical instruments, in praise to God. And while the voices, in harmony with instruments of music, resounded through the temple and were borne upon the air through Jerusalem, the cloud of God's glory took possession of the house, as it had formerly filled the tabernacle. "And it came to pass, when the priests were come out of the holy place, that the cloud filled the house of the Lord, so that the priests could not stand to minister because of the cloud; for the glory of the Lord had filled the house of the Lord."

King Solomon stood upon a brazen scaffold before the altar and blessed the people. He then knelt down and, with his hands raised upward, poured forth earnest and solemn prayer to God while the congregation were bowed with their faces to the ground. After Solomon had ended his prayer, a miraculous fire came from heaven and consumed the sacrifice.

Because of the sins of Israel the calamity which God said should come upon the temple if His people departed from Him was fulfilled some hundreds of years after the temple was built. God promised Solomon, if he would remain faithful, and his people would obey all His commandments, that that glorious temple should stand forever in all its splendor, as an evidence of the prosperity and exalted blessings resting upon Israel for their obedience.

The Captivity of Israel

Because of Israel's transgression of the commandments of God and their wicked acts, God suffered them to go into captivity, to humble and punish them. Before the temple was destroyed, God made known to a few of His faithful servants the fate of the temple, which was the pride of Israel, and which they regarded with idolatry, while they were sinning against God. He also revealed to them the captivity of Israel. These righteous men, just before the destruction of the temple, removed the sacred ark containing the tables of stone, and with mourning and sadness secreted it in a cave where it was to be hidden from the people of Israel because of their sins, and was to be no more restored to them. That sacred ark is yet hidden. It has never been disturbed since it was secreted.

Chapter 25—The First Advent of Christ

This chapter is based on Genesis 32 and 33.

I was carried down to the time when Jesus was to take upon Himself man's nature, humble Himself as a man, and suffer the temptations of Satan.

His birth was without worldly grandeur. He was born in a stable and cradled in a manger; yet His birth was honored far above that of any of the sons of men. Angels from heaven informed the shepherds of the advent of Jesus, and light and glory from God accompanied their testimony. The heavenly host touched their harps and glorified God. They triumphantly heralded the advent of the Son of God to a fallen world to accomplish the work of redemption, and by His death to bring peace, happiness, and everlasting life to man. God honored the advent of His Son. Angels worshiped Him.

The Baptism of Jesus

Angels of God hovered over the scene of His baptism; the Holy Spirit descended in the form of a dove and lighted upon Him, and as the people stood greatly amazed, with their eyes fastened upon Him, the Father's voice was heard from heaven, saying, Thou art My beloved Son; in Thee I am well pleased.

John was not certain that it was the Saviour who came to be baptized of him in Jordan. But God had promised him a sign by which he should know the Lamb of God. That sign was given as the heavenly dove rested upon Jesus and the glory of God shone round about Him. John reached forth his hand, pointing to Jesus, and with a loud voice cried out, "Behold the Lamb of God, which taketh away the sin of the world!" John 1:29.

Ministry of John

John informed his disciples that Jesus was the promised Messiah, the Saviour of the world. As his work was closing, he taught his disciples to look to Jesus and follow Him as the Great Teacher. John's life was sorrowful and self-denying. He heralded the first advent of Christ but was not permitted to witness His miracles and enjoy the power manifested by Him. When Jesus should establish Himself as a teacher, John knew that he himself must die. His voice was seldom heard, except in the wilderness. His life was lonely. He did not cling to his father's family, to enjoy their society, but left them in order to fulfill his mission.

Multitudes left the busy cities and villages, and flocked to the wilderness to hear the words of the wonderful prophet. John laid the ax to the root of the tree. He reproved sin, fearless of consequences, and prepared the way for the Lamb of God.

Herod was affected as he listened to the powerful, pointed testimonies of John, and with deep interest he inquired what he must do to become his disciple. John was acquainted with the fact that he was about to marry his brother's wife, while her husband was yet living, and faithfully told Herod that this was not lawful. Herod was unwilling to make any sacrifice. He married his brother's wife and, through her influence, seized John and put him in prison, intending, however, to release him. While there confined, John heard through his disciples of the mighty works of Jesus. He could not listen to His gracious words, but the disciples informed him and comforted him with what they had heard. Soon John was beheaded, through the influence of Herod's wife. I saw that the humblest disciples who followed Jesus, witnessed His miracles, and heard the comforting words which fell from His lips, were greater than John the Baptist; that is, they were more exalted and honored, and had more pleasure in their lives.

John came in the spirit and power of Elijah to proclaim the first advent of Jesus. I was pointed down to the last days and saw that John represented those who should go forth in the spirit and power of Elijah to herald the day of wrath and the second advent of Jesus.

The Temptation

After the baptism of Jesus in Jordan, He was led by the Spirit into the wilderness, to be tempted of the devil. The Holy Spirit had prepared Him for that special scene of fierce temptations. Forty days He was tempted of Satan, and in those days He ate nothing. Everything around Him was unpleasant, from which human nature would be led to shrink. He was with the wild beasts and the devil, in a desolate, lonely place. The Son of God was pale and emaciated, through fasting and suffering. But His course was marked out, and He must fulfill the work which He came to do.

Satan took advantage of the sufferings of the Son of God and prepared to beset Him with manifold temptations, hoping to obtain the victory over Him, because He had humbled Himself as a man. Satan came with this temptation: "If Thou be the Son of God, command this stone that it be made bread." He tempted Jesus to condescend to give him proof of His being the Messiah, by exercising

His divine power. Jesus mildly answered him, "It is written, That man shall not live by bread alone, but by every word of God." Luke 4:3, 4.

Satan was seeking a dispute with Jesus concerning His being the Son of God. He referred to His weak, suffering condition and boastingly affirmed that he was stronger than Jesus. But the word spoken from heaven, "Thou art My beloved Son; in Thee I am well pleased" (Luke 3:22), was sufficient to sustain Jesus through all His sufferings. I saw that Christ had nothing to do in convincing Satan of His power or of His being the Saviour of the world. Satan has sufficient evidence of the exalted station and authority of the Son of God. His unwillingness to yield to Christ's authority had shut him out of heaven.

Satan, to manifest his power, carried Jesus to Jerusalem and set Him upon a pinnacle of the temple, and there tempted Him to give evidence that He was the Son of God, by casting Himself down from that dizzy height. Satan came with the words of inspiration: "For it is written, He shall give His angels charge over Thee, to keep Thee: and in their hands they shall bear Thee up, lest at any time Thou dash Thy foot against a stone." Jesus answering said unto him, "It is said, Thou shalt not tempt the Lord thy God." Luke 4:10-12. Satan wished to cause Jesus to presume upon the mercy of His Father and risk His life before the fulfillment of His mission. He had hoped that the plan of salvation would fail; but the plan was laid too deep to be overthrown or marred by Satan.

Christ is the example for all Christians. When they are tempted, or their rights are disputed, they should bear it patiently. They should not feel that they have a right to call upon the Lord to display His power that they may obtain a victory over their enemies, unless God can be directly honored and glorified thereby. If Jesus had cast Himself from the pinnacle of the temple, it would not have glorified His Father, for none would have witnessed the act but Satan and the angels of God. And it would have been tempting the Lord to display His power to His bitterest foe. It would have been condescending to the one whom Jesus came to conquer.

"And the devil, taking Him up into a high mountain, shewed unto Him all the kingdoms of the world in a moment of time. And the devil said unto Him, All this power will I give Thee, and the glory of them: for that is delivered unto me; and to whomsoever I will I give it. If Thou therefore wilt worship me, all shall be Thine. And Jesus answered and said unto him, Get thee behind Me, Satan: for it is written, Thou shalt worship the Lord Thy God, and Him only shalt thou serve." Luke 4:5-8.

Satan presented before Jesus the kingdoms of the world in the most attractive light. If Jesus would there worship him, he offered to relinquish his claims to the possessions of earth. If the plan of salvation should be carried out and Jesus should die to redeem man, Satan knew that his own power must be limited and finally taken away, and that he would be destroyed. Therefore it was his studied plan to prevent, if possible, the completion of the great work which had been commenced by the Son of God. If the plan of man's redemption should fail, Satan would retain the kingdom which he then claimed. And if he should succeed, he flattered himself that he would reign in opposition to the God of heaven.

The Tempter Rebuked

Satan exulted when Jesus laid aside His power and glory, and left heaven. He thought that the Son of God was then placed in his power. The temptation took so easily with the holy pair in Eden that he hoped by his satanic power and cunning to overthrow even the Son of God, and thereby save his own life and kingdom. If he could tempt Jesus to depart from the will of His Father, his object would be gained. But Jesus met the tempter with the rebuke, "Get thee behind Me, Satan." He was to bow only to His Father.

Satan claimed the kingdom of earth as his and insinuated to Jesus that all His sufferings might be saved: that He need not die to obtain the kingdoms of this world; if He would worship him He might have all the possessions of earth and the glory of reigning over them. But Jesus was steadfast. He knew that the time was to come when He would, by His own life, redeem the kingdom from Satan, and that, after a season, all in heaven and earth would submit to Him. He chose His life of suffering and His dreadful death as the way appointed by His Father that He might become a lawful heir to the kingdoms of earth and have them given into His hands as an everlasting possession. Satan also will be given into His hands to be destroyed by death, nevermore to annoy Jesus or the saints in glory.

Chapter 26—The Ministry of Christ

This chapter is based on Genesis 32 and 33.

After Satan had ended his temptations he departed from Jesus for a season, and angels prepared Him food in the wilderness and strengthened Him, and the blessing of His Father rested upon Him. Satan had failed in his fiercest temptations; yet he looked forward to the period of Jesus' ministry, when he should at different times try his cunning against Him. He still hoped to prevail against Him by stirring up those who would not receive Jesus, to hate and seek to destroy Him.

Satan held a special council with his angels. They were disappointed and enraged that they had prevailed nothing against the Son of God. They decided that they must be more cunning and use their power to the utmost to inspire unbelief in the minds of His own nation as to His being the Saviour of the world, and in this way discourage Jesus in His mission. No matter how exact the Jews might be in their ceremonies and sacrifices, if they could be kept blinded as to the prophecies and be made to believe that the Messiah was to appear as a mighty worldly king, they might be led to despise and reject Jesus.

I was shown that Satan and his angels were very busy during Christ's ministry, inspiring men with unbelief, hate, and scorn. Often when Jesus uttered some cutting truth, reproving their sins, the people would become enraged. Satan and his angels urged them on to take the life of the Son of God. More than once they took up stones to cast at Him, but angels guarded Him and bore Him away from the angry multitude to a place of safety. Again, as the plain truth dropped from His holy lips, the multitude laid hold of Him and led Him to the brow of a hill, intending to cast Him down. A contention arose among themselves as to what they should do with Him, when the angels again hid Him from the sight of the multitudes, and He, passing through the midst of them, went His way.

Satan still hoped that the great plan of salvation would fail. He exerted all his power to make the hearts of the people hard and their feelings bitter against Jesus. He hoped that so few would receive Him as the Son of God that He would consider His sufferings and sacrifice too great to make for so small a company.

But I saw that if there had been but two who would have accepted Jesus as the Son of God and believed on Him to the saving of their souls, He would have carried out the plan.

Relieving the Suffering

Jesus began His work by breaking Satan's power over the suffering. He restored the sick to health, gave sight to the blind, and healed the lame, causing them to leap for joy and to glorify God. He restored to health those who had been infirm and bound in Satan's cruel power many years. With gracious words He comforted the weak, the trembling, and the desponding. The feeble, suffering ones whom Satan held in triumph, Jesus wrenched from his grasp, bringing to them soundness of body and great joy and happiness. He raised the dead to life, and they glorified God for the mighty display of His power. He wrought mightily for all who believed on Him.

The life of Christ was filled with words and acts of benevolence, sympathy, and love. He was ever attentive to listen to and relieve the woes of those who came to Him. Multitudes carried in their own persons the evidence of His divine power. Yet after the work had been accomplished, many were ashamed of the humble yet mighty Preacher. Because the rulers did not believe on Him, the people were not willing to accept Jesus. He was a man of sorrows and acquainted with grief. They could not endure to be governed by His sober, self-denying life. They wished to enjoy the honor which the world bestows. Yet many followed the Son of God and listened to His instructions, feasting upon the words which fell so graciously from His lips. His words were full of meaning, yet so plain that the weakest could understand them.

Ineffective Opposition

Satan and his angels blinded the eyes and darkened the understanding of the Jews, and stirred up the chief of the people and the rulers to take the Saviour's life. Others were sent to bring Jesus unto them, but as they came near where He was they were greatly amazed. They saw Him filled with sympathy and compassion, as He witnessed human woe. They heard Him in love and tenderness speak encouragingly to the weak and afflicted. They also heard Him, in a voice of authority, rebuke the power of Satan and bid his captives go free. They listened to the words of wisdom that fell from His lips, and they were captivated; they could not lay hands on Him. They returned to the priests and elders without Jesus.

When asked, "Why have ye not brought Him?" they related what they had witnessed of His miracles, and the holy words of wisdom, love, and knowledge which they had heard, and ended with saying, "Never man spake like this Man." The chief priests accused them of being also deceived, and some of the officers were ashamed that they had not taken Him. The priests inquired in a scornful manner if any of the rulers had believed on Him. I saw that many of the magistrates and elders did believe on Jesus, but Satan kept them from acknowledging it; they feared the reproach of the people more than they feared God.

Thus far the cunning and hatred of Satan had not broken up the plan of salvation. The time for the accomplishment of the object for which Jesus came into the world was drawing near. Satan and his angels consulted together and decided to inspire Christ's own nation to cry eagerly for His blood and heap upon Him cruelty and scorn. They hoped that Jesus would resent such treatment and fail to maintain His humility and meekness.

While Satan was laying his plans, Jesus was carefully opening to His disciples the sufferings through which He must pass—that He would be crucified and that He would rise again the third day. But their understanding seemed dull, and they could not comprehend what He told them.

The Transfiguration

The faith of the disciples was greatly strengthened at the transfiguration, when they were permitted to behold Christ's glory and to hear the voice from heaven testifying to His divine character. God chose to give the followers of Jesus strong proof that He was the promised Messiah, that in their bitter sorrow and disappointment at His crucifixion, they would not entirely cast away their confidence. At the transfiguration the Lord sent Moses and Elijah to talk with Jesus concerning His sufferings and death. Instead of choosing angels to converse with His Son, God chose those who had themselves experienced the trials of earth.

Elijah had walked with God. His work had been painful and trying, for the Lord through him had reproved the sins of Israel. Elijah was a prophet of God; yet he was compelled to flee from place to place to save his life. His own nation hunted him like a wild beast that they might destroy him. But God translated Elijah. Angels bore him in glory and triumph to heaven.

Moses was greater than any who had lived before him. He had been highly honored of God, being privileged to talk with the Lord face to face, as a man speaks with a friend. He was permitted to see the bright light and excellent glory that enshrouded the Father. The Lord through Moses delivered the children of Israel from Egyptian bondage. Moses was a mediator for his people, often standing between them and the wrath of God. When the anger of the Lord was greatly kindled against Israel for their unbelief, their murmurings, and their grievous sins, Moses' love for them was tested. God proposed to destroy them and to make of him a mighty nation. Moses showed his love for Israel by his earnest pleading in their behalf. In his distress he prayed God to turn from His fierce anger and forgive Israel, or blot his name out of His book.

Moses passed through death, but Michael came down and gave him life before his body had seen corruption. Satan tried to hold the body, claiming it as his; but Michael resurrected Moses and took him to heaven. Satan railed bitterly against God, denouncing Him as unjust in permitting his prey to be taken from him; but Christ did not rebuke His adversary, though it was through his temptation that the servant of God had fallen. He meekly referred him to His Father, saying, "The Lord rebuke thee." Jude 1:9.

Jesus had told His disciples that there were some standing with Him who should not taste of death till they should see the kingdom of God come with power. At the transfiguration this promise was fulfilled. The countenance of Jesus was there changed and shone like the sun. His raiment was white and glistening. Moses was present to represent those who will be raised from the dead at the second appearing of Jesus. And Elijah, who was translated without seeing death, represented those who will be changed to immortality at Christ's second coming and will be translated to heaven without seeing death. The disciples beheld with astonishment and fear the excellent majesty of Jesus and the cloud that overshadowed them, and heard the voice of God in terrible majesty, saying, "This is My beloved Son: hear Him."

Chapter 27—The Betrayal of Christ

I was carried down to the time when Jesus ate the Passover supper with His disciples. Satan had deceived Judas and led him to think that he was one of Christ's true disciples; but his heart had ever been carnal. He had seen the mighty works of Jesus, he had been with Him through His ministry, and had yielded to the overpowering evidence that He was the Messiah; but Judas was close and covetous; he loved money. He complained in anger of the costly ointment poured upon Jesus.

Mary loved her Lord. He had forgiven her sins, which were many, and had raised from the dead her much-loved brother, and she felt that nothing was too dear to bestow upon Jesus. The more precious the ointment, the better she could express her gratitude to her Saviour by devoting it to Him.

Judas, as an excuse for his covetousness, urged that the ointment might have been sold and given to the poor. But it was not because he had any care for the poor; for he was selfish, and often appropriated to his own use that which was entrusted to his care to be given unto the poor. Judas had been inattentive to the comfort and even to the wants of Jesus, and to excuse his covetousness he often referred to the poor. This act of generosity on the part of Mary was a most cutting rebuke of his covetous disposition. The way was prepared for Satan's temptation to find a ready reception in the heart of Judas.

The priests and rulers of the Jews hated Jesus, but multitudes thronged to listen to His words of wisdom and to witness His mighty works. The people were stirred with the deepest interest and anxiously followed Jesus to hear the instructions of this wonderful Teacher. Many of the rulers believed on Him, but dared not confess their faith lest they should be put out of the synagogue. The priests and elders decided that something must be done to draw the attention of the people from Jesus. They feared that all men would believe on Him. They could see no safety for themselves. They must lose their position or put Jesus to death. And after they should put Him to death, there would still be those who were living monuments of His power.

Jesus had raised Lazarus from the dead, and they feared that if they should kill Jesus, Lazarus would testify of His mighty power. The people were flocking to see him who was raised from the dead, and the rulers determined to slay Lazarus also, and put down the excitement. Then they would turn the people to the traditions and doctrines of men, to tithe mint and rue, and again have influence over them. They agreed to take Jesus when He was alone, for if they should attempt to take Him in a crowd, when the minds of the people were all interested in Him, they would be stoned.

Judas knew how anxious they were to obtain Jesus and offered to betray Him to the chief priests and elders for a few pieces of silver. His love of money led him to agree to betray his Lord into the hands of His bitterest enemies. Satan was working directly through Judas, and in the midst of the impressive scene of the last supper the traitor was devising plans to betray his Master. Jesus sorrowfully told His disciples that all of them would be offended because of Him that night. But Peter ardently affirmed that although all others should be offended because of Him, he would not be offended. Jesus said to Peter, "Satan hath desired to have you, that he may sift you as wheat: but I have prayed for thee, that thy faith fail not: and when thou art converted, strengthen thy brethren." Luke 22:31, 32.

In the Garden

I beheld Jesus in the garden with His disciples. In deep sorrow He bade them watch and pray, lest they should enter into temptation. He knew that their faith was to be tried and their hopes disappointed, and that they would need all the strength which they could obtain by close watching and fervent prayer. With strong cries and weeping, Jesus prayed, "Father, if Thou be willing, remove this cup from Me: nevertheless not My will, but Thine, be done." Luke 22:42. The Son of God prayed in agony. Great drops of blood gathered upon His face and fell to the ground. Angels were hovering over the place, witnessing the scene, but only one was commissioned to go and strengthen the Son of God in His agony. There was no joy in heaven. The angels cast their crowns and harps from them and with the deepest interest silently watched Jesus. They wished to surround the Son of God, but the commanding angels suffered them not, lest, as they should behold His betrayal, they should deliver Him; for the plan had been laid, and it must be fulfilled.

After Jesus had prayed He came to His disciples, but they were sleeping. In that dreadful hour He had not the sympathy and prayers of even His disciples. Peter, who was so zealous a short time before, was heavy with sleep. Jesus reminded him of his positive declarations and said to him, "What, could ye not watch with Me one hour?" Matthew 26:40. Three times the Son of God prayed in agony.

Judas Betrays Jesus

Then Judas, with his band of armed men, appeared. He approached His Master as usual, to salute Him. The band surrounded Jesus; but there He manifested His divine power, as He said, "Whom seek ye?" "I am He." They fell backward to the ground. Jesus made this inquiry that they might witness His power and have evidence that He could deliver Himself from their hands if He would.

The disciples began to hope as they saw the multitude with their staves and swords fall so quickly. As they arose and again surrounded the Son of God, Peter drew his sword and smote a servant of the high priest and cut off an ear. Jesus bade him to put up the sword, saying, "Thinkest thou that I cannot now pray to My Father, and He shall presently give Me more than twelve legions of angels?" Matthew 26:53. I saw that as these words were spoken, the countenances of the angels were animated with hope. They wished then and there to surround their Commander and disperse that angry mob. But again sadness settled upon them, as Jesus added, "But how then shall the Scriptures be fulfilled, that thus it must be?" Matthew 26:54. The hearts of the disciples also sank in despair and bitter disappointment as Jesus suffered Himself to be led away by His enemies.

The disciples feared for their own lives, and they all forsook Him and fled. Jesus was left alone in the hands of the murderous mob. Oh, what a triumph of Satan then! And what sadness and sorrow with the angels of God! Many companies of holy angels, each with a tall commanding angel at their head, were sent to witness the scene. They were to record every insult and cruelty imposed upon the Son of God, and to register every pang of anguish which Jesus should suffer; for the very men who joined in this dreadful scene are to see it all again in living characters.

Chapter 28—The Trial of Christ

The angels, as they left heaven, in sadness laid off their glittering crowns. They could not wear them while their Commander was suffering and was to wear a crown of thorns. Satan and his angels were busy in the judgment hall to destroy human feeling and sympathy. The very atmosphere was heavy and polluted by their influence. The chief priests and elders were inspired by them to insult and abuse Jesus in a manner the most difficult for human nature to bear. Satan hoped that such mockery and violence would call forth from the Son of God some complaint or murmur; or that He would manifest His divine power and wrench Himself from the grasp of the multitude, and that thus the plan of salvation might at last fail.

Peter's Denial

Peter followed his Lord after His betrayal. He was anxious to see what would be done with Jesus. But when he was accused of being one of His disciples, fear for his own safety led him to declare that he knew not the Man. The disciples were noted for the purity of their language, and Peter, to convince his accusers that he was not one of Christ's disciples, denied the charge the third time with cursing and swearing. Jesus, who was at some distance from Peter, turned a sorrowful, reproving gaze upon him. Then the disciple remembered the words which Jesus had spoken to him in the upper chamber, and also his own zealous assertion, "Though all men shall be offended because of Thee, yet will I never be offended." Matthew 26:33. He had denied his Lord, even with cursing and swearing; but that look of Jesus' melted Peter's heart and saved him. He wept bitterly and repented of his great sin, and was converted, and then was prepared to strengthen his brethren.

In the Judgment Hall

The multitude were clamorous for the blood of Jesus. They cruelly scourged Him, and put upon Him an old purple kingly robe, and bound His sacred head with a crown of thorns. They put a reed into His hand, and bowed to Him, and mockingly saluted Him, "Hail, king of the Jews!" John 19:3. They then took the reed from His hand and smote Him with it upon the head, causing the thorns to penetrate His temples, sending the blood trickling down His face and beard.

It was difficult for the angels to endure the sight. They would have delivered Jesus, but the commanding angels forbade them, saying that it was a great ransom which was to be paid for man; but it would be complete and would cause the death of him who had the power of death. Jesus knew that angels were witnessing the scene of His humiliation. The weakest angel could have caused that mocking throng to fall powerless and could have delivered Jesus. He knew that if He should desire it of His Father, angels would instantly release Him. But it was necessary that He should suffer the violence of wicked men, in order to carry out the plan of salvation.

Jesus stood meek and humble before the infuriated multitude, while they offered Him the vilest abuse. They spat in His face—that face from which they will one day desire to hide, which will give light to the city of God and shine brighter than the sun. Christ did not cast upon the offenders an angry look. They covered His head with an old garment, blindfolding Him, and then struck Him in the face and cried out, "Prophesy, who was it that smote Thee?" Luke 22:64. There was commotion among the angels. They would have rescued Him instantly, but their commanding angels restrained them.

Some of the disciples had gained confidence to enter where Jesus was and witness His trial. They expected that He would manifest His divine power, and deliver Himself from the hands of His enemies, and punish them for their cruelty toward Him. Their hopes would rise and fall as the different scenes transpired. Sometimes they doubted, and feared that they had been deceived. But the voice heard at the mount of transfiguration, and the glory they there beheld, strengthened their faith that He was the Son of God. They called to mind the scenes which they had witnessed, the miracles which they had seen Jesus perform in healing the sick, opening the eyes of the blind, unstopping the deaf ears, rebuking and casting out devils, raising the dead to life, and even calming the wind and the sea.

They could not believe that He would die. They hoped that He would yet rise in power, and with His commanding voice disperse that bloodthirsty multitude, as when He entered the temple and drove out those who were making the house of God a place of merchandise, when they fled before Him as if pursued by a company of armed soldiers. The disciples hoped that Jesus would manifest His power and convince all that He was the King of Israel.

Judas's Confession

Judas was filled with bitter remorse and shame at his treacherous act in betraying Jesus. And when he witnessed the abuse which the Saviour endured, he was overcome. He had loved Jesus, but had loved money more. He had not thought that Jesus would suffer Himself to be taken by the mob which he led on. He had expected Him to work a miracle and deliver Himself from them. But when he saw the infuriated multitude in the judgment hall, thirsting for blood, he deeply felt his guilt; and while many were vehemently accusing Jesus, Judas rushed through the multitude, confessing that he had sinned in betraying innocent blood. He offered the priests the money which they had paid him, and entreated them to release Jesus, declaring that He was entirely innocent.

For a short time vexation and confusion kept the priests silent. They did not wish the people to know that they had hired one of the professed followers of Jesus to betray Him into their hands. Their hunting Jesus like a thief and taking Him secretly, they wished to hide. But the confession of Judas and his haggard, guilty appearance exposed the priests before the multitude, showing that it was hatred that had caused them to take Jesus. As Judas loudly declared Jesus to be innocent, the priests replied, "What is that to us? see thou to that." Matthew 27:4. They had Jesus in their power, and were determined to make sure of Him. Judas, overwhelmed with anguish, threw the money that he now despised at the feet of those who had hired him, and, in anguish and horror, went and hanged himself.

Jesus had many sympathizers in the company about Him, and His answering nothing to the many questions put to Him amazed the throng. Under all the mockery and violence of the mob, not a frown, not a troubled expression, rested upon His features. He was dignified and composed. The spectators looked upon Him with wonder. They compared His perfect form and firm, dignified bearing with the appearance of those who sat in judgment against Him, and said to one another that He appeared more like a king than any of the rulers. He bore no marks of being a criminal. His eye was mild, clear, and undaunted, His forehead broad and high. Every feature was strongly marked with benevolence and noble principle. His patience and forbearance were so unlike man that many trembled. Even Herod and Pilate were greatly troubled at His noble, Godlike bearing.

Jesus Before Pilate

From the first, Pilate was convinced that Jesus was no common man. He believed Him to be an excellent character and entirely innocent of the charges brought against Him. The angels who were witnessing the scene marked the convictions of the Roman governor, and to save him from engaging in the awful act of delivering Christ to be crucified, an angel was sent to Pilate's wife, and gave her information through a dream that it was the Son of God in whose trial her husband was engaged, and that He was an innocent sufferer. She immediately sent a message to Pilate, stating that she had suffered many things in a dream on account of Jesus and warning him to have nothing to do with that holy Man. The messenger, pressing hastily through the crowd, placed the letter in the hands of Pilate. As he read, he trembled and turned pale, and at once determined to have nothing to do with putting Christ to death. If the Jews would have the blood of Jesus, he would not give his influence to it, but would labor to deliver Him.

Sent to Herod

When Pilate heard that Herod was in Jerusalem, he was greatly relieved, for he hoped to free himself from all responsibility in the trial and condemnation of Jesus. He at once sent Him, with His accusers, to Herod. This ruler had become hardened in sin. The murder of John the Baptist had left upon his conscience a stain from which he could not free himself. When he heard of Jesus and the mighty works wrought by Him, he feared and trembled, believing Him to be John the Baptist risen from the dead. When Jesus was placed in his hands by Pilate, Herod considered the act an acknowledgment of his power, authority, and judgment. This had the effect to make friends of the two rulers, who had before been enemies. Herod was pleased to see Jesus, expecting Him to work some mighty miracle for his satisfaction. But it was not the work of Jesus to gratify curiosity or to seek His own safety. His divine, miraculous power was to be exercised for the salvation of others, but not in His own behalf.

Jesus answered nothing to the many questions put to Him by Herod; neither did He reply to His enemies, who were vehemently accusing Him. Herod was enraged because Jesus did not appear to fear his power, and with his men of war he derided, mocked, and abused the Son of God. Yet he was astonished at the noble, Godlike appearance of Jesus when shamefully abused, and, fearing to condemn Him, he sent Him again to Pilate.

Satan and his angels were tempting Pilate and trying to lead him on to his own ruin. They suggested to him that if he did not take part in condemning Jesus others would; the multitude were thirsting for His blood; and if he did not deliver Him to be crucified, he would lose his power and worldly honor, and would be denounced as a believer on the impostor. Through fear of losing his power and authority, Pilate consented to the death of Jesus. And notwithstanding he placed the blood of Jesus upon His accusers, and the multitude received it, crying, "His blood be on us, and on our children" (Matthew 27:25), yet Pilate was not clear; he was guilty of the blood of Christ. For his own selfish interest, his love of honor from the great men of earth, he delivered an innocent man to die. If Pilate had followed his own convictions he would have had nothing to do with condemning Jesus.

The appearance and words of Jesus during His trial made a deep impression upon the minds of many who were present on that occasion. The result of the influence thus exerted was apparent after His resurrection. Among those who were then added to the church, there were many whose conviction dated from the time of Jesus' trial.

Satan's rage was great as he saw that all the cruelty which he had led the Jews to inflict on Jesus had not called forth from Him the slightest murmur. Although He had taken upon Himself man's nature, He was sustained by a Godlike fortitude, and departed not in the least from the will of His Father.

Chapter 29—The Crucifixion of Christ

Christ, the precious Son of God, was led forth and delivered to the people to be crucified. The disciples and believers from the region round about joined the throng that followed Jesus to Calvary. The mother of Jesus was also there, supported by John, the beloved disciple. Her heart was stricken with unutterable anguish; yet she, with the disciples, hoped that the painful scene would change, and Jesus would assert His power, and appear before His enemies as the Son of God. Then again her mother heart would sink as she remembered words in which He had briefly referred to the things which were that day being enacted.

Jesus had scarcely passed the gate of Pilate's house when the cross which had been prepared for Barabbas was brought out and laid upon His bruised and bleeding shoulders. Crosses were also placed upon the companions of Barabbas, who were to suffer death at the same time with Jesus. The Saviour had borne His burden but a few rods when, from loss of blood and excessive weariness and pain, He fell fainting to the ground.

When Jesus revived, the cross was again placed upon His shoulders and He was forced forward. He staggered on for a few steps, bearing His heavy load, then fell as one lifeless to the ground. He was at first pronounced to be dead, but finally he again revived. The priests and rulers felt no compassion for their suffering victim; but they saw that it was impossible for Him to carry the instrument of torture farther. While they were considering what to do, Simon, a Cyrenian, coming from an opposite direction, met the crowd, was seized at the instigation of the priests, and compelled to carry the cross of Christ. The sons of Simon were disciples of Jesus, but he himself had never been connected with Him.

A great multitude followed the Saviour to Calvary, many mocking and deriding; but some were weeping and recounting His praise. Those whom He had healed of various infirmities, and those whom He had raised from the dead, declared His marvelous works with earnest voice, and demanded to know what Jesus had done that He should be treated as a malefactor. Only a few days before, they had attended Him with joyful hosannas, and the waving of palm branches, as He rode triumphantly to Jerusalem. But many who had then shouted His praise, because it was popular to do so, now swelled the cry of "Crucify Him! Crucify Him!"

Nailed to the Cross

Upon arriving at the place of execution, the condemned were bound to the instruments of torture. While the two thieves wrestled in the hands of those who stretched them upon the cross, Jesus made no resistance. The mother of Jesus looked on with agonizing suspense, hoping that He would work a miracle to save Himself. She saw His hands stretched upon the cross—those dear hands that had ever dispensed blessings, and had been reached forth so many times to heal the suffering. And now the hammer and nails were brought, and as the spikes were driven through the tender flesh and fastened to the cross, the heart-stricken disciples bore away from the cruel scene the fainting form of the mother of Christ.

Jesus made no murmur of complaint; His face remained pale and serene, but great drops of sweat stood upon His brow. There was no pitying hand to wipe the death dew from His face, nor words of sympathy and unchanging fidelity to stay His human heart. He was treading the winepress all alone; and of all the people there was none with Him. While the soldiers were doing their fearful work, and He was enduring the most acute agony, Jesus prayed for His enemies—"Father, forgive them; for they know not what they do." Luke 23:34. That prayer of Christ for His enemies embraced the world, taking in every sinner who should live, until the end of time.

After Jesus was nailed to the cross, it was lifted by several powerful men and thrust with great violence into the place prepared for it, causing the most excruciating agony to the Son of God. And now a terrible scene was enacted. Priests, rulers, and scribes forgot the dignity of their sacred offices, and joined with the rabble in mocking and jeering the dying Son of God, saying, "If Thou be the King of the Jews, save Thyself." Luke 23:37. And some deridingly repeated among themselves, "He saved others; Himself He cannot save." Mark 15:31. The dignitaries of the temple, the hardened soldiers, the vile thief upon the cross, and the base and cruel among the multitude—all united in their abuse of Christ.

The thieves who were crucified with Jesus suffered like physical torture with Him: but one was only hardened and rendered desperate and defiant by his pain. He took up the mocking of the priests, and railed upon Jesus, saying, "If Thou be Christ, save Thyself and us." Luke 23:39. The other malefactor was not a hardened criminal. When he heard the sneering words of his companion in crime, he "rebuked him, saying, Dost thou not fear God, seeing thou art in the same condemnation? And we indeed justly; for we receive the due reward of our deeds; but this Man hath done nothing amiss." Luke 23:40, 41. Then, as his heart went out to Christ, heavenly illumination flooded his mind. In Jesus, bruised, mocked, and hanging upon the cross, he saw his Redeemer, his only hope, and appealed to Him in humble faith: "Lord, remember me when Thou comest into Thy kingdom. And Jesus said unto him, Verily I say unto thee today, [By placing the comma after the word today, instead of after the word thee, as in the common versions, the true meaning of the text is more apparent.] shalt thou be with me in paradise." Luke 23:42, 43.

With amazement the angels beheld the infinite love of Jesus, who, suffering the most excruciating agony of mind and body, thought only of others, and encouraged the penitent soul to believe. While pouring out His life in death, He exercised a love for man stronger than death. Many who witnessed those scenes on Calvary were afterward established by them in the faith of Christ.

The enemies of Jesus now awaited His death with impatient hope. That event they imagined would forever hush the rumors of His divine power and the wonders of His miracles. They flattered themselves that they should then no longer tremble because of His influence. The unfeeling soldiers who had stretched the body of Jesus on the cross, divided His clothing among themselves, contending over one garment, which was woven without seam. They finally decided the matter by casting lots for it. The pen of inspiration had accurately described this scene hundreds of years before it took place: "For dogs have compassed Me: the assembly of the wicked have inclosed Me: they pierced My hands and My feet.... They part My garments among them, and cast lots upon My vesture." Psalm 22:16, 18.

A Lesson in Filial Love

The eyes of Jesus wandered over the multitude that had collected together to witness His death, and He saw at the foot of the cross John supporting Mary, the mother of Christ. She had returned to the terrible scene, not being able to longer remain away from her Son. The last lesson of Jesus was one of filial love. He looked upon the grief-stricken face of His mother, and then upon John; said He, addressing the former: "Woman, behold thy son!" Then, to the disciple: "Behold thy mother!" John 19:27. John well understood the words of Jesus, and the sacred trust which was committed to him. He immediately removed the mother of Christ from the fearful scene of Calvary. From that hour he cared for her as would a dutiful son, taking her to his own home. The perfect example of Christ's filial love shines forth with undimmed luster from the mist of ages. While enduring the keenest torture, He was not forgetful of His mother, but made all provision necessary for her future.

The mission of Christ's earthly life was now nearly accomplished. His tongue was parched, and He said, "I thirst." They saturated a sponge with vinegar and gall, and offered it Him to drink; and when He had tasted it, He refused it. And now the Lord of life and glory was dying, a ransom for the race. It was the sense of sin, bringing the Father's wrath upon Him as man's substitute, that made the cup He drank so bitter, and broke the heart of the Son of God.

As man's substitute and surety, the iniquity of men was laid upon Christ; He was counted a transgressor that He might redeem them from the curse of the law. The guilt of every descendant of Adam of every age was pressing upon His heart; and the wrath of God and the terrible manifestation of His displeasure because of iniquity, filled the soul of His Son with consternation. The withdrawal of the divine countenance from the Saviour in this hour of supreme anguish pierced His heart with a sorrow that can never be fully understood by man. Every pang endured by the Son of God upon the cross, the blood drops that flowed from His head, His hands and feet, the convulsions of agony which racked His frame, and the unutterable anguish that filled His soul at the hiding of His Father's face from Him, speak to man, saying, It is for love of thee that the Son of God consents to have these heinous crimes laid upon Him; for thee He spoils the domain of death, and opens the gates of Paradise and immortal life. He who stilled the angry waves by His word and walked the foam-capped billows, who made devils tremble and disease flee from His touch, who raised the dead to life and opened the eyes of the blind, offers Himself upon the cross as the last sacrifice for man. He, the sin-bearer, endures judicial punishment for iniquity and becomes sin itself for man.

Satan, with his fierce temptations, wrung the heart of Jesus. Sin, so hateful to His sight, was heaped upon Him till He groaned beneath its weight. No wonder that His humanity trembled in that fearful hour. Angels witnessed with amazement the despairing agony of the Son of God, so much greater than His physical pain that the latter was hardly felt by Him. The hosts of heaven veiled their faces from the fearful sight.

Inanimate nature expressed a sympathy with its insulted and dying Author. The sun refused to look upon the awful scene. Its full, bright rays were illuminating the earth at midday, when suddenly it seemed to be blotted out. Complete darkness enveloped the cross and all the vicinity about, like a funeral pall. The darkness lasted three full hours. At the ninth hour the terrible darkness lifted from the people, but still wrapt the Saviour as in a mantle. The angry lightnings seemed to be hurled at Him as He hung upon the cross. Then "Jesus cried with a loud voice, saying, Eloi, Eloi, lama sabachthani? which is, being interpreted, My God, My God, why hast Thou forsaken Me?" Mark 15:34.

It Is Finished

In silence the people watch for the end of this fearful scene. Again the sun shines forth, but the cross is enveloped in darkness. Suddenly the gloom is lifted from the cross, and in clear trumpet tones, that seem to resound throughout creation, Jesus cries, "It is finished." "Father, into Thy hands I commend My spirit." Luke 23:46. A light encircled the cross, and the face of the Saviour shone with a glory like unto the sun. He then bowed His head upon His breast and died.

At the moment in which Christ died, there were priests ministering in the temple before the veil which separated the holy from the most holy place. Suddenly they felt the earth tremble beneath them, and the veil of the temple, a strong rich drapery that had been renewed yearly, was rent in twain from top to bottom by the same bloodless hand that wrote the words of doom upon the walls of Belshazzar's palace.

Jesus did not yield up His life till He had accomplished the work which He came to do; and He exclaimed with His parting breath, "It is finished!" Angels rejoiced as the words were uttered, for the great plan of redemption was being triumphantly carried out. There was joy in heaven that the sons of Adam could now, through a life of obedience, be exalted finally to the presence of God. Satan was defeated, and knew that his kingdom was lost.

The Burial

John was at a loss to know what measures he should take in regard to the body of his beloved Master. He shuddered at the thought of its being handled by rough and unfeeling soldiers, and placed in a dishonored burial place. He knew he could obtain no favors from the Jewish authorities, and he could hope little from Pilate. But Joseph and Nicodemus came to the front in this emergency. Both of these men were members of the Sanhedrin, and acquainted with Pilate. Both were men of wealth and influence. They were determined that the body of Jesus should have an honorable burial.

Joseph went boldly to Pilate, and begged from him the body of Jesus for burial. Pilate then gave an official order that the body of Jesus should be given to Joseph. While the disciple John was anxious and troubled about the sacred remains of his beloved Master, Joseph of Arimathea returned with the commission from the governor; and Nicodemus, anticipating the result of Joseph's interview with Pilate, came with a costly mixture of myrrh and aloes of about one hundred pounds' weight. The most honored in all Jerusalem could not have been shown more respect in death.

Gently and reverently they removed with their own hands the body of Jesus from the instrument of torture, their sympathetic tears falling fast as they looked upon His bruised and lacerated form, which they carefully bathed and cleansed from the stain of blood. Joseph owned a new tomb, hewn from stone, which he was reserving for himself; it was near Calvary, and he now prepared this sepulcher for Jesus. The body, together with the spices brought by Nicodemus, was carefully wrapped in a linen sheet, and the three disciples bore their precious burden to the new sepulcher, wherein man had never before lain. There they straightened those mangled limbs, and folded the bruised hands upon the pulseless breast. The Galilean women drew near, to see that all had been done that could be done for the lifeless form of their beloved Teacher. Then they saw the heavy stone rolled against the entrance of the sepulcher, and the Son of God was left at rest. The women were last at the cross, and last at the tomb of Christ.

Although the Jewish rulers had carried out their fiendish purpose in putting to death the Son of God, their apprehensions were not quieted, nor was their jealousy of Christ dead. Mingled with the joy of gratified revenge, there was an ever-present fear that His dead body, lying in Joseph's tomb, would come forth to life. Therefore "the chief priests and Pharisees came together unto Pilate, saying, Sir, we remember that that deceiver said, while He was yet alive, After three days I will rise again. Command therefore that the sepulchre be made sure until the third day, lest His disciples come by night, and steal Him away, and say unto the people, He is risen from the dead: so the last error shall be worse than the first." Matthew 27:63, 64. Pilate was as unwilling as were the Jews that Jesus should rise with power to punish the guilt of those who had destroyed Him, and he placed a band of Roman soldiers at the command of the priests. Said he, "Ye have a watch: go your way, make it as sure as ye can. So they went, and made the sepulchre sure, sealing the stone, and setting a watch." Matthew 27:65, 66.

The Jews realized the advantage of having such a guard about the tomb of Jesus. They placed a seal upon the stone that closed the sepulcher, that it might not be disturbed without the fact being known, and took every precaution against the disciples' practicing any deception in regard to the body of Jesus. But all their plans and precautions only served to make the triumph of the resurrection more complete and to more fully establish its truth.

Chapter 30—The Resurrection of Christ

The disciples rested on the Sabbath, sorrowing for the death of their Lord, while Jesus, the King of glory, lay in the tomb. As night drew on, soldiers were stationed to guard the Saviour's resting place, while angels, unseen, hovered above the sacred spot. The night wore slowly away, and while it was yet dark the watching angels knew that the time for the release of God's dear Son, their loved Commander, had nearly come. As they were waiting with the deepest emotion the hour of His triumph, a mighty angel came flying swiftly from heaven. His face was like the lightning, and his garments white as snow. His light dispersed the darkness from his track and caused the evil angels, who had triumphantly claimed the body of Jesus, to flee in terror from his brightness and glory. One of the angelic host who had witnessed the scene of Christ's humiliation, and was watching His resting place, joined the angel from heaven, and together they came down to the sepulcher. The earth trembled and shook as they approached, and there was a great earthquake.

Terror seized the Roman guard. Where was now their power to keep the body of Jesus? They did not think of their duty or of the disciples' stealing Him away. As the light of the angels shone around, brighter than the sun, that Roman guard fell as dead men to the ground. One of the angels laid hold of the great stone and rolled it away from the door of the sepulcher and seated himself upon it. The other entered the tomb and unbound the napkin from the head of Jesus.

"Thy Father Calls Thee"

Then the angel from heaven, with a voice that caused the earth to quake, cried out, "Thou Son of God, Thy Father calls Thee! Come forth." Death could hold dominion over Him no longer. Jesus arose from the dead, a triumphant conqueror. In solemn awe the angelic host gazed upon the scene. And as Jesus came forth from the sepulcher, those shining angels prostrated themselves to the earth in worship and hailed Him with songs of victory and triumph.

Satan's angels had been compelled to flee before the bright, penetrating light of the heavenly angels, and they bitterly complained to their king that their prey had been violently taken from them, and that He whom they so much hated had risen from the dead. Satan and his hosts had exulted that their power over fallen man had caused the Lord of life to be laid in the grave, but short was their hellish triumph. For as Jesus walked forth from His prison house a majestic conqueror, Satan knew that after a season he must die, and his kingdom pass unto Him whose right it was. He lamented and raged that, notwithstanding all his efforts, Jesus had not been overcome but had opened a way of salvation for man, and whosoever would might walk in it and be saved.

The evil angels and their commander met in council to consider how they could still work against the government of God. Satan bade his servants go to the chief priests and elders. Said he, "We succeeded in deceiving them, blinding their eyes and hardening their hearts against Jesus. We made them believe that He was an imposter. That Roman guard will carry the hateful news that Christ has risen. We led the priests and elders on to hate Jesus and to murder Him. Now hold it before them that if it becomes known that Jesus is risen, they will be stoned by the people for putting to death an innocent man."

The Report of the Roman Guard

As the host of heavenly angels departed from the sepulcher and the light and glory passed away, the Roman guard ventured to raise their heads and look about them. They were filled with amazement as they saw that the great stone had been rolled from the door of the sepulcher and that the body of Jesus was gone. They hastened to the city to make known to the priests and elders what they had seen. As those murderers listened to the marvelous report, paleness sat upon every face. Horror seized them at the thought of what they had done. If the report was correct, they were lost. For a time they sat in silence, looking upon one another's faces, not knowing what to do or what to say. To accept the report would be to condemn themselves. They went aside to consult as to what should be done. They reasoned that if the report brought by the guard should be circulated among the people, those who put Christ to death would be slain as His murderers.

It was decided to hire the soldiers to keep the matter secret. The priests and elders offered them a large sum of money, saying, "Say ye, His disciples came by night, and stole Him away while we slept." Matthew 28:13. And when the guard inquired what would be done with them for sleeping at their post, the Jewish officers promised to persuade the governor and secure their safety. For the sake of money the Roman guard sold their honor and agreed to follow the counsel of the priests and elders.

The First Fruits of Redemption

When Jesus, as He hung upon the cross, cried out, "It is finished", the rocks rent, the earth shook, and some of the graves were opened. When He arose a victor over death and the grave, while the earth was reeling and the glory of heaven shone around the sacred spot, many of the righteous dead, obedient to His call, came forth as witnesses that He had risen. Those favored, risen saints came forth glorified. They were chosen and holy ones of every age, from creation down even to the days of Christ. Thus while the Jewish leaders were seeking to conceal the fact of Christ's resurrection, God chose to bring up a company from their graves to testify that Jesus had risen, and to declare His glory.

Those risen ones differed in stature and form, some being more noble in appearance than others. I was informed that the inhabitants of earth had been degenerating, losing their strength and comeliness. Satan has the power of disease and death, and with every age the effects of the curse have been more visible, and the power of Satan more plainly seen. Those who lived in the days of Noah and Abraham resembled the angels in form, comeliness, and strength. But every succeeding generation have been growing weaker and more subject to disease, and their life has been of shorter duration. Satan has been learning how to annoy and enfeeble the race.

Those who came forth after the resurrection of Jesus appeared to many, telling them that the sacrifice for man was completed, that Jesus, whom the Jews crucified, had risen from the dead; and in proof of their words they declared, "We be risen with Him." They bore testimony that it was by His mighty power that they had been called forth from their graves. Notwithstanding the lying reports circulated, the resurrection of Christ could not be concealed by Satan, his angels, or the chief priests; for this holy company, brought forth from their graves, spread the wonderful, joyful news; also Jesus showed Himself to His sorrowing, heartbroken disciples, dispelling their fears and causing them joy and gladness.

The Women at the Sepulcher

Early in the morning of the first day of the week, before it was yet light, holy women came to the sepulcher, bringing sweet spices to anoint the body of Jesus. They found that the heavy stone had been rolled away from the door of the sepulcher, and the body of Jesus was not there. Their hearts sank within them, and they feared that their enemies had taken away the body. Suddenly they beheld two angels in white apparel, their faces bright and shining. These heavenly beings understood the errand of the women and immediately told them that Jesus was not there; He had risen, but they could behold the place where He had lain. They bade them go and tell His disciples that He would go before them into Galilee. With fear and great joy the women hurried back to the sorrowing disciples and told them the things which they had seen and heard.

The disciples could not believe that Christ had risen, but, with the women who had brought the report, ran hastily to the sepulcher. They found that Jesus was not there; they saw His linen clothes, but could not believe the good news that He had risen from the dead. They returned home, marveling at what they had seen, also at the report brought them by the women.

But Mary chose to linger around the sepulcher, thinking of what she had seen and distressed with the thought that she might have been deceived. She felt that new trials awaited her. Her grief was renewed, and she broke forth in bitter weeping. She stooped down to look again into the sepulcher, and beheld two angels clothed in white. One was sitting where the head of Jesus had lain, the other where His feet had been. They spoke to her tenderly and asked her why she wept. She replied, "They have taken away my Lord, and I know not where they have laid Him." John 20:13.

"Touch Me Not"

As she turned from the sepulcher she saw Jesus standing near, but knew Him not. He spoke to her tenderly, inquiring the cause of her sorrow and asking whom she was seeking. Supposing that He was the gardener, she begged Him, if He had borne away her Lord, to tell her where He had laid Him, that she might take Him away. Jesus spoke to her with his own heavenly voice, saying, "Mary!" She was acquainted with the tones of that dear voice, and quickly answered, "Master!" and in her joy was about to embrace Him; but Jesus said, "Touch Me not; for I am not yet ascended to My Father: but go to My brethren, and say unto them, I ascend unto My Father, and your Father; and to My God, and your God." John 20:17. Joyfully she hastened to the disciples with the good news. Jesus quickly ascended to His Father to hear from His lips that He accepted the sacrifice, and to receive all power in heaven and on earth.

Angels like a cloud surrounded the Son of God and bade the everlasting gates be lifted up, that the King of glory might come in. I saw that while Jesus was with that bright heavenly host, in the presence of God, and surrounded by His glory, He did not forget His disciples upon the earth, but received power from His

Father, that He might return and impart power to them. The same day He returned and showed Himself to His disciples. He suffered them then to touch Him, for He had ascended to His Father and had received power.

Doubting Thomas

At this time Thomas was not present. He would not humbly receive the report of the disciples, but firmly and self-confidently affirmed that he would not believe unless he should put his fingers in the prints of the nails and his hand in the side where the cruel spear was thrust. In this he showed a lack of confidence in his brethren. If all should require the same evidence, none would now receive Jesus and believe in His resurrection. But it was the will of God that the report of the disciples should be received by those who could not themselves see and hear the risen Saviour.

God was not pleased with the unbelief of Thomas. When Jesus again met with His disciples, Thomas was with them; and when he beheld Jesus, he believed. But he had declared that he would not be satisfied without the evidence of feeling added to sight, and Jesus gave him the evidence which he had desired. Thomas cried out, "My Lord and my God!" But Jesus reproved him for his unbelief, saying, "Thomas, because thou hast seen Me, thou hast believed: blessed are they that have not seen, and yet have believed." John 20:28, 29.

The Discomfiture of Christ's Slayer

As the news spread from city to city and from town to town, the Jews in their turn feared for their lives and concealed the hatred which they cherished toward the disciples. Their only hope was to spread their lying report. And those who wished this lie to be true accepted it. Pilate trembled as he heard that Christ had risen. He could not doubt the testimony given, and from that hour peace left him forever. For the sake of worldly honor, for fear of losing his authority and his life, he had delivered Jesus to die. He was now fully convinced that it was not merely an innocent man of whose blood he was guilty, but the Son of God. Miserable to its close was the life of Pilate. Despair and anguish crushed every hopeful, joyful feeling. He refused to be comforted and died a most miserable death.

Forty Days With the Disciples

Jesus remained with His disciples forty days, causing them joy and gladness of heart as He opened to them more fully the realities of the kingdom of God. He commissioned them to bear testimony to the things which they had seen and heard concerning His sufferings, death, and resurrection, that He had made a sacrifice for sin, and that all who would might come unto Him and find life. With faithful tenderness He told them that they would be persecuted and distressed, but they would find relief in recalling their experience and remembering the words which He had spoken to them. He told them that He had overcome the temptations of Satan and obtained the victory through trials and suffering. Satan could have no more power over Him, but would bring his temptations to bear more directly upon them and upon all who should believe in His name. But they could overcome as He had overcome. Jesus endowed His disciples with power to work miracles, and told them that although they should be persecuted by wicked men, He would from time to time send His angels to deliver them; their lives could not be taken until their mission should be accomplished; then they might be required to seal with their blood the testimonies which they had borne.

His anxious followers gladly listened to His teachings, eagerly feasting upon every word which fell from His holy lips. Now they certainly knew that He was the Saviour of the world. His words sank deep into their hearts, and they sorrowed that they must soon be parted from their heavenly Teacher and no longer hear comforting, gracious words from His lips. But again their hearts were warmed with love and exceeding joy, as Jesus told them that He would go and prepare mansions for them and come again and receive them, that they might be ever with Him. He promised also to send the Comforter, the Holy Spirit, to guide them into all truth. "And He lifted up His hands, and blessed them." Luke 24:50.

Chapter 31—The Ascension of Christ

All heaven was waiting the hour of triumph when Jesus should ascend to His Father. Angels came to receive the King of glory and to escort Him triumphantly to heaven. After Jesus had blessed His disciples, He was parted from them and taken up. And as He led the way upward, the multitude of captives who were raised at His resurrection followed. A multitude of the heavenly host were in attendance, while in heaven an innumerable company of angels awaited His coming.

As they ascended to the Holy City, the angels who escorted Jesus cried out, "Lift up your heads, O ye gates; and be ye lift up, ye everlasting doors; and the King of glory shall come in." The angels in the city cried out with rapture, "Who is this King of glory?" The escorting angels answered in triumph, "The Lord strong and mighty, the Lord mighty in battle! Lift up your heads, O ye gates; even lift them up, ye everlasting doors; and the King of glory shall come in." Again the waiting angels asked, "Who is this King of glory?" and the escorting angels answered in melodious strains, "The Lord of hosts, He is the King of glory." Psalm 24:7-10. And the heavenly train passed into the city of God.

Then all the heavenly host surrounded their majestic Commander, and with the deepest adoration bowed before Him and cast their glittering crowns at His feet. And then they touched their golden harps, and in sweet, melodious strains filled all heaven with rich music and songs to the Lamb who was slain, yet lives again in majesty and glory.

The Promise of Return

As the disciples gazed sorrowfully toward heaven to catch the last glimpse of their ascending Lord, two angels clothed in white apparel stood by them and said to them, "Ye men of Galilee, why stand ye gazing up into heaven? this same Jesus, which is taken up from you into heaven, shall so come in like manner as ye have seen Him go into heaven." Acts 1:11. The disciples and the mother of Jesus, who with them had witnessed the ascension of the Son of God, spent the following night in talking over His wonderful acts and the strange and glorious events which had taken place within a short time.

The Wrath of Satan

Satan again counseled with his angels, and with bitter hatred against God's government told them that while he retained his power and authority upon earth their efforts must be tenfold stronger against the followers of Jesus. They had prevailed nothing against Christ but must overthrow His followers, if possible. In every generation they must seek to ensnare those who would believe in Jesus. He related to his angels that Jesus had given His disciples power to rebuke them and cast them out, and to heal those whom they should afflict. Then Satan's angels went forth like roaring lions, seeking to destroy the followers of Jesus.

Chapter 32—Pentecost

This chapter is based on Acts 2:1.

When Jesus opened the understanding of the disciples to the meaning of the prophecies concerning Himself, He assured them that all power was given Him in heaven and on earth, and bade them go preach the gospel to every creature. The disciples, with a sudden revival of their old hope that Jesus would take His place upon the throne of David at Jerusalem, inquired, "Wilt Thou at this time restore again the kingdom to Israel?" Acts 1:6. The Saviour threw an uncertainty over their minds in regard to the subject by replying that it was not for them "to know the times or the seasons, which the Father hath put in His own power." Acts 1:7.

The disciples began to hope that the wonderful descent of the Holy Ghost would influence the Jewish people to accept Jesus. The Saviour forbore to further explain, for He knew that when the Holy Spirit should come upon them in full measure their minds would be illuminated and they would fully understand the work before them, and take it up just where He had left it.

The disciples assembled in the upper chamber, uniting in supplications with the believing women, with Mary the mother of Jesus, and with His brethren. These brethren, who had been unbelieving, were now fully established in their faith by the scenes attending the crucifixion and by the resurrection and ascension of the Lord. The number assembled was about one hundred and twenty.

The Descent of the Holy Spirit

"And when the day of Pentecost was fully come, they were all with one accord in one place. And suddenly there came a sound from heaven as of a rushing mighty wind, and it filled all the house where they were sitting. And there appeared unto them cloven tongues like as of fire, and it sat upon each of them. And they were all filled with the Holy Ghost, and began to speak with other tongues, as the Spirit gave them utterance." The Holy Ghost, assuming the form of tongues of fire divided at the tips, and resting upon those assembled, was an emblem of the gift which was bestowed upon them of speaking with fluency several different languages, with which they had formerly been unacquainted. And the appearance of fire signified the fervent zeal with which they would labor and the power which would attend their words.

Under this heavenly illumination the scriptures which Christ had explained to them stood forth in their minds with the vivid luster and loveliness of clear and powerful truth. The veil which had prevented them from seeing the end of that which was abolished was now removed, and the object of Christ's mission and the nature of His kingdom were comprehended with perfect clearness.

In the Power of Pentecost

The Jews had been scattered to almost every nation, and spoke various languages. They had come long distances to Jerusalem, and had temporarily taken up their abode there, to remain through the religious festivals then in progress and to observe their requirements. When assembled, they were of every known tongue. This diversity of languages was a great obstacle to the labors of God's servants in publishing the doctrine of Christ to the uttermost parts of the earth. That God should supply the deficiency of the apostles in a miraculous manner was to the people the most perfect confirmation of the testimony of these witnesses for Christ. The Holy Spirit had done for them that which they could not have accomplished for themselves in a lifetime; they could now spread the truth of the gospel abroad, speaking with accuracy the language of those for whom they were laboring. This miraculous gift was the highest evidence they could present to the world that their commission bore the signet of Heaven.

"And there were dwelling at Jerusalem Jews, devout men, out of every nation under heaven. Now when this was noised abroad, the multitude came together, and were confounded, because that every man heard them speak in his own language. And they were all amazed and marvelled, saying one to another, Behold, are not all these which speak Galileans? And how hear we every man in our own tongue, wherein we were born?"

The priests and rulers were greatly enraged at this wonderful manifestation, which was reported throughout all Jerusalem and the vicinity, but they dared not give way to their malice, for fear of exposing themselves to the hatred of the people. They had put the Master to death, but here were His servants, unlearned men of Galilee, tracing out the wonderful fulfillment of prophecy and teaching the doctrine of Jesus in all the languages then spoken. They spoke with power of the wonderful works of the Saviour, and unfolded to their hearers the plan of salvation in the mercy and sacrifice of the Son of God. Their words convicted and converted thousands who listened. The traditions and superstitions inculcated by the priests were swept away from their minds and they accepted the pure teachings of the Word of God.

Peter's Sermon

Peter showed them that this manifestation was the direct fulfillment of the prophecy of Joel, wherein he foretold that such power would come upon men of God to fit them for a special work.

Peter traced back the lineage of Christ in a direct line to the honorable house of David. He did not use any of the teachings of Jesus to prove His true position, because he knew their prejudices were so great that it would be of no effect. But he referred them to David, whom the Jews regarded as a venerable patriarch of their nation. Said Peter:

"For David speaketh concerning Him, I foresaw the Lord always before my face, for He is on my right hand, that I should not be moved: therefore did my heart rejoice, and my tongue was glad; moreover also my flesh shall rest in hope: because Thou wilt not leave My soul in hell, neither wilt Thou suffer Thine Holy One to see corruption."

Peter here shows that David could not have spoken in reference to himself, but definitely of Jesus Christ. David died a natural death like other men; his sepulcher, with the honored dust it contained, had been preserved with great care until that time. David, as king of Israel, and also as a prophet, had been specially honored by God. In prophetic vision he was shown the future life and ministry of Christ. He saw His rejection, His trial, crucifixion, burial, resurrection, and ascension.

David testified that the soul of Christ was not to be left in hell (the grave), nor was His flesh to see corruption. Peter shows the fulfillment of this prophecy in Jesus of Nazareth. God had actually raised Him up from the tomb before His body saw corruption. He was now the exalted One in the heaven of heavens.

On that memorable occasion large numbers who had heretofore ridiculed the idea of so unpretending a person as Jesus being the Son of God, became thoroughly convinced of the truth and acknowledged Him as their Saviour. Three thousand souls were added to the church. The apostles spoke by the power of the Holy Ghost; and their words could not be controverted, for they were confirmed by mighty miracles, wrought by them through the outpouring of the Spirit of God. The disciples were themselves astonished at the results of this visitation, and the quick and abundant harvest of souls. All the people were filled with amazement. Those who did not yield their prejudice and bigotry were so overawed that they dared not by voice or violence attempt to stay the mighty work, and, for the time being, their opposition ceased.

The arguments of the apostles alone, although clear and convincing, would not have removed the prejudice of the Jews which had withstood so much evidence. But the Holy Ghost sent those arguments home with divine power to their hearts. They were as sharp arrows of the Almighty, convicting them of their terrible guilt in rejecting and crucifying the Lord of glory. "Now when they heard this, they were pricked in their heart, and said unto Peter and to the rest of the apostles, Men and brethren, what shall we do? Then Peter said unto them, Repent, and be baptized every one of you in the name of Jesus Christ for the remission of sins, and ye shall receive the gift of the Holy Ghost."

Peter urged home upon the convicted people the fact that they had rejected Christ because they had been deceived by the priests and rulers; and if they continued to look to them for counsel, and waited for those leaders to acknowledge Christ before they dared to do so, they would never accept Him. Those powerful men, although they made a profession of sanctity, were ambitious, and zealous for riches and earthly glory. They would never come to Christ to receive light. Jesus had foretold a terrible retribution to come upon that people for their obstinate unbelief, notwithstanding the most powerful evidences given them that Jesus was the Son of God.

From this time forth the language of the disciples was pure, simple, and accurate in word and accent, whether they spoke their native tongue or a foreign language. These humble men, who had never learned in the school of the prophets, presented truths so elevated and pure as to astonish those who heard them. They could not go personally to the uttermost parts of the earth; but there were men at the feast from every quarter of the world, and the truths received by them were carried to their various homes and published among their people, winning souls to Christ.

A Lesson for Our Day

This testimony in regard to the establishment of the Christian church is given us not only as an important portion of sacred history but also as a lesson. All who profess the name of Christ should be waiting, watching, and praying with one heart. All differences should be put away, and unity and tender love one for another pervade the whole. Then our prayers may go up together to our heavenly Father with strong, earnest faith. Then we may wait with patience and hope the fulfillment of the promise.

The answer may come with sudden velocity and overpowering might, or it may be delayed for days and weeks, and our faith receive a trial. But God knows how and when to answer our prayer. It is our part of the work to put ourselves in connection with the divine channel. God is responsible for His part of the work. He is faithful who hath promised. The great and important matter with us is to be of one heart and mind, putting aside all envy and malice, and, as humble supplicants, to watch and wait. Jesus, our Representative and Head, is ready to do for us what He did for the praying, watching ones on the day of Pentecost.

Chapter 33—The Healing of the Cripple

This chapter is based on Acts 3 and 4.

A short time after the descent of the Holy Spirit, and immediately after a season of fervent prayer, Peter and John, going up to the temple to worship, saw a distressed and poverty-stricken cripple, forty years of age, who had known no other life than one of pain and infirmity. This unfortunate man had long desired to go to Jesus and be healed, but he was almost helpless, and was removed far from the scene of the Great Physician's labors. Finally his earnest pleadings induced some kind persons to bear him to the gate of the temple. But upon arriving there he discovered that the Healer, upon whom his hopes were centered, had been put to a cruel death.

His disappointment excited the pity of those who knew how long he had eagerly hoped and expected to be healed by Jesus, and they daily brought him to the temple, that the passers-by might be moved to give him a trifle to relieve his present wants. As Peter and John passed, he begged charity from them. The disciples regarded him with compassion. "And Peter, fastening his eyes upon him with John, said, Look on us." "Silver and gold have I none; but such as I have give I thee: in the name of Jesus Christ of Nazareth rise up and walk."

The poor man's countenance had fallen when Peter declared his own poverty, but grew bright with hope and faith as the disciple continued. "And he took him by the right hand, and lifted him up: and immediately his feet and ankle bones received strength. And he leaping up stood, and walked, and entered with them into the temple, walking, and leaping, and praising God. And all the people saw him walking and praising God: and they knew that it was he which sat for alms at the Beautiful gate of the temple: and they were filled with wonder and amazement at that which had happened unto him."

The Jews were astonished that the disciples could perform miracles similar to those of Jesus. He, they supposed, was dead, and they had expected all such wonderful manifestations to cease with Him. Yet here was this man who had been a helpless cripple for forty years, now rejoicing in the full use of his limbs, free from pain, and happy in believing on Jesus.

The apostles saw the amazement of the people, and questioned them why they should be astonished at the miracle which they had witnessed, and regard them with awe as though it were through their own power they had done this thing. Peter assured them it was done through the merits of Jesus of Nazareth, whom they had rejected and crucified, but whom God had raised from the dead the third day. "And His name through faith hath made this man strong, whom ye see and know: yea, the faith which is by Him hath given him this perfect soundness in the presence of you all. And now, brethren, I wot that through ignorance ye did it, as did also your rulers. But those things, which God before had shewed by the mouth of all His prophets that Christ should suffer He hath so fulfilled."

After the performance of this miracle the people flocked together in the temple, and Peter addressed them in one part of the temple, while John spoke to them in another part. The apostles, having spoken plainly of the great crime of the Jews, in rejecting and putting to death the Prince of life, were careful not to drive them to madness or despair. Peter was willing to lessen the atrocity of their guilt as much as possible, by presuming that they did the deed ignorantly. He declared to them that the Holy Ghost was calling for them to repent of their sins and to be converted; that there was no hope for them except through the mercy of that Christ whom they had crucified; through faith in Him only could their sins be cancelled by His blood.

Arrest and Trial of the Apostles

This preaching the resurrection of Christ, and that through His death and resurrection He would finally bring up all the dead from their graves, deeply stirred the Sadducees. They felt that their favorite doctrine was in danger and their reputation at stake. Some of the officials of the temple, and the captain of the temple, were Sadducees. The captain, with the help of a number of Sadducees, arrested the two apostles and put them in prison, as it was too late for their cases to be examined that night.

The following day Annas and Caiaphas, with the other dignitaries of the temple, met together for the trial of the prisoners, who were then brought before them. In that very room, and before those very men, Peter had shamefully denied his Lord. All this came distinctly before the mind of the disciple as he now appeared for his own trial. He had now an opportunity of redeeming his former wicked cowardice.

The company present remembered the part Peter had acted at the trial of his Master, and they flattered themselves that he could be intimidated by the threat of imprisonment and death. But the Peter who denied Christ in the hour of His greatest need was the impulsive, self-confident disciple, differing widely from the Peter who was before the Sanhedrin for examination that day. He had been converted; he was distrustful of self, and no longer a proud boaster. He was filled with the Holy Spirit, and through its power he had become firm as a rock, courageous, yet modest, in magnifying Christ. He was ready to remove the stain of his apostasy by honoring the name he had once disowned.

Peter's Bold Defense

Hitherto the priests had avoided having the crucifixion or resurrection of Jesus mentioned; but now, in fulfillment of their purpose, they were forced to inquire of the accused by what power they had accomplished the remarkable cure of the impotent man. Then Peter, filled with the Holy Ghost, addressed the priests and elders respectfully, and declared: "Be it known unto you all, and to all the people of Israel, that by the name of Jesus Christ of Nazareth, whom ye crucified, whom God raised from the dead, even by Him doth this man stand here before you whole. This is the stone which was set at nought of you builders, which is become the head of the corner. Neither is there salvation in any other: for there is none other name under heaven given among men, whereby we must be saved."

The seal of Christ was on the words of Peter, and his countenance was illuminated by the Holy Spirit. Close beside him, as a convincing witness, stood the man who had been so miraculously cured. The appearance of this man, who but a few hours before was a helpless cripple, now restored to soundness of body, and being enlightened concerning Jesus of Nazareth, added a weight of testimony to the words of Peter. Priests, rulers, and people were silent. The rulers had no power to refute his statement. They had been obliged to hear that which they most desired not to hear: the fact of the resurrection of Jesus Christ, and His power in heaven to perform miracles through the medium of His apostles on earth.

The defense of Peter, in which he boldly avowed from whence his strength was obtained, appalled them. He had referred to the stone set at nought by the builders—meaning the authorities of the church, who should have perceived the value of Him whom they rejected—but which had nevertheless become the head of the corner. In those words he directly referred to Christ, who was the foundation stone of the church.

The people were amazed at the boldness of the disciples. They supposed, because they were ignorant fishermen, they would be overcome with embarrassment when confronted by the priests, scribes, and elders. But they took knowledge that they had been with Jesus. The apostles spoke as He had spoken, with a convincing power that silenced their adversaries. In order to conceal their perplexity, the priests and rulers ordered the apostles to be taken away, that they might counsel among themselves.

They all agreed that it would be useless to deny that the man had been healed through power given the apostles in the name of the crucified Jesus. They would gladly have covered up the miracle by falsehoods; but the work was done in the full light of day and before a crowd of people, and had already come to the knowledge of thousands. They felt that the work must be immediately stopped, or Jesus would gain many believers, their own disgrace would follow, and they would be held guilty of the murder of the Son of God.

But notwithstanding their disposition to destroy the disciples, they dared not do worse than threaten them with the severest punishment if they continued to teach or work in the name of Jesus. Thereupon Peter and John boldly declared that their work had been given them of God, and they could not but speak the things which they had seen and heard. The priests would gladly have punished these noble men for their unswerving fidelity to their sacred calling, but they feared the people, "for all men glorified God for that which was done." So, with repeated threats and injunctions, the apostles were set at liberty.

Chapter 34—Loyalty to God Under Persecution

This chapter is based on Acts 5:12-42.

The apostles continued their work of mercy, in healing the afflicted and in proclaiming a crucified and risen Saviour, with great power. Numbers were continually added to the church by baptism, but none dared join them who were not united heart and mind with the believers in Christ. Multitudes flocked to Jerusalem, bringing their sick and those who were vexed by unclean spirits. Many sufferers were laid in the streets as Peter and John passed by, that their shadows might fall upon and heal them. The power of the risen Saviour had indeed fallen upon the apostles, and they worked signs and miracles that daily increased the number of believers.

These things greatly perplexed the priests and rulers, especially those among them who were Sadducees. They saw that if the apostles were allowed to preach a resurrected Saviour, and to do miracles in His name, their doctrine that there was no resurrection of the dead would be rejected by all, and their sect would soon become extinct. The Pharisees saw that the tendency of their preaching would be to undermine the Jewish ceremonies and make the sacrificial offerings of none effect. Their former efforts to suppress these preachers had been in vain, but they now felt determined to put down the excitement.

Delivered by an Angel

The apostles were accordingly arrested and imprisoned, and the Sanhedrin was called to try their case. A large number of learned men, in addition to the council, were summoned, and they counseled together what should be done with these disturbers of the peace. "But the angel of the Lord by night opened the prison doors, and brought them forth, and said, Go, stand and speak in the temple to the people all the words of this life. And when they heard that, they entered into the temple early in the morning, and taught."

When the apostles appeared among the believers and recounted how the angel had led them directly through the band of soldiers guarding the prison and bade them resume the work which had been interrupted by the priests and rulers, the brethren were filled with joy and amazement.

The priests and rulers in council had decided to fix upon them the charge of insurrection and accuse them of murdering Ananias and Sapphira (Acts 5:1-11), and of conspiring to deprive the priests of their authority and put them to death. They trusted that the mob would then be excited to take the matter in hand and to deal by the apostles as they had dealt by Jesus. They were aware that many who did not accept the doctrine of Christ were weary of the arbitrary rule of the Jewish authorities and were anxious for some decided change. If these persons became interested in, and embraced, the belief of the apostles, acknowledging Jesus as the Messiah, they feared the anger of the entire people would be raised against the priests, who would be made to answer for the murder of Christ. They decided to take strong measures to prevent this. They finally sent for the supposed prisoners to be brought before them. Great was their amazement when the report was brought back that the prison doors were found securely bolted and the guard stationed before them, but that the prisoners were nowhere to be found.

Soon the report was brought: "Behold, the men whom ye put in prison are standing in the temple, and teaching the people." Although the apostles were miraculously delivered from prison, they were not saved from examination and punishment. Christ had said when He was with them, "Take heed to yourselves: for they shall deliver you up to councils." God had given them a token of His care and an assurance of His presence by sending the angel to them; it was now their part to suffer for the sake of that Jesus whom they preached. The people were so wrought upon by what they had seen and heard that the priests and rulers knew it would be impossible to excite them against the apostles.

The Second Trial

"Then went the captain with the officers, and brought them without violence: for they feared the people, lest they should have been stoned. And when they had brought them, they set them before the council: and the high priest asked them, saying, Did not we straitly command you that ye should not teach in this name? and, behold, ye have filled Jerusalem with your doctrine, and intend to bring this Man's blood upon us." They were not as willing to bear the blame of slaying Jesus as when they swelled the cry with the debased mob: "His blood be on us, and on our children."

Peter, with the other apostles, took up the same line of defense he had followed at his former trial: "Then Peter and the other apostles answered and said, We ought to obey God rather than men." It was the angel sent by God who delivered them from prison, and who commanded them to teach in the temple. In following his directions they were obeying the divine command, which they must continue to do at any cost to themselves. Peter continued: "The God of our fathers raised up Jesus, whom ye slew and hanged on a tree. Him hath God exalted with His right hand to be a Prince and a Saviour, for to give repentance to Israel, and forgiveness of sins. And we are His witnesses of these things; and so is also the Holy Ghost, whom God hath given to them that obey Him."

The Spirit of inspiration was upon the apostles, and the accused became the accusers, charging the murder of Christ upon the priests and rulers who composed the council. The Jews were so enraged at this that they decided, without any further trial and without authority from the Roman officers, to take the law into their own hands and put the prisoners to death. Already guilty of the blood of Christ, they were now eager to imbrue their hands in the blood of His apostles. But there was one man of learning and high position whose clear intellect saw that this violent step would lead to terrible consequences. God raised up a man of their own council to stay the violence of the priests and rulers.

Gamaliel, the learned Pharisee and doctor, a man of great reputation, was a person of extreme caution, who, before speaking in behalf of the prisoners, requested them to be removed. He then spoke with great deliberation and calmness: "Ye men of Israel, take heed to yourselves what we intend to do as touching these men. For before these days rose up Theudas, boasting himself to be somebody; to whom a number of men, about four hundred, joined themselves: who was slain; and all, as many as obeyed him, were scattered, and brought to nought. After this man rose up Judas of Galilee in the days of the taxing, and drew away much people after him: he also perished; and all, even as many as obeyed him, were dispersed. And now I say unto you, Refrain from these men, and let them alone: for if this counsel or this work be of men, it will come to nought: but if it be of God, ye cannot overthrow it; lest haply ye be found even to fight against God."

The priests could not but see the reasonableness of his views; they were obliged to agree with him, and very reluctantly released the prisoners, after beating them with rods and charging them again and again to preach no more in the name of Jesus, or their lives would pay the penalty of their boldness. "And they departed from the presence of the council, rejoicing that they were counted worthy to suffer shame for His name. And daily in the temple, and in every house, they ceased not to teach and preach Jesus Christ."

Well might the persecutors of the apostles be troubled when they saw their inability to overthrow these witnesses for Christ, who had faith and courage to turn their shame into glory and their pain into joy for the sake of their Master, who had borne humiliation and agony before them. Thus these brave disciples continued to teach in public, and secretly in private houses, by the request of the occupants who dared not openly confess their faith, for fear of the Jews.

Chapter 35—Gospel Order

This chapter is based on Acts 6:1-7.

"And in those days, when the number of the disciples multiplied, there arose a murmuring of the Grecians against the Hebrews, because their widows were neglected in the daily ministration." These Grecians were residents of other countries, where the Greek language was spoken. By far the larger number of converts were Jews who spoke Hebrew; but these had lived in the Roman Empire, and spoke only Greek. Murmurings began to rise among them that the Grecian widows were not so liberally supplied as the needy among the Hebrews. Any partiality of this kind would have been grievous to God; and prompt measures were taken to restore peace and harmony to the believers.

The Holy Spirit suggested a method whereby the apostles might be relieved from the task of apportioning to the poor, and similar burdens, so that they could be left free to preach Christ. "Then the twelve called the multitude of the disciples unto them, and said, It is not reason that we should leave the word of God, and serve tables. Wherefore, brethren, look ye out among you seven men of honest report, full of the Holy Ghost and wisdom, whom we may appoint over this business. But we will give ourselves continually to prayer, and to the ministry of the word."

The church accordingly selected seven men full of faith and the wisdom of the Spirit of God, to attend to the business pertaining to the cause. Stephen was chosen first; he was a Jew by birth and religion, but spoke the Greek language, and was conversant with the customs and manners of the Greeks. He was therefore considered the most proper person to stand at the head and have supervision of the disbursement of the funds appropriated to the widows, orphans, and the worthy poor. This selection met the minds of all, and the dissatisfaction and murmuring were quieted.

The seven chosen men were solemnly set apart for their duties by prayer and the laying on of hands. Those who were thus ordained were not thereby excluded from teaching the faith. On the contrary, it is recorded that "Stephen, full of faith and power, did great wonders and miracles among the people." They were fully qualified to instruct in the truth. They were also men of calm judgment and discretion, well calculated to deal with difficult cases of trial, of murmuring or jealousy.

This choosing of men to transact the business of the church, so that the apostles could be left free for their special work of teaching the truth, was greatly blessed of God. The church advanced in numbers and strength. "And the word of God increased; and the number of the disciples multiplied in Jerusalem greatly; and a great company of the priests were obedient to the faith."

It is necessary that the same order and system should be maintained in the church now as in the days of the apostles. The prosperity of the cause depends very largely upon its various departments being conducted by men of ability, who are qualified for their positions. Those who are chosen of God to be leaders in the cause of God, having the general oversight of the spiritual interest of the church, should be relieved, as far as possible, from cares and perplexities of a temporal nature. Those whom God has called to minister in word and doctrine should have time for meditation, prayer, and study of the Scriptures. Their clear spiritual discernment is dimmed by entering into the lesser details of business and dealing with the various temperaments of those who meet together in church capacity. It is proper for all matters of a temporal nature to come before the proper officers and be by them adjusted. But if they are of so difficult a character as to baffle their wisdom, they should be carried into the council of those who have the oversight of the entire church.

Chapter 36—Death of Stephen

This chapter is based on Acts 6:8 to 7:60.

Stephen was very active in the cause of God and declared his faith boldly. "Then there arose certain of the synagogue, which is called the synagogue of the Libertines, and Cyrenians, and Alexandrians, and of them of Cilicia and of Asia, disputing with Stephen. And they were not able to resist the wisdom and the spirit by which he spake." These students of the great rabbis had felt confident that in a public discussion they could obtain a complete victory over Stephen, because of his supposed ignorance. But he not only spoke with the power of the Holy Ghost, but it was plain to all the vast assembly that he was also a student of the prophecies and learned in all matters of the law. He ably defended the truths he advocated, and utterly defeated his opponents.

The priests and rulers who witnessed the wonderful manifestation of the power that attended the ministration of Stephen were filled with bitter hatred. Instead of yielding to the weight of evidence he presented, they determined to silence his voice by putting him to death.

They therefore seized Stephen and brought him before the Sanhedrin council for trial.

Learned Jews from the surrounding countries were summoned for the purpose of refuting the arguments of the accused. Saul, who had distinguished himself as a zealous opponent of the doctrine of Christ, and a persecutor of all who believed on Him, was also present. This learned man took a leading part against Stephen. He brought the weight of eloquence and the logic of the rabbis to bear upon the case, and convince the people that Stephen was preaching delusive and dangerous doctrines.

But Saul met in Stephen one as highly educated as himself, and one who had a full understanding of the purpose of God in the spreading of the gospel to other nations. He believed in the God of Abraham, Isaac, and Jacob, and was fully established in regard to the privileges of the Jews; but his faith was broad, and he knew the time had come when the true believers should worship not alone in temples made with hands; but, throughout the world, men might worship

God in Spirit and in truth. The veil had dropped from the eyes of Stephen, and he discerned to the end of that which was abolished by the death of Christ.

The priests and rulers prevailed nothing against his clear, calm wisdom, though they were vehement in their opposition. They determined to make an example of Stephen and, while they thus satisfied their revengeful hatred, prevent others, through fear, from adopting his belief. Charges were preferred against him in a most imposing manner. False witnesses were hired to testify that they had heard him speak blasphemous words against the temple and the law. Said they, "For we have heard him say, that this Jesus of Nazareth shall destroy this place, and shall change the customs which Moses delivered us."

As Stephen stood face to face with his judges, to answer to the crime of blasphemy, a holy radiance shone upon his countenance. "And all that sat in the council, looking stedfastly on him, saw his face as it had been the face of an angel." Many who beheld the lighted countenance of Stephen trembled and veiled their faces, but stubborn unbelief and prejudice never faltered.

Stephen's Defense

Stephen was questioned as to the truth of the charges against him, and took up his defense in a clear, thrilling voice that rang through the council hall. He proceeded to rehearse the history of the chosen people of God in words that held the assembly spellbound. He showed a thorough knowledge of the Jewish economy, and the spiritual interpretation of it now made manifest through Christ. He began with Abraham and traced down through history from generation to generation, going through all the national records of Israel to Solomon, taking up the most impressive points to vindicate his cause.

He made plain his own loyalty to God and to the Jewish faith, while he showed that the law in which they trusted for salvation had not been able to preserve Israel from idolatry. He connected Jesus Christ with all the Jewish history. He referred to the building of the temple by Solomon, and to the words of both Solomon and Isaiah: "Howbeit the Most High dwelleth not in temples made with hands." "Heaven is My throne, and earth is My footstool: what house will ye build Me? saith the Lord: or what is the place of My rest? Hath not my hand made all these things?" The place of God's highest worship was in heaven.

When Stephen had reached this point, there was a tumult among the people. The prisoner read his fate in the countenances before him. He perceived the resistance that met his words, which were spoken at the dictation of the Holy

Ghost. He knew that he was giving his last testimony. Few who read this address of Stephen properly appreciate it. The occasion, the time and place, should be borne in mind to make his words convey their full significance.

When he connected Jesus Christ with the prophecies and spoke of the temple as he did, the priest, affecting to be horror stricken, rent his robe. This act was to Stephen a signal that his voice would soon be silenced forever. Although he was just in the midst of his sermon, he abruptly concluded it by suddenly breaking away from the chain of history, and, turning upon his infuriated judges, said, "Ye stiffnecked and uncircumcised in heart and ears, ye do always resist the Holy Ghost: as your fathers did, so do ye. Which of the prophets have not your fathers persecuted? and they have slain them which shewed before of the coming of the Just One; of whom ye have been now the betrayers and murderers: who have received the law by the disposition of angels, and have not kept it."

A Martyr's Death

At this priests and rulers were beside themselves with anger. They were more like wild beasts of prey than like human beings. They rushed upon Stephen, gnashing their teeth. But he was not intimidated; he had expected this. His face was calm, and shone with an angelic light. The infuriated priests and the excited mob had no terrors for him. "But he, being full of the Holy Ghost, looked up stedfastly into heaven, and saw the glory of God, and Jesus standing on the right hand of God, and said, Behold, I see the heavens opened, and the Son of man standing on the right hand of God."

The scene about him faded from his vision; the gates of heaven were ajar, and Stephen, looking in, saw the glory of the courts of God, and Christ, as if just risen from His throne, standing ready to sustain His servant, who was about to suffer martyrdom for His name. When Stephen proclaimed the glorious scene opened before him, it was more than his persecutors could endure. They stopped their ears, that they might not hear his words, and, uttering loud cries, ran furiously upon him with one accord. "And they stoned Stephen, calling upon God, and saying, Lord Jesus, receive my spirit. And he kneeled down, and cried with a loud voice, Lord, lay not this sin to their charge. And when he had said this, he fell asleep."

Amid the agonies of this most cruel death the faithful martyr, like his divine Master, prayed for his murderers. The witnesses who had accused Stephen were required to cast the first stones. These persons laid down their clothes at the feet of Saul, who had taken an active part in the disputation and had consented to the prisoner's death.

The martyrdom of Stephen made a deep impression upon all who witnessed it. It was a sore trial to the church, but resulted in the conversion of Saul. The faith, constancy, and glorification of the martyr could not be effaced from his memory. The signet of God upon his face, his words, that reached to the very soul of all who heard them, except those who were hardened by resisting the light, remained in the memory of the beholders, and testified to the truth of that which he had proclaimed.

There had been no legal sentence passed upon Stephen, but the Roman authorities were bribed by large sums of money to make no investigation of the case. Saul seemed to be imbued with a frenzied zeal at the scene of Stephen's trial and death. He seemed to be angered at his own secret convictions that Stephen was honored of God at the very period when he was dishonored of men.

He continued to persecute the church of God, hunting them down, seizing them in their houses, and delivering them up to the priests and rulers for imprisonment and death. His zeal in carrying forward the persecution was a terror to the Christians in Jerusalem. The Roman authorities made no special effort to stay the cruel work, and secretly aided the Jews in order to conciliate them and secure their favor.

The learned Saul was a mighty instrument in the hands of Satan to carry out his rebellion against the Son of God; but a mightier than Satan had selected Saul to take the place of the martyred Stephen, and to labor and suffer for His name. Saul was a man of much esteem among the Jews, for both his learning and his zeal in persecuting the believers. He was not a member of the Sanhedrin council until after the death of Stephen, when he was elected to that body in consideration of the part he had acted on that occasion.

Chapter 37—The Conversion of Saul

This chapter is based on Acts 9:1-22.

The mind of Saul was greatly stirred by the triumphant death of Stephen. He was shaken in his prejudice; but the opinions and arguments of the priests and rulers finally convinced him that Stephen was a blasphemer; that Jesus Christ whom he preached was an imposter, and that those ministering in holy offices must be right. Being a man of decided mind and strong purpose, he became very bitter in his opposition to Christianity, after having once entirely settled in his mind that the views of the priests and scribes were right. His zeal led him to voluntarily engage in persecuting the believers. He caused holy men to be dragged before the councils, and to be imprisoned or condemned to death without evidence of any offense, save their faith in Jesus. Of a similar character, though in a different direction, was the zeal of James and John when they would have called down fire from heaven to consume those who slighted and scorned their Master.

Saul was about to journey to Damascus on his own business; but he was determined to accomplish a double purpose, by searching out, as he went, all the believers in Christ. For this purpose he obtained letters from the high priest to read in the synagogues, which authorized him to seize all those who were suspected of being believers in Jesus, and to send them by messengers to Jerusalem, there to be tried and punished. He set out on his way, full of the strength and vigor of manhood and the fire of a mistaken zeal.

As the weary travelers neared Damascus, the eyes of Saul rested with pleasure upon the fertile land, the beautiful gardens, the fruitful orchards, and the cool streams that ran murmuring amid the fresh green shrubbery. It was very refreshing to look upon such a scene after a long, wearisome journey over a desolate waste. While Saul, with his companions, was gazing and admiring, suddenly a light above the brightness of the sun shone round about him, "and he fell to the earth, and heard a voice saying unto him, Saul, Saul, why persecutest thou Me? And he said, Who art Thou, Lord? And the Lord said, I am Jesus whom thou persecutest: it is hard for thee to kick against the pricks."

The Vision of Christ

The scene was one of the greatest confusion. The companions of Saul were stricken with terror, and almost blinded by the intensity of the light. They heard the voice, but saw no one, and to them all was unintelligible and mysterious. But Saul, lying prostrate upon the ground, understood the words that were spoken, and saw clearly before him the Son of God. One look upon that glorious Being imprinted His image forever upon the soul of the stricken Jew. The words struck home to his heart with appalling force. A flood of light poured in upon the darkened chambers of his mind, revealing his ignorance and error. He saw that, while imagining himself to be zealously serving God in persecuting the followers of Christ, he had in reality been doing the work of Satan.

He saw his folly in resting his faith upon the assurances of the priests and rulers, whose sacred office had given them great influence over his mind and caused him to believe that the story of the resurrection was an artful fabrication of the disciples of Jesus. Now that Christ was revealed to Saul, the sermon of Stephen was brought forcibly to his mind. Those words which the priests had pronounced blasphemy, now appeared to him as truth and verity. In that time of wonderful illumination his mind acted with remarkable rapidity. He traced down through prophetic history and saw that the rejection of Jesus by the Jews, His crucifixion, resurrection, and ascension had been foretold by the prophets, and proved Him to be the promised Messiah. He remembered the words of Stephen: "I see the heavens opened, and the Son of man standing on the right hand of God" (Acts 7:56), and he knew that the dying saint had looked upon the kingdom of glory.

What a revelation was all this to the persecutor of the believers. Clear but terrible light had broken in upon his soul. Christ was revealed to him as having come to earth in fulfillment of His mission, being rejected, abused, condemned, and crucified by those whom He came to save, and as having risen from the dead and ascended into the heavens. In that terrible moment he remembered that the holy Stephen had been sacrificed by his consent, and that through his instrumentality many worthy saints had met their death by cruel persecution.

"And he trembling and astonished said, Lord, what wilt Thou have me to do? And the Lord said unto him, Arise, and go into the city, and it shall be told thee what thou must do." No doubt entered the mind of Saul that this was the veritable Jesus of Nazareth who spoke to him, and that He was indeed the long-looked-for Messiah, the Consolation and Redeemer of Israel.

When the effulgent glory was withdrawn, and Saul arose from the earth, he found himself totally deprived of sight. The brightness of Christ's glory had been too intense for his mortal sight, and when it was removed, the blackness of night settled upon his vision. He believed that his blindness was the punishment of God for his cruel persecution of the followers of Jesus. He groped about in terrible darkness, and his companions, in fear and amazement, led him by the hand into Damascus.

Directed to the Church

The answer to Saul's question is, "Arise, and go into the city, and it shall be told thee what thou must do." Jesus sends the inquiring Jew to His church, to obtain from them a knowledge of his duty. Christ performed the work of revelation and conviction; and now the penitent was in a condition to learn of those whom God had ordained to teach His truth. Thus Jesus gave sanction to the authority of His organized church, and placed Saul in connection with His representatives on earth. The light of heavenly illumination deprived Saul of sight, but Jesus, the great Healer, did not at once restore it. All blessings flow from Christ, but He had now established a church as His representative on earth, and to it belonged the work of directing the repentant sinner in the way of life. The very men whom Saul had purposed to destroy were to be his instructors in the religion he had despised and persecuted.

The faith of Saul was severely tested during the three days of fasting and prayer at the house of Judas, in Damascus. He was totally blind, and in utter darkness of mind as to what was required of him. He had been directed to go to Damascus, where it would be told him what he was to do. In his uncertainty and distress he cried earnestly to God. "And there was a certain disciple at Damascus, named Ananias; and to him said the Lord in a vision, Ananias. And he said, Behold, I am here, Lord. And the Lord said unto him, Arise, and go into the street which is called Straight, and enquire in the house of one Judas for one called Saul, of Tarsus: for, behold, he prayeth, and hath seen a vision of a man named Ananias coming in, and putting his hand on him, that he might receive his sight."

Ananias could hardly credit the words of the angel messenger, for Saul's bitter persecution of the saints at Jerusalem had spread far and near. He presumed to expostulate; said he, "Lord, I have heard by many of this man, how much evil he hath done to Thy saints at Jerusalem. And here he hath authority from the chief priests to bind all that call on Thy name." But the command to

Ananias was imperative: "Go thy way: for he is a chosen vessel unto Me, to bear My name before the Gentiles, and kings, and the children of Israel."

The disciple, obedient to the direction of the angel, sought out the man who had but recently breathed out threatenings against all who believed on the name of Jesus. He addressed him: "Brother Saul, the Lord, even Jesus, that appeared unto thee in the way as thou camest, hath sent me, that thou mightest receive thy sight, and be filled with the Holy Ghost. And immediately there fell from his eyes as it had been scales: and he received sight forthwith, and arose, and was baptized."

Christ here gives an example of His manner of working for the salvation of men. He might have done all this work directly for Saul; but this was not in accordance with His plan. His blessings were to come through the agencies which He had ordained. Saul had something to do in the line of confession to those whose destruction he had meditated; and God had a responsible work for the men to do whom He had authorized to act in His stead.

Saul becomes a learner of the disciples. In the light of the law he sees himself a sinner. He sees that Jesus, whom in his ignorance he had considered an impostor, is the author and foundation of the religion of God's people from the days of Adam, and the finisher of the faith now so clear to his enlightened vision; the vindicator of the truth, and the fulfiller of the prophecies. He had regarded Jesus as making of none effect the law of God; but when his spiritual vision was touched by the finger of God, he learned that Christ was the originator of the entire Jewish system of sacrifices; that He came into the world for the express purpose of vindicating His Father's law; and that in His death the typical law had met its antitype. By the light of the moral law, which he had believed himself to be zealously keeping, Saul saw himself a sinner of sinners.

From Persecutor to Apostle

Paul was baptized by Ananias in the river of Damascus. He was then strengthened by food, and immediately began to preach Jesus to the believers in the city, the very ones whom he had set out from Jerusalem with the purpose of destroying. He also taught in the synagogues that Jesus who had been put to death was indeed the Son of God. His arguments from prophecy were so conclusive, and his efforts were so attended by the power of God, that the opposing Jews were confounded and unable to answer him. Paul's rabbinical and Pharisaic education was now to be used to good account in preaching the gospel and in sustaining the cause he had once used every effort to destroy.

The Jews were thoroughly surprised and confounded by the conversion of Paul. They were aware of his position at Jerusalem, and knew what was his principal errand to Damascus, and that he was armed with a commission from the high priest that authorized him to take the believers in Jesus and to send them as prisoners to Jerusalem; yet now they beheld him preaching the gospel of Jesus, strengthening those who were already its disciples and continually making new converts to the faith he had once so zealously opposed. Paul demonstrated to all who heard him that his change of faith was not from impulse nor fanaticism, but was brought about by overwhelming evidence.

As he labored in the synagogues his faith grew stronger; his zeal in maintaining that Jesus was the Son of God increased in the face of the fierce opposition of the Jews. He could not remain long in Damascus, for after the Jews had recovered from their surprise at his wonderful conversion and subsequent labors, they turned resolutely from the overwhelming evidence thus brought to bear in favor of the doctrine of Christ. Their astonishment at the conversion of Paul was changed into an intense hatred of him like unto that which they had manifested against Jesus.

Preparation for Service

Paul's life was in peril, and he received a commission from God to leave Damascus for a time. He went into Arabia; and there, in comparative solitude, he had ample opportunity for communion with God and for contemplation. He wished to be alone with God, to search his own heart, to deepen his repentance, and to prepare himself by prayer and study to engage in a work which appeared to him too great and too important for him to undertake. He was an apostle, not chosen of men, but chosen of God, and his work was plainly stated to be among the Gentiles.

While in Arabia he did not communicate with the apostles; he sought God earnestly with all his heart, determining not to rest till he knew for a certainty that his repentance was accepted and his great sin pardoned. He would not give up the conflict until he had the assurance that Jesus would be with him in his coming ministry. He was ever to carry about with him in the body the marks of Christ's glory, in his eyes, which had been blinded by the heavenly light, and he desired also to bear with him constantly the assurance of Christ's sustaining grace. Paul came into close connection with Heaven, and Jesus communed with him, and established him in his faith, bestowing upon him His wisdom and grace.

Chapter 38—The Early Ministry of Paul

This chapter is based on Acts 9:23-31 and 22:17-21.

Paul now returned to Damascus and preached boldly in the name of Jesus. The Jews could not withstand the wisdom of his arguments, and they therefore counseled together to silence his voice by force—the only argument left to a sinking cause. They decided to assassinate him. The apostle was made acquainted with their purpose. The gates of the city were vigilantly guarded, day and night, to cut off his escape. The anxiety of the disciples drew them to God in prayer; there was little sleeping among them, as they were busy in devising ways and means for the escape of the chosen apostle. Finally they conceived a plan by which he was let down from a window and lowered over the wall in a basket at night. In this humiliating manner Paul made his escape from Damascus.

He now proceeded to Jerusalem, wishing to become acquainted with the apostles there, and especially with Peter. He was very anxious to meet the Galilean fishermen who had lived, and prayed, and conversed with Christ upon earth. It was with a yearning heart that he desired to meet the chief of apostles. As Paul entered Jerusalem, he regarded with changed views the city and the temple. He now knew that the retributive judgment of God was hanging over them.

The grief and anger of the Jews because of the conversion of Paul knew no bounds. But he was firm as a rock, and flattered himself that when he related his wonderful experience to his friends, they would change their faith as he had done, and believe on Jesus. He had been strictly conscientious in his opposition to Christ and His followers, and when he was arrested and convicted of his sin, he immediately forsook his evil ways and professed the faith of Jesus. He now fully believed that when his friends and former associates heard the circumstances of his marvelous conversion, and saw how changed he was from the proud Pharisee who persecuted and delivered unto death those who believed in Jesus as the Son of God, they would also become convicted of their error and join the ranks of the believers.

He attempted to join himself to his brethren, the disciples; but great was his grief and disappointment when he found that they would not receive him as one of their number. They remembered his former persecutions, and suspected him of acting a part to deceive and destroy them. True, they had heard of his wonderful conversion, but as he had immediately retired into Arabia, and they had heard nothing definite of him further, they had not credited the rumor of his great change.

Meeting With Peter and James

Barnabas, who had liberally contributed his money to sustain the cause of Christ and to relieve the necessities of the poor, had been acquainted with Paul when he opposed the believers. He now came forward and renewed that acquaintance, heard the testimony of Paul in regard to his miraculous conversion and his experience from that time. He fully believed and received Paul, took him by the hand and led him into the presence of the apostles. He related his experience which he had just heard—that Jesus had personally appeared to Paul while on his way to Damascus; that He had talked with him; that Paul had recovered his sight in answer to the prayers of Ananias, and had afterward maintained that Jesus was the Son of God in the synagogues of that city.

The apostles no longer hesitated; they could not withstand God. Peter and James, who at that time were the only apostles in Jerusalem, gave the right hand of fellowship to the once fierce persecutor of their faith; and he was now as much beloved and respected as he had formerly been feared and avoided. Here the two grand characters of the new faith met—Peter, one of the chosen companions of Christ while He was upon earth, and Paul, the Pharisee, who, since the ascension of Jesus, had met Him face to face and had talked with Him, and had also seen Him in vision, and the nature of His work in heaven.

This first interview was of great consequence to both these apostles, but it was of short duration, for Paul was eager to get about his Master's business. Soon the voice which had so earnestly disputed with Stephen was heard in the same synagogue fearlessly proclaiming that Jesus was the Son of God— advocating the same cause that Stephen had died to vindicate. He related his own wonderful experience, and with a heart filled with yearning for his brethren and former associates, presented the evidences from prophecy, as Stephen had done, that Jesus, who had been crucified, was the Son of God.

But Paul had miscalculated the spirit of his Jewish brethren. The same fury that had burst forth upon Stephen was visited upon himself. He saw that he must separate from his brethren, and sorrow filled his heart. He would willingly have yielded up his life if by that means they might have been brought to a knowledge of the truth. The Jews began to lay plans to take his life, and the disciples urged him to leave Jerusalem; but he lingered, unwilling to leave the place, and anxious to labor a little longer for his Jewish brethren. He had taken so active a part in the martyrdom of Stephen that he was deeply anxious to wipe out the stain by boldly vindicating the truth which had cost Stephen his life. It looked to him like cowardice to flee from Jerusalem.

Flight From Jerusalem

While Paul, braving all the consequences of such a step, was praying earnestly to God in the temple, the Saviour appeared to him in vision, saying, "Make haste, and get thee quickly out of Jerusalem: for they will not receive thy testimony concerning Me." Paul even then hesitated to leave Jerusalem without convincing the obstinate Jews of the truth of his faith; he thought that, even if his life should be sacrificed for the truth, it would not more than settle the fearful account which he held against himself for the death of Stephen. He answered, "Lord, they know that I imprisoned and beat in every synagogue them that believed on Thee: and when the blood of Thy martyr Stephen was shed, I also was standing by, and consenting unto his death, and kept the raiment of them that slew him." But the reply was more decided than before: "Depart: for I will send thee far hence unto the Gentiles."

When the brethren learned of the vision of Paul, and the care which God had over him, their anxiety on his behalf was increased; for they realized that he was indeed a chosen vessel of the Lord, to bear the truth to the Gentiles. They hastened his secret escape from Jerusalem, for fear of his assassination by the Jews. The departure of Paul suspended for a time the violent opposition of the Jews, and the church had a period of rest, in which many were added to the number of believers.

Chapter 39—The Ministry of Peter

This chapter is based on Acts 9:32 to 11:18.

Peter, in pursuance of his work, visited the saints at Lydda. There he healed Aeneas, who had been confined to his bed for eight years with the palsy. "And Peter said unto him, Aeneas, Jesus Christ maketh thee whole: arise, and make thy bed. And he arose immediately. And all that dwelt at Lydda and Saron saw him, and turned to the Lord."

Joppa was near Lydda, and at that time Tabitha—called Dorcas by interpretation—lay there dead. She had been a worthy disciple of Jesus Christ, and her life had been characterized by deeds of charity and kindness to the poor and sorrowful, and by zeal in the cause of truth. Her death was a great loss; the infant church could not well spare her noble efforts. When the believers heard of the marvelous cures which Peter had performed in Lydda, they greatly desired him to come to Joppa. Messengers were sent to him to solicit his presence there.

"Then Peter arose and went with them. When he was come, they brought him into the upper chamber: and all the widows stood by him weeping, and shewing the coats and garments which Dorcas made, while she was with them." Peter had the weeping and wailing friends sent from the room. He then knelt down and prayed fervently to God to restore life and health to the pulseless body of Dorcas; "and turning him to the body said, Tabitha, arise. And she opened her eyes: and when she saw Peter, she sat up. And he gave her his hand, and lifted her up, and when he had called the saints and widows, presented her alive." This great work of raising the dead to life was the means of converting many in Joppa to the faith of Jesus.

The Centurion

"There was a certain man of Caesarea called Cornelius, a centurion of the band called the Italian band, a devout man, and one that feared God with all his house, which gave much alms to the people, and prayed to God alway." Though Cornelius was a Roman, he had become acquainted with the true God and had renounced idolatry. He was obedient to the will of God and worshiped Him with a true heart. He had not connected himself with the Jews, but was acquainted with, and obedient to, the moral law. He had not been circumcised, nor did he take part in the sacrificial offerings; he was therefore accounted by the Jews as unclean. He, however, sustained the Jewish cause by liberal donations, and was known far and near for his deeds of charity and benevolence. His righteous life made him of good repute among both Jews and Gentiles.

Cornelius had not an understanding faith in Christ, although he believed the prophecies and was looking for Messiah to come. Through his love and obedience to God, he was brought nigh unto Him, and was prepared to receive the Saviour when He should be revealed to him. Condemnation comes by rejecting the light given. The centurion was a man of noble family and held a position of high trust and honor; but these circumstances had not tended to subvert the noble attributes of his character. True goodness and greatness united to make him a man of moral worth. His influence was beneficial to all with whom he was brought in contact.

He believed in the one God, the Creator of heaven and earth. He revered Him, acknowledged His authority, and sought counsel of Him in all the business of his life. He was faithful in his home duties as well as in his official responsibilities, and had erected the altar of God in his family. He dared not venture to carry out his plans, and bear the burden of his weighty responsibilities, without the help of God; therefore he prayed much and earnestly for that help. Faith marked all his works, and God regarded him for the purity of his actions, and his liberalities, and came near to him in word and Spirit.

The Angel Visits Cornelius

While Cornelius was praying, God sent a celestial messenger to him, who addressed him by name. The centurion was afraid, yet knew that the angel was sent of God to instruct him, and said, "What is it, Lord? And he said unto him, Thy prayers and thine alms are come up for a memorial before God. And now send men to Joppa, and call for one Simon, whose surname is Peter: he lodgeth with one Simon a tanner, whose house is by the sea side: he shall tell thee what thou oughtest to do."

Here again God showed His regard for the gospel ministry, and for His organized church. His angel was not the one to tell the story of the cross to Cornelius. A man, subject as himself to human frailties and temptations, was to instruct him concerning the crucified, risen, and ascended Saviour. The heavenly messenger was sent for the express purpose of putting Cornelius in connection with the minister of God, who would teach him how he and his house could be saved.

Cornelius was gladly obedient to the message, and sent messengers at once to seek out Peter, according to the directions of the angel. The explicitness of these directions, in which was even named the occupation of the man with whom Peter was then making his home, evidences that Heaven is well acquainted with the history and business of men in every grade of life. God is cognizant of the daily employment of the humble laborer, as well as of that of the king upon his throne. And the avarice, cruelty, secret crimes, and selfishness of men are known to him, as well as their good deeds, charity, liberality, and kindness. Nothing is hidden from God.

Peter's Vision

Immediately after this interview with Cornelius the angel went to Peter, who, very weary and hungry from journeying, was praying on the housetop. While praying he was shown a vision, "and saw heaven opened, and a certain vessel descending unto him, as it had been a great sheet knit at the four corners, and let down to the earth: wherein were all manner of four-footed beasts of the earth, and wild beasts, and creeping things, and fowls of the air.

"And there came a voice to him, Rise, Peter; kill and eat. But Peter said, Not so, Lord; for I have never eaten any thing that is common or unclean. And the voice spake unto him again the second time, What God hath cleansed, that call not thou common. This was done thrice: and the vessel was received again into heaven."

Here we may perceive the workings of God's plan to set the machinery in motion, whereby His will may be done on earth as it is done in heaven. Peter had not yet preached the gospel to the Gentiles. Many of them had been interested listeners to the truths which he taught; but the middle wall of partition, which the death of Christ had broken down, still existed in the minds of the apostles, and excluded the Gentiles from the privileges of the gospel. The Greek Jews had received the labors of the apostles, and many of them had responded to those efforts by embracing the faith of Jesus; but the conversion of Cornelius was to be the first one of importance among the Gentiles.

By the vision of the sheet and its contents, let down from heaven, Peter was to be divested of his settled prejudices against the Gentiles; to understand that, through Christ, heathen nations were made partakers of the blessings and privileges of the Jews, and were to be thus benefited equally with them. Some have urged that this vision was to signify that God had removed His prohibition from the use of the flesh of animals which he had formerly pronounced unclean; and that therefore swines' flesh was fit for food. This is a very narrow and altogether erroneous interpretation, and is plainly contradicted in the Scriptural account of the vision and its consequences.

The vision of all manner of live beasts, which the sheet contained, and of which Peter was commanded to kill and eat, being assured that what God had cleansed should not be called common or unclean by him, was simply an illustration presenting to his mind the true position of the Gentiles; that by the death of Christ they were made fellow heirs with the Israel of God. It conveyed to Peter both reproof and instruction. His labors had heretofore been confined entirely to the Jews; and he had looked upon the Gentiles as an unclean race, and excluded from the promises of God. His mind was now being led to comprehend the world-wide extent of the plan of God.

Even while he pondered over the vision, it was explained to him. "Now while Peter doubted in himself what this vision which he had seen should mean, behold, the men which were sent from Cornelius had made enquiry for Simon's house, and stood before the gate, and called, and asked whether Simon, which was surnamed Peter, were lodged there. While Peter thought on the vision, the Spirit said unto him, Behold, three men seek thee. Arise, therefore, and get thee down, and go with them, doubting nothing: for I have sent them."

It was a trying command to Peter; but he dared not act according to his own feelings, and therefore went down from his chamber and received the messengers sent to him from Cornelius. They communicated their singular errand to the apostle, and, according to the direction he had just received from God, he at once agreed to accompany them on the morrow. He courteously entertained them that night, and in the morning set out with them for Caesarea, accompanied by six of his brethren, who were to be witnesses of all he should say or do while visiting the Gentiles; for he knew that he should be called to account for so direct an opposition to the Jewish faith and teachings.

It was nearly two days before the journey was ended and Cornelius had the glad privilege of opening his doors to a gospel minister, who, according to the assurance of God, should teach him and his house how they might be saved. While the messengers were on their errand, the centurion had gathered together as many of his relatives as were accessible, that they, as well as he, might be instructed in the truth. When Peter arrived, a large company were gathered, eagerly waiting to listen to his words.

The Visit to Cornelius

As Peter entered the house of the Gentile, Cornelius did not salute him as an ordinary visitor, but as one honored of Heaven, and sent to him by God. It is an Eastern custom to bow before a prince or other high dignitary, and for children to bow before their parents who are honored with positions of trust. But Cornelius, overwhelmed with reverence for the apostle who had been delegated by God, fell at his feet and worshiped him.

Peter shrank with horror from this act of the centurion, and lifted him to his feet, saying, "Stand up; I myself also am a man." He then commenced to converse with him familiarly, in order to remove the sense of awe and extreme reverence with which the centurion regarded him.

Had Peter been invested with the authority and position accorded to him by the Roman Catholic Church, he would have encouraged, rather than have checked, the veneration of Cornelius. The so-called successors of Peter require kings and emperors to bow at their feet, but Peter himself claimed to be only an erring and fallible man.

Peter spoke with Cornelius and those assembled in his house, concerning the custom of the Jews; that it was considered unlawful for them to mingle socially with Gentiles, and involved ceremonial defilement. It was not prohibited by the law of God, but the tradition of men had made it a binding custom. Said he, "Ye know how that it is an unlawful thing for a man that is a Jew to keep company, or come unto one of another nation; but God hath shewed me that I should not call any man common or unclean. Therefore came I unto you without gainsaying, as soon as I was sent for: I ask therefore for what intent ye have sent for me."

Cornelius thereupon related his experience, and the words of the angel that had appeared to him in vision. In conclusion he said, "Immediately therefore I sent to thee; and thou hast well done that thou art come. Now therefore are we all here present before God, to hear all things that are commanded thee of God. Then Peter opened his mouth, and said, Of a truth I perceive that God is no respecter of persons: but in every nation he that feareth Him, and worketh righteousness, is accepted with Him." Although God had favored the Jews above all other nations, yet if they rejected light and did not live up to their profession, they were no more exalted in His esteem than other nations. Those among the Gentiles who, like Cornelius, feared God, and worked righteousness, living up to what light they had, were kindly regarded by God, and their sincere service was accepted.

But the faith and righteousness of Cornelius could not be perfect without a knowledge of Christ; therefore God sent that light and knowledge to him for the further development of his righteous character. Many refuse to receive the light which the providence of God sends them, and, as an excuse for so doing, quote the words of Peter to Cornelius and his friends: "But in every nation he that feareth Him, and worketh righteousness, is accepted with Him." They maintain that it is of no consequence what men believe, so long as their works are good. Such ones are wrong; faith must unite with their works. They should advance with the light that is given them. If God brings them in connection with His servants who have received new truth, substantiated by the Word of God, they should accept it with joy. Truth is onward. Truth is upward. On the other hand, those who claim that their faith alone will save them are trusting to a rope of sand, for faith is strengthened and made perfect by works only.

The Gentiles Receive the Holy Spirit

Peter preached Jesus to that company of attentive hearers; His life, ministry, miracles, betrayal, crucifixion, resurrection, and ascension, and His work in heaven, as man's Representative and Advocate, to plead in the sinner's behalf. As the apostle spoke, his heart glowed with the Spirit of God's truth which he was presenting to the people. His hearers were charmed by the doctrine they heard, for their hearts had been prepared to receive the truth. The apostle was interrupted by the descent of the Holy Ghost, as was manifested on the day of Pentecost. "And they of the circumcision which believed were astonished, as many as came with Peter, because that on the Gentiles also was poured out the gift of the Holy Ghost. For they heard them speak with tongues, and magnify God. Then answered Peter, Can any man forbid water, that these should not be baptized, which have received the Holy Ghost as well as we? And he commanded them to be baptized in the name of the Lord. Then prayed they him to tarry certain days."

The descent of the Holy Ghost upon the Gentiles was not an equivalent for baptism. The requisite steps in conversion, in all cases, are faith, repentance, and baptism. Thus the true Christian church are united in one Lord, one faith, one baptism. Diverse temperaments are modified by sanctifying grace, and the same distinguishing principles regulate the lives of all. Peter yielded to the entreaties of the believing Gentiles, and remained with them for a time, preaching Jesus to all the Gentiles thereabout.

When the brethren in Judea heard that Peter had preached to the Gentiles, and had met with them and eaten with them in their houses, they were surprised and offended by such strange movements on his part. They feared that such a course, which looked presumptuous to them, would tend to contradict his own teachings. As soon as Peter visited them, they met him with severe censure, saying, "Thou wentest in to men uncircumcised, and didst eat with them."

The Vision of the Church Enlarged

Then Peter candidly laid the whole matter before them. He related his experience in regard to the vision, and pleaded that it admonished him no longer to keep up the ceremonial distinction of circumcision and uncircumcision, nor to look upon the Gentiles as unclean, for God was not a respecter of persons. He informed them of the command of God to go to the Gentiles, the coming of the messengers, his journey to Caesarea, and the meeting with Cornelius and the company collected at his house. His caution was made manifest to his brethren from the fact that, although commanded by God to go to the Gentile's house, he had taken with him six of the disciples then present, as witnesses of all he should say or do while there. He recounted the substance of his interview with Cornelius, in which the latter had told him of his vision, wherein he had been directed to send messengers to Joppa to bring Peter to him, who would tell him words whereby he, and all his house, might be saved.

He recounted the events of this first meeting with the Gentiles, saying, "And as I began to speak, the Holy Ghost fell on them, as on us at the beginning. Then remembered I the word of the Lord, how that He said, John indeed baptized with water; but ye shall be baptized with the Holy Ghost. Forasmuch then as God gave them the like gift as He did unto us, who believed on the Lord Jesus Christ, what was I, that I could withstand God?"

The disciples, upon hearing this account, were silenced, and convinced that Peter's course was in direct fulfillment of the plan of God, and that their old prejudices and exclusiveness were to be utterly destroyed by the gospel of Christ. "When they heard these things, they held their peace, and glorified God, saying, Then hath God also to the Gentiles granted repentance unto life."

Chapter 40—Peter Delivered From Prison

This chapter is based on Acts 12:1-23.

Herod was professedly a proselyte to the Jewish faith, and apparently very zealous in perpetuating the ceremonies of the law. The government of Judea was in his hands, subject to Claudius, the Roman emperor; he also held the position of tetrarch of Galilee. Herod was anxious to obtain the favor of the Jews, hoping thus to make secure his offices and honors. He therefore proceeded to carry out the desires of the Jews in persecuting the church of Christ. He began his work by spoiling the houses and goods of the believers; he then began to imprison the leading ones. He seized upon James and cast him into prison, and there sent an executioner to kill him with a sword, as another Herod had caused the prophet John to be beheaded. He then became bolder, seeing that the Jews were well pleased with his acts, and imprisoned Peter. These cruelties were performed during the sacred occasion of the Passover.

The people applauded the act of Herod in causing the death of James, though some of them complained of the private manner in which it was accomplished, maintaining that a public execution would have had the effect to more thoroughly intimidate all believers and sympathizers. Herod therefore held Peter in custody for the purpose of gratifying the Jews by the public spectacle of his death. But it was suggested to the ruler that it would not be safe to bring the veteran apostle out for execution before all the people who were assembled in Jerusalem for the Passover. It was feared that his venerable appearance might excite their pity and respect; they also dreaded lest he should make one of those powerful appeals which had frequently roused the people to investigate the life and character of Jesus Christ, and which they, with all their artifice, were totally unable to controvert. In such case, the Jews apprehended that his release would be demanded at the hands of the king.

While the execution of Peter was being delayed, upon various pretexts, until after the Passover, the church of Christ had time for deep searching of heart and earnest prayer. Strong petitions, tears, and fasting were mingled together. They prayed without ceasing for Peter; they felt that he could not be spared from the Christian work; and they felt that they had arrived at a point where, without the special help of God, the church of Christ would become extinct.

The day of Peter's execution was at last appointed; but still the prayers of the believers ascended to Heaven. And while all their energies and sympathies were called out in fervent appeals, angels of God were guarding the imprisoned apostle. Man's extremity is God's opportunity. Peter was placed between two soldiers, and was bound by two chains, each chain being fastened to the wrist of one of his guards. He was therefore unable to move without their knowledge. The prison doors were securely fastened, and a strong guard was placed before them. All chance of rescue or escape, by human means, was thus cut off.

The apostle was not intimidated by his situation. Since his reinstatement after his denial of Christ, he had unflinchingly braved danger and manifested a noble courage and boldness in preaching a crucified, risen, and ascended Saviour. He believed the time had now come when he was to yield up his life for Christ's sake.

The night before his appointed execution, Peter, bound with chains, slept between the two soldiers, as usual. Herod, remembering the escape of Peter and John from prison, where they had been confined because of their faith, took double precautions on this occasion. The soldiers on guard, in order to secure their extra vigilance, were made answerable for the safekeeping of the prisoner. He was bound, as has been described, in a cell of massive rock, the doors of which were bolted and barred. Sixteen men were detailed to guard this cell, relieving each other at regular intervals. Four comprised the watch at one time. But the bolts and bars and Roman guard, which effectually cut off from the prisoner a possibility of human aid, were only to result in making the triumph of God more complete in Peter's deliverance from prison. Herod was lifting his hand against Omnipotence, and he was to be utterly humiliated and defeated in his attempt upon the life of the servant of God.

Delivered by an Angel

On this last night before the execution a mighty angel, commissioned from heaven, descended to rescue him. The strong gates which shut in the saint of God open without the aid of human hands; the angel of the Most High enters, and they close again noiselessly behind him. He enters the cell, hewn from the solid rock, and there lies Peter, sleeping the blessed, peaceful sleep of innocence and perfect trust in God, while chained to a powerful guard on either side of him. The light which envelopes the angel illuminates the prison, but does not waken the sleeping apostle. His is the sound repose that invigorates and renews and that comes of a good conscience.

Peter is not awakened until he feels the stroke of the angel's hand and hears his voice saying, "Arise up quickly." He sees his cell, which had never been blessed by a ray of sunshine, illuminated by the light of heaven, and an angel of great glory standing before him. He mechanically obeys the voice of the angel; and in rising lifts his hands, and finds that the chains have been broken from his wrists. Again the voice of the angel is heard: "Gird thyself, and bind on thy sandals."

Again Peter mechanically obeys, keeping his wondering gaze riveted upon his heavenly visitant, and believing himself to be dreaming, or in a vision. The armed soldiers are passive as if chiseled from marble, as the angel again commands, "Cast thy garment about thee, and follow me." Thereupon the heavenly being moves toward the door, and the usually talkative Peter follows, dumb from amazement. They step over the motionless guard and reach the heavily bolted and barred door, which swings open of its own accord and closes again immediately; while the guard within and outside the door are motionless at their posts.

The second gate, which is also guarded within and without, is reached; it opens as did the first, with no creaking of hinges or rattling of iron bolts; they pass without, and it closes again as noiselessly. They pass through the third gateway in the same manner, and at last find themselves in the open street. No word is spoken; there is no sound of footstep; the angel glides on before, encircled by a light of dazzling brightness, and Peter follows his deliverer, bewildered, and believing himself to be in a dream. Street after street is threaded thus, and then, the mission of the angel being completed, he suddenly disappears.

As the heavenly light faded away, Peter felt himself to be in profound darkness; but gradually the darkness seemed to decrease, as he became accustomed to it, and he found himself alone in the silent street, with the cool night air upon his brow. He now realized that it was no dream or vision that had visited him. He was free, in a familiar part of the city; he recognized the place as one which he had often frequented, and had expected to pass for the last time on the morrow, when on the way to the scene of his prospective death. He tried to recall the events of the last few moments. He remembered falling asleep, bound between the two soldiers, with his sandals and outer garment removed. He examined his person and found himself fully dressed, and girded.

His wrists, swollen from wearing the cruel irons, were now free from the manacles, and he realized that his freedom was no delusion, but a blessed reality. On the morrow he was to have been led forth to die; but lo, an angel had delivered him from prison and from death. "And when Peter was come to himself, he said, Now I know of a surety, that the Lord hath sent His angel, and hath delivered me out of the hand of Herod and from all the expectation of the people of the Jews."

The Answer to Prayer

The apostle made his way direct to the house where his brethren were assembled together for prayer; he found them engaged in earnest prayer for him at that moment. "And as Peter knocked at the door of the gate, a damsel came to hearken, named Rhoda. And when she knew Peter's voice, she opened not the gate for gladness, but ran in, and told how Peter stood before the gate. And they said unto her, Thou art mad. But she constantly affirmed that it was even so. Then said they, It is his angel. But Peter continued knocking: and when they had opened the door, and saw him, they were astonished. But he, beckoning unto them with the hand to hold their peace, declared unto them how the Lord had brought him out of the prison. And he said, Go shew these things unto James, and to the brethren. And he departed, and went into another place."

Joy and praise filled the hearts of the fasting, praying believers, that God had heard and answered their prayers, and delivered Peter from the hand of Herod. In the morning the people gathered together to witness the execution of the apostle. Herod sent officers to bring Peter from prison with great display of arms and guard, in order to ensure against his escape, to intimidate all sympathizers, and to exhibit his own power. There was the guard at the door of the prison, the bolts and bars of the door still fast and strong, the guard inside, the chains attached to the wrists of the two soldiers; but the prisoner was gone.

Herod's Retribution

When the report of these things was brought to Herod, he was exasperated, and charged the keepers of the prison with unfaithfulness. They were accordingly put to death for the alleged crime of sleeping at their post. At the same time Herod knew that no human power had rescued Peter. But he was determined not to acknowledge that a divine power had been at work to thwart his base designs. He would not humiliate himself thus, but set himself boldly in defiance of God.

Herod, not long after Peter's deliverance from prison, went down from Judea to Caesarea and there abode. He there made a grand festival, designed to excite the admiration and applause of the people. Pleasure lovers from all quarters were assembled together, and there was much feasting and wine drinking. Herod made a most gorgeous appearance before the people. He was clad in a robe, sparkling with silver and gold, that caught the rays of the sun in its glittering folds, and dazzled the eyes of the beholders. With great pomp and ceremony he stood before the multitude, and addressed them in an eloquent oration.

The majesty of his appearance and the power of his well-chosen language swayed the assembly with a mighty influence. Their senses were already perverted by feasting and wine; they were dazzled by his glittering decorations and charmed by his grand deportment and eloquent words; and, wild with enthusiasm, they showered upon him adulation, and proclaimed him a god, declaring that mortal man could not present such an appearance or command such startling eloquence of language. They further declared that they had ever respected him as a ruler, but from henceforth they should worship him as a god.

Herod knew that he deserved none of this praise and homage; yet he did not rebuke the idolatry of the people, but accepted it as his due. The glow of gratified pride was on his countenance as he heard the shout ascend: "It is the voice of a god, and not of a man." The same voices which now glorified a vile sinner had, but a few years before, raised the frenzied cry of, Away with Jesus! Crucify Him! crucify Him! Herod received this flattery and homage with great pleasure, and his heart bounded with triumph; but suddenly a swift and terrible change came over him. His countenance became pallid as death and distorted with agony; great drops of sweat started from his pores. He stood a moment as if transfixed with pain and terror; then, turning his blanched and livid face to his horror-stricken friends, he cried in hollow, despairing tones, He whom you have exalted as a God is struck with death!

He was borne in a state of the most excruciating anguish from the scene of wicked revelry, the mirth, and pomp, and display of which he now loathed in his soul. A moment before, he had been the proud recipient of the praise and worship of that vast throng—now he felt himself in the hands of a Ruler mightier than himself. Remorse seized him; he remembered his cruel command to slay the innocent James; he remembered his relentless persecution of the followers of Christ, and his design to put to death the apostle Peter, whom God had delivered out of his hand; he remembered how, in his mortification and disappointed rage, he had wreaked his unreasoning revenge upon the keepers of the prisoner and executed them without mercy. He felt that God, who had rescued the apostle from death, was now dealing with him, the relentless persecutor. He found no relief from pain of body or anguish of mind, and he expected none. Herod was acquainted with the law of God, which says, "Thou shalt have no other gods before Me," and he knew that in accepting the worship of the people he had filled up the measure of his iniquity and had brought upon himself the just wrath of God.

The same angel who had left the royal courts of heaven to rescue Peter from the power of his persecutor, had been the messenger of wrath and judgment to Herod. The angel smote Peter to arouse him from slumber; but it was with a different stroke that he smote the wicked king, bringing mortal disease upon him. God poured contempt upon Herod's pride, and his person, which he had exhibited decked in shining apparel before the admiring gaze of the people, was eaten by worms, and putrefied while yet alive. Herod died in great agony of mind and body, under the retributive justice of God.

This demonstration of divine judgment had a mighty influence upon the people. While the apostle of Christ had been miraculously delivered from prison and death, his persecutor had been stricken down by the curse of God. The news was borne to all lands, and was the means of bringing many to believe on Christ.

Chapter 41—In the Regions Beyond

This chapter is based on Acts 13:1-4 and 15:1-31.

The apostles and disciples who left Jerusalem during the fierce persecution that raged there after the martyrdom of Stephen, preached Christ in the cities round about, confining their labors to the Hebrew and Greek Jews. "And the hand of the Lord was with them: and a great number believed, and turned unto the Lord." Acts 11:21.

When the believers in Jerusalem heard the good tidings they rejoiced; and Barnabas, "a good man, and full of the Holy Ghost and of faith," was sent to Antioch, the metropolis of Syria, to help the church there. He labored there with great success. As the work increased, he solicited and obtained the help of Paul; and the two disciples labored together in that city for a year, teaching the people and adding to the numbers of the church of Christ.

Antioch had both a large Jewish and Gentile population; it was a great resort for lovers of ease and pleasure, because of the healthfulness of its situation, its beautiful scenery, and the wealth, culture, and refinement that centered there. Its extensive commerce made it a place of great importance, where people of all nationalities were found. It was therefore a city of luxury and vice. The retribution of God finally came upon Antioch, because of the wickedness of its inhabitants.

It was here that the disciples were first called Christians. This name was given them because Christ was the main theme of their preaching, teaching, and conversation. They were continually recounting the incidents of His life during the time in which His disciples were blessed with His personal company. They dwelt untiringly upon His teachings, His miracles of healing the sick, casting out devils, and raising the dead to life. With quivering lips and tearful eyes they spoke of His agony in the garden, His betrayal, trial, and execution, the forbearance and humility with which He endured the contumely and torture imposed upon Him by His enemies, and the Godlike pity with which He prayed for those who persecuted Him. His resurrection and ascension and his work in heaven as a Mediator for fallen man were joyful topics with them. The heathen might well call them Christians, since they preached of Christ and addressed their prayers to God through Him.

Paul found, in the populous city of Antioch, an excellent field of labor, where his great learning, wisdom, and zeal, combined, wielded a powerful influence over the inhabitants and frequenters of that city of culture.

Meanwhile the work of the apostles was centered at Jerusalem, where Jews of all tongues and countries came to worship at the temple during the stated festivals. At such times the apostles preached Christ with unflinching courage, though they knew that in so doing their lives were in constant jeopardy. Many converts to the faith were made, and these, scattering to their homes in different parts of the country, dispersed the seeds of truth throughout all nations and among all classes of society.

Peter, James, and John felt confident that God had appointed them to preach Christ among their own countrymen at home. But Paul had received his commission from God, while praying in the temple, and his broad missionary field had been presented before him with remarkable distinctness. To prepare him for his extensive and important work, God had brought him into close connection with Himself, and had opened before his enraptured vision a glimpse of the beauty and glory of heaven.

Ordination of Paul and Barnabas

God communicated with the devout prophets and teachers in the church at Antioch. "As they ministered to the Lord, and fasted, the Holy Ghost said, Separate me Barnabas and Saul for the work whereunto I have called them." Acts 13:2. These apostles were therefore dedicated to God in a most solemn manner by fasting and prayer and the laying on of hands; and they were sent forth to their field of labor among the Gentiles.

Both Paul and Barnabas had been laboring as ministers of Christ, and God had abundantly blessed their efforts, but neither of them had previously been formally ordained to the gospel ministry by prayer and the laying on of hands. They were now authorized by the church not only to teach the truth but to baptize and to organize churches, being invested with full ecclesiastical authority. This was an important era for the church. Though the middle wall of partition between Jew and Gentile had been broken down by the death of Christ, letting the Gentiles into the full privileges of the gospel, the veil had not yet been torn away from the eyes of many of the believing Jews, and they could not clearly discern to the end of that which was abolished by the Son of God. The work was now to be prosecuted with vigor among the Gentiles, and was to result in strengthening the church by a great ingathering of souls.

The apostles, in this, their special work, were to be exposed to suspicion, prejudice, and jealousy. As a natural consequence of their departure from the exclusiveness of the Jews, their doctrine and views would be subject to the charge of heresy; and their credentials as ministers of the gospel would be questioned by many zealous, believing Jews. God foresaw all these difficulties which His servants would undergo, and, in His wise providence, caused them to be invested with unquestionable authority from the established church of God, that their work should be above challenge.

The ordination by the laying on of hands was, at a later date, greatly abused; unwarrantable importance was attached to the act, as though a power came at once upon those who received such ordination, which immediately qualified them for any and all ministerial work, as though virtue lay in the act of laying on of hands. We have, in the history of these two apostles, only a simple record of the laying on of hands, and its bearing upon their work. Both Paul and Barnabas had already received their commission from God Himself; and the ceremony of the laying on of hands added no new grace or virtual qualification. It was merely setting the seal of the church upon the work of God—an acknowledged form of designation to an appointed office.

The First General Conference

Certain Jews from Judea raised a general consternation among the believing Gentiles by agitating the question of circumcision. They asserted, with great assurance, that none could be saved without being circumcised and keeping the entire ceremonial law.

This was an important question, and one which affected the church in a very great degree. Paul and Barnabas met it with promptness, and opposed introducing the subject to the Gentiles. They were opposed in this by the believing Jews of Antioch, who favored the position of those from Judea. The matter resulted in much discussion and want of harmony in the church, until finally the church at Antioch, apprehending that a division among them would occur from any further discussion of the question, decided to send Paul and Barnabas, together with some responsible men of Antioch, to Jerusalem, to lay the matter before the apostles and elders. There they were to meet delegates from the different churches, and those who had come to attend the approaching annual festivals. Meanwhile all controversy was to cease, until a final decision should be made by the responsible men of the church. This decision was then to be universally accepted by the various churches throughout the country.

Upon arriving at Jerusalem the delegates from Antioch related before the assembly of the churches the success that had attended the ministry with them, and the confusion that had resulted from the fact that certain converted Pharisees declared that the Gentile converts must be circumcised and keep the law of Moses in order to be saved.

The Jews had prided themselves upon their divinely appointed services; and they concluded that as God once specified the Hebrew manner of worship, it was impossible that He should ever authorize a change in any of its specifications. They decided that Christianity must connect itself with the Jewish laws and ceremonies. They were slow to discern to the end of that which had been abolished by the death of Christ, and to perceive that all their sacrificial offerings had but prefigured the death of the Son of God, in which type had met its antitype, rendering valueless the divinely appointed ceremonies and sacrifices of the Jewish religion.

Paul had prided himself upon his Pharisaical strictness; but after the revelation of Christ to him on the road to Damascus the mission of the Saviour and his own work in the conversion of the Gentiles were plain to his mind, and he fully comprehended the difference between a living faith and a dead formalism. Paul still claimed to be one of the children of Abraham, and kept the Ten Commandments in letter and in spirit as faithfully as he had ever done before his conversion to Christianity. But he knew that the typical ceremonies must soon altogether cease, since that which they had shadowed forth had come to pass, and the light of the gospel was shedding its glory upon the Jewish religion, giving a new significance to its ancient rites.

Evidence of Cornelius' Experience

The question thus brought under the consideration of the council seemed to present insurmountable difficulties, viewed in whatever light. But the Holy Ghost had, in reality, already settled this problem, upon the decision of which depended the prosperity, and even the existence, of the Christian church. Grace, wisdom, and sanctified judgment were given to the apostles to decide the vexed question.

Peter reasoned that the Holy Ghost had decided the matter by descending with equal power upon the uncircumcised Gentiles and the circumcised Jews. He recounted his vision, in which God had presented before him a sheet filled with all manner of four-footed beasts, and had bidden him kill and eat; that when he had refused, affirming that he had never eaten that which was common or unclean, God had said, "What God hath cleansed, that call not thou common."

He said, "God, which knoweth the hearts, bare them witness, giving them the Holy Ghost, even as He did unto us; and put no difference between us and them, purifying their hearts by faith. Now therefore why tempt ye God, to put a yoke upon the neck of the disciples, which neither our fathers nor we were able to bear?"

This yoke was not the law of the Ten Commandments, as those who oppose the binding claim of the law assert; but Peter referred to the law of ceremonies, which was made null and void by the crucifixion of Christ. This address of Peter brought the assembly to a point where they could listen with reason to Paul and Barnabas, who related their experience in working among the Gentiles.

The Decision

James bore his testimony with decision—that God designed to bring in the Gentiles to enjoy all the privileges of the Jews. The Holy Ghost saw good not to impose the ceremonial law on the Gentile converts; and the apostles and elders, after careful investigation of the subject, saw the matter in the same light, and their mind was as the mind of the Spirit of God. James presided at the council, and his final decision was, "Wherefore my sentence is, that we trouble not them, which from among the Gentiles are turned to God."

It was his sentence that the ceremonial law, and especially the ordinance of circumcision, be not in any wise urged upon the Gentiles, or even recommended to them. James sought to impress the fact upon his brethren that the Gentiles, in turning to God from idolatry, made a great change in their faith; and that much caution should be used not to trouble their minds with perplexing and doubtful questions, lest they be discouraged in following Christ.

The Gentiles, however, were to take no course which should materially conflict with the views of their Jewish brethren, or which would create prejudice in their minds against them. The apostles and elders therefore agreed to instruct the Gentiles by letter to abstain from meats offered to idols, from fornication, from things strangled, and from blood. They were required to keep the commandments and to lead holy lives. The Gentiles were assured that the men who had urged circumcision upon them were not authorized to do so by the apostles.

Paul and Barnabas were recommended to them as men who had hazarded their lives for the Lord. Judas and Silas were sent with these apostles to declare to the Gentiles, by word of mouth, the decision of the council. The four servants of God were sent to Antioch with the epistle and message, which put an end to all controversy; for it was the voice of the highest authority upon earth.

The council which decided this case was composed of the founders of the Jewish and Gentile Christian churches. Elders from Jerusalem and deputies from Antioch were present, and the most influential churches were represented. The council did not claim infallibility in their deliberations, but moved from the dictates of enlightened judgment and with the dignity of a church established by the divine will. They saw that God Himself had decided this question by favoring the Gentiles with the Holy Ghost, and it was left for them to follow the guidance of the Spirit.

The entire body of Christians were not called to vote upon the question. The apostles and elders—men of influence and judgment—framed and issued the decree, which was thereupon generally accepted by the Christian churches. All were not pleased, however, with this decision; there was a faction of false brethren who assumed to engage in a work on their own responsibility. They indulged in murmuring and faultfinding, proposing new plans and seeking to pull down the work of the experienced men whom God had ordained to teach the doctrine of Christ. The church has had such obstacles to meet from the first, and will ever have them to the close of time.

Chapter 42—Paul's Years of Ministry

Paul was an unwearied worker. He traveled constantly from place to place, sometimes through inhospitable regions, sometimes on the water, through storm and tempest. He allowed nothing to hinder him from doing his work. He was the servant of God and must carry out His will. By word of mouth and by letter he bore a message that ever since has brought help and strength to the church of God. To us, living at the close of this earth's history, the message that he bore speaks plainly of the dangers that will threaten the church, and of the false doctrines that the people of God will have to meet.

From country to country and from city to city Paul went, preaching of Christ and establishing churches. Wherever he could find a hearing, he labored to counterwork error and to turn the feet of men and women into the path of right. Those who by his labors in any place were led to accept Christ, he organized into a church. No matter how few in number they might be, this was done. And Paul did not forget the churches thus established. However small a church might be, it was the object of his care and interest.

Paul's calling demanded of him service of varied kinds—working with his hands to earn his living, establishing churches, writing letters to the churches already established. Yet in the midst of these varied labors he declared, "This one thing I do." (Philippians 3:13.) One aim he kept steadfastly before him in all his work—to be faithful to Christ, who, when he was blaspheming His name and using every means in his power to make others blaspheme it, had revealed Himself to him. The one great purpose of his life was to serve and honor Him whose name had once filled him with contempt. His one desire was to win souls to the Saviour. Jew and Gentile might oppose and persecute him, but nothing could turn him from his purpose.

Paul Reviews His Experience

Writing to the Philippians, he describes his experience before and after his conversion. "If any other man thinketh that he hath whereof he might trust in the flesh," he says, "I more: circumcised the eighth day, of the stock of Israel, of the tribe of Benjamin, an Hebrew of the Hebrews; as touching the law, a

Pharisee; concerning zeal, persecuting the church; touching the righteousness which is in the law, blameless." Philippians 3:4-6.

After his conversion his testimony was:

"Yea verily, and I count all things to be loss for the excellency of the knowledge of Christ Jesus my Lord: for whom I suffered the loss of all things, and do count them but refuse, that I may gain Christ, and be found in Him, not having a righteousness of mine own, even that which is of the law, but that which is through faith in Christ, the righteousness which is from God by faith." Philippians 3:8, 9, A.R.V.

The righteousness that heretofore he had thought of so much worth was now worthless in his sight. The longing of his soul was: "That I may know Him, and the power of His resurrection, and the fellowship of His sufferings, being made conformable unto His death; if by any means I might attain unto the resurrection of the dead. Not as though I had already attained, either were already perfect: but I follow after, if that I may apprehend that for which also I am apprehended of Christ Jesus. Brethren I count not myself to have apprehended: but this one thing I do, forgetting those things which are behind, and reaching forth unto those things which are before, I press toward the mark for the prize of the high calling of God in Christ Jesus." Philippians 3:10-14.

An Adaptable Worker

See him in the dungeon at Philippi, where, despite his pain-racked body, his song of praise breaks the silence of midnight. After the earthquake has opened the prison doors, his voice is again heard, in words of cheer to the heathen jailer, "Do thyself no harm: for we are all here"—every man in his place, restrained by the presence of one fellow prisoner. And the jailer, convicted of the reality of that faith which sustains Paul, inquires the way of salvation, and with his whole household unites with the persecuted band of Christ's disciples.

See Paul at Athens before the council of the Areopagus, as he meets science with science, logic with logic, and philosophy with philosophy. Mark how, with the tact born of divine love, he points to Jehovah as the "Unknown God," whom his hearers have ignorantly worshiped; and in words quoted from a poet of their own, he pictures Him as a Father whose children they are. Hear him, in that age of caste, when the rights of man as man were wholly unrecognized, as he sets forth the great truth of human brotherhood, declaring that God "hath made of one blood all nations of men for to dwell on all the face of the earth."

Then he shows how, through all the dealings of God with man, run like a thread of gold His purposes of grace and mercy. He "hath determined the times before appointed, and the bounds of their habitation; that they should seek the Lord, if haply they might feel after Him, and find Him, though He be not far from every one of us." Hear him in the court of Festus, when King Agrippa, convicted of the truth of the gospel, exclaims, "Almost thou persuadest me to be a Christian." With what gentle courtesy does Paul, pointing to his own chain, make answer, "I would to God, that not only thou, but also all that hear me this day, were both almost, and altogether such as I am, except these bonds."

Thus passed his life, as described in his own words, "in journeyings often, in perils of waters, in perils of robbers, in perils by mine own countrymen, in perils by the heathen, in perils in the city, in perils in the wilderness, in perils in the sea, in perils among false brethren; in weariness and painfulness, in watchings often, in hunger and thirst, in fastings often, in cold and nakedness." 2 Corinthians 11:26, 27.

"Being reviled," he said, "we bless; being persecuted, we suffer it: being defamed, we intreat"; "as sorrowful, yet alway rejoicing; as poor, yet making many rich; as having nothing, and yet possessing all things." 1 Corinthians 4:12, 13; 2 Corinthians 6:10.

Ministry in Bonds

Although he was a prisoner for a great length of time, yet the Lord carried forward His special work through him. His bonds were to be the means of spreading the knowledge of Christ and thus glorifying God. As he was sent from city to city for his trial, his testimony concerning Jesus and the interesting incidents of his own conversion were related before kings and governors, that they should be left without excuse concerning Jesus. Thousands believed on Him and rejoiced in His name.

I saw that God's special purpose was fulfilled in the journey of Paul upon the sea; He designed that the ship's crew might thus witness the power of God through Paul, and that the heathen also might hear the name of Jesus, and that many might be converted through the teaching of Paul and by witnessing the miracles he wrought. Kings and governors were charmed by his reasoning, and as with zeal and the power of the Holy Spirit he preached Jesus and related the interesting events of his experience, conviction fastened upon them that Jesus was the Son of God.

Chapter 43—Martyrdom of Paul and Peter

The apostles Paul and Peter were for many years widely separated in their labors, it bcing thc work of Paul to carry the gospel to the Gentiles, while Peter labored especially for the Jews. But in the providence of God, both were to bear witness for Christ in the world's metropolis, and upon its soil both were to shed their blood as the seed of a vast harvest of saints and martyrs.

About the time of Paul's second arrest Peter also was apprehended and thrust into prison. He had made himself especially obnoxious to the authorities by his zeal and success in exposing the deceptions and defeating the plots of Simon Magus, the sorcerer, who had followed him to Rome to oppose and hinder the work of the gospel. Nero was a believer in magic, and had patronized Simon. He was therefore greatly incensed against the apostle, and was thus prompted to order his arrest.

The emperor's malice against Paul was heightened by the fact that members of the imperial household, and also other persons of distinction, had been converted to Christianity during his first imprisonment. For this reason he made the second imprisonment much more severe than the first, granting him little opportunity to preach the gospel; and he determined to cut short his life as soon as a plausible pretext could be found for so doing. Nero's mind was so impressed with the force of the apostle's words at his last trial that he deferred the decision of the case, neither acquitting nor condemning him. But the sentence was only deferred. It was not long before the decision was pronounced which consigned Paul to a martyr's grave. Being a Roman citizen, he could not be subjected to torture, and was therefore sentenced to be beheaded.

Peter, as a Jew and a foreigner, was condemned to be scourged and crucified. In prospect of this fearful death, the apostle remembered his great sin in denying Jesus in the hour of trial, and his only thought was that he was unworthy of so great an honor as to die in the same manner as did his Master. Peter had sincerely repented of that sin, and had been forgiven by Christ, as is shown by the high commission given him to feed the sheep and lambs of the flock. But he could never forgive himself. Not even the thought of the agonies of the last terrible scene could lessen the bitterness of his sorrow and repentance. As a last favor he entreated his executioners that he might be nailed to the cross with his head downward. The request was granted, and in this manner died the great apostle Peter.

Paul's Final Witness

Paul was led in a private manner to the place of execution. His persecutors, alarmed at the extent of his influence, feared that converts might be won to Christianity even by the scene of his death. Hence few spectators were allowed to be present. But the hardened soldiers appointed to attend him listened to his words, and with amazement saw him cheerful and even joyous in prospect of such a death. His spirit of forgiveness toward his murderers and unwavering confidence in Christ to the very last proved a savor of life unto life to some who witnessed his martyrdom. More than one erelong accepted the Saviour whom Paul preached, and fearlessly sealed their faith with their blood.

The life of Paul, to its very latest hour, testified to the truth of his words in the second epistle to the Corinthians: "For God, who commanded the light to shine out of darkness, hath shined in our hearts, to give the light of the knowledge of the glory of God in the face of Jesus Christ. But we have this treasure in earthen vessels, that the excellency of the power may be of God, and not of us. We are troubled on every side, yet not distressed; we are perplexed, but not in despair; persecuted, but not forsaken; cast down, but not destroyed; always bearing about in the body the dying of the Lord Jesus, that the life also of Jesus might be made manifest in our body." 2 Corinthians 4:6-10. His sufficiency was not in himself but in the presence and agency of the divine Spirit that filled his soul and brought every thought into subjection to the will of Christ. The fact that his own life exemplified the truth he proclaimed gave convincing power to both his preaching and his deportment. Says the prophet, "Thou wilt keep him in perfect peace, whose mind is stayed on Thee: because he trusteth in Thee." Isaiah 26:3. It was this heaven-born peace, expressed upon the countenance, that won many a soul to the gospel.

The apostle was looking into the great beyond, not with uncertainty or in dread, but with joyful hope and longing expectation. As he stood at the place of martyrdom he saw not the gleaming sword of the executioner or the green earth so soon to receive his blood; he looked up through the calm blue heaven of that summer's day to the throne of the Eternal. His language was, O Lord, Thou art my comfort and my portion. When shall I embrace Thee? When shall I behold Thee for myself, without a dimming veil between?

Paul carried with him through his life on earth the very atmosphere of heaven. All who associated with him felt the influence of his connection with Christ and companionship with angels. Here lies the power of the truth. The unstudied, unconscious influence of a holy life is the most convincing sermon that can be given in favor of Christianity. Argument, even when unanswerable, may provoke only opposition; but a godly example has a power which it is impossible to wholly resist.

While the apostle lost sight of his own near sufferings, he felt a deep solicitude for the disciples whom he was about to leave to cope with prejudice, hatred, and persecution. He endeavored to strengthen and encourage the few Christians who accompanied him to the place of execution, by repeating the exceeding precious promises given for those who are persecuted for righteousness' sake. He assured them that nothing shall fail of all that the Lord hath spoken concerning His tried and faithful ones. They shall arise and shine; for the light of the Lord shall arise upon them. They shall put on their beautiful garments when the glory of the Lord shall be revealed. For a little season they may be in heaviness through manifold temptations, they may be destitute of earthly comfort; but they must encourage their hearts by saying, I know in whom I have believed. He is able to keep that which I have committed to His trust. His rebuke will come to an end, and the glad morning of peace and perfect day will come.

The Captain of our salvation has prepared His servant for the last great conflict. Ransomed by the sacrifice of Christ, washed from sin in His blood, and clothed in His righteousness, Paul has the witness in himself that his soul is precious in the sight of his Redeemer. His life is hid with Christ in God, and he is persuaded that He who has conquered death is able to keep that which is committed to his trust. His mind grasps the Saviour's promise, "I will raise him up at the last day." John 6:40. His thoughts and hopes are centered in the second advent of his Lord. And as the sword of the executioner descends and the shadows of death gather about the martyr's soul, his latest thought springs forward, as will his earliest thought in the great awakening, to meet the Lifegiver who shall welcome him to the joy of the blest.

Well-nigh a score of centuries have passed since Paul the aged poured out his blood as a witness for the Word of God and for the testimony of Christ. No faithful hand recorded for the generations to come the last scenes in the life of this holy man; but inspiration has preserved for us his dying testimony. Like a trumpet peal has his voice rung out through all the ages, nerving with his own courage thousands of witnesses for Christ, and wakening in thousands of sorrow-stricken hearts the echo of his own triumphant joy: "I am now ready to be offered, and the time of my departure is at hand. I have fought a good fight, I have finished my course, I have kept the faith: henceforth there is laid up for me a crown of righteousness, which the Lord, the righteous Judge, shall give me at that day: and not to me only, but unto all them also that love His appearing." 2 Timothy 4:6-8.

Chapter 44—The Great Apostasy

When Jesus revealed to His disciples the fate of Jerusalem and the scenes of the second advent, He foretold also the experience of His people from the time when He should be taken from them to His return in power and glory for their deliverance. From Olivet the Saviour beheld the storms about to fall upon the apostolic church, and, penetrating deeper into the future, His eye discerned the fierce, wasting tempests that were to beat upon His followers in the coming ages of darkness and persecution. In a few brief utterances, of awful significance, He foretold the portion which the rulers of this world would mete out to the church of God. The followers of Christ must tread the same path of humiliation, reproach, and suffering which their Master trod. The enmity that burst forth against the world's Redeemer would be manifested against all who should believe on His name.

The history of the early church testified to the fulfillment of the Saviour's words. The powers of earth and hell arrayed themselves against Christ in the person of His followers. Paganism foresaw that should the gospel triumph, her temples and altars would be swept away; therefore she summoned her forces to destroy Christianity. The fires of persecution were kindled. Christians were stripped of their possessions and driven from their homes. They "endured a great fight of afflictions." They "had trial of cruel mockings and scourgings, yea, moreover of bonds and imprisonment." Hebrews 11:36. Great numbers sealed their testimony with their blood. Noble and slave, rich and poor, learned and ignorant, were alike slain without mercy.

In vain were Satan's efforts to destroy the church of Christ by violence. The great controversy in which the disciples of Jesus yielded up their lives did not cease when these faithful standard-bearers fell at their post. By defeat they conquered. God's workmen were slain, but His work went steadily forward. The gospel continued to spread, and the number of its adherents to increase. It penetrated into regions that were inaccessible, even to the eagles of Rome. Said a Christian, expostulating with the heathen rulers who were urging forward the persecution: You may "kill us, torture us, condemn us.... Your injustice is the proof that we are innocent.... Nor does your cruelty ... avail you." It was but a stronger invitation to bring others to their persuasion. "The oftener we are mown down by you, the more in number we grow; the blood of Christians is seed."

Thousands were imprisoned and slain; but others sprang up to fill their places. And those who were martyred for their faith were secured to Christ, and accounted of Him as conquerors. They had fought the good fight, and they were to receive the crown of glory when Christ should come. The sufferings which they endured brought Christians nearer to one another and to their Redeemer. Their living example and dying testimony were a constant witness for the truth; and, where least expected, the subjects of Satan were leaving his service and enlisting under the banner of Christ.

The Compromise With Paganism

Satan therefore laid his plans to war more successfully against the government of God, by planting his banner in the Christian church. If the followers of Christ could be deceived and led to displease God, then their strength, fortitude, and firmness would fail, and they would fall an easy prey.

The great adversary now endeavored to gain by artifice what he had failed to secure by force. Persecution ceased, and in its stead were substituted the dangerous allurements of temporal prosperity and worldly honor. Idolaters were led to receive a part of the Christian faith, while they rejected other essential truths. They professed to accept Jesus as the Son of God and to believe in His death and resurrection; but they had no conviction of sin and felt no need of repentance or of a change of heart. With some concessions on their part, they proposed that Christians should make concessions, that all might unite on the platform of belief in Christ.

Now was the church in fearful peril. Prison, torture, fire, and sword were blessings in comparison with this. Some of the Christians stood firm, declaring that they could make no compromise. Others reasoned that if they should yield or modify some features of their faith, and unite with those who had accepted a part of Christianity, it might be the means of their full conversion. That was a time of deep anguish to the faithful followers of Christ. Under a cloak of pretended Christianity, Satan was insinuating himself into the church, to corrupt their faith and turn their minds from the word of truth.

At last the larger portion of the Christian company lowered their standard, and a union was formed between Christianity and paganism. Although the worshipers of idols professed to be converted, and united with the church, they still clung to their idolatry, only changing the objects of their worship to images of Jesus, and even of Mary and the saints. The foul leaven of idolatry, thus introduced into the church, continued its baleful work. Unsound doctrines, superstitious rites, and idolatrous ceremonies were incorporated into her faith and worship. As the followers of Christ united with idolaters, the Christian religion became corrupted and the church lost her purity and power. There were some, however, who were not misled by these delusions. They still maintained their fidelity to the Author of truth and worshiped God alone.

There have ever been two classes among those who profess to be followers of Christ. While one class study the Saviour's life and earnestly seek to correct their defects and to conform to the Pattern, the other class shun the plain, practical truths which expose their errors. Even in her best estate the church was not composed wholly of the true, pure, and sincere. Our Saviour taught that those who willfully indulge in sin are not to be received into the church; yet He connected with Himself men who were faulty in character, and granted them the benefits of His teachings and example, that they might have an opportunity to see and correct their errors.

But there is no union between the Prince of light and the prince of darkness, and there can be no union between their followers. When Christians consented to unite with those who were but half converted from paganism, they entered upon a path which led farther and farther from the truth. Satan exulted that he had succeeded in deceiving so large a number of the followers of Christ. He then brought his power to bear more fully upon them, and inspired them to persecute those who remained true to God. None could so well understand how to oppose the true Christian faith as could those who had once been its defenders; and these apostate Christians, uniting with their half-pagan companions, directed their warfare against the most essential features of the doctrines of Christ.

It required a desperate struggle for those who would be faithful to stand firm against the deceptions and abominations which were disguised in sacerdotal garments and introduced into the church. The Bible was not accepted as the standard of faith. The doctrine of religious freedom was termed heresy, and its upholders were hated and proscribed.

Withdrawal of the Faithful

After a long and severe conflict the faithful few decided to dissolve all union with the apostate church if she still refused to free herself from falsehood and idolatry. They saw that separation was an absolute necessity if they would obey the Word of God. They dared not tolerate errors fatal to their own souls and set an example which would imperil the faith of their children and children's children. To secure peace and unity they were ready to make any concession consistent with fidelity to God; but they felt that even peace would be too dearly purchased at the sacrifice of principle. If unity could be secured only by the compromise of truth and righteousness, then let there be difference, and even war. Well would it be for the church and the world if the principles that actuated those steadfast souls were revived in the hearts of God's professed people.

The apostle Paul declares that "all that will live godly in Christ Jesus shall suffer persecution." 2 Timothy 3:12. Why is it, then, that persecution seems in a great degree to slumber? The only reason is that the church has conformed to the world's standard, and therefore awakens no opposition. The religion current in our day is not of the pure and holy character which marked the Christian faith in the days of Christ and His apostles. It is only because of the spirit of compromise with sin, because the great truths of the Word of God are so indifferently regarded, because there is so little vital godliness in the church, that Christianity is apparently so popular with the world. Let there be a revival of the faith and power of the early church, and the spirit of persecution will be revived and the fires of persecution will be rekindled.

Chapter 45—The Mystery of Iniquity

The apostle Paul, in his second letter to the Thessalonians, foretold the great apostasy which would result in the establishment of the papal power. He declared that the day of Christ should not come, "except there come a falling away first, and that man of sin be revealed, the son of perdition; who opposeth and exalteth himself above all that is called God, or that is worshiped; so that he as God sitteth in the temple of God, shewing himself that he is God." And furthermore, the apostle warns his brethren that "the mystery of iniquity doth already work." 2 Thessalonians 2:3, 4, 7. Even at that early date he saw, creeping into the church, errors that would prepare the way for the development of the Papacy.

Little by little, at first in stealth and silence and then more openly as it increased in strength and gained control of the minds of men, the mystery of iniquity carried forward its deceptive and blasphemous work. Almost imperceptibly the customs of heathenism found their way into the Christian church. The spirit of compromise and conformity was restrained for a time by the fierce persecutions which the church endured under paganism. But as persecution ceased, and Christianity entered the courts and palaces of kings, she laid aside the humble simplicity of Christ and His apostles for the pomp and pride of pagan priests and rulers; and in place of the requirements of God, she substituted human theories and traditions. The nominal conversion of Constantine in the early part of the fourth century caused great rejoicing; and the world, arrayed in robes of righteousness, walked into the church. Now the work of corruption rapidly progressed. Paganism, while appearing to be vanquished, became the conqueror. Her spirit controlled the church. Her doctrines, ceremonies, and superstitions were incorporated into the faith and worship of the professed followers of Christ.

This compromise between paganism and Christianity resulted in the development of the man of sin foretold in prophecy as opposing and exalting himself above God. That gigantic system of false religion is a masterpiece of Satan's power—a monument of his efforts to seat himself upon the throne to rule the earth according to his will.

To secure worldly gains and honors, the church was led to seek the favor and support of the great men of earth, and having thus rejected Christ, she was induced to yield allegiance to the representative of Satan—the Bishop of Rome.

It is one of the leading doctrines of Romanism that the pope is the visible head of the universal church of Christ, invested with supreme authority over bishops and pastors in all parts of the world. More than this, the pope has arrogated the very titles of Deity.

Satan well knew that the Holy Scriptures would enable men to discern his deceptions and withstand his power. It was by the Word that even the Saviour of the world had resisted his attacks. At every assault Christ presented the shield of eternal truth, saying, "It is written." To every suggestion of the adversary he opposed the wisdom and power of the Word. In order for Satan to maintain his sway over men and establish the authority of the papal usurper, he must keep them in ignorance of the Scriptures. The Bible would exalt God and place finite men in their true position; therefore its sacred truths must be concealed and suppressed. This logic was adopted by the Roman church. For hundreds of years the circulation of the Bible was prohibited. The people were forbidden to read it, or to have it in their houses, and unprincipled priests and prelates interpreted its teachings to sustain their pretensions. Thus the pope came to be almost universally acknowledged as the vicegerent of God on earth, endowed with supreme authority over church and state.

Times and Laws Changed

The detector of error having been removed, Satan worked according to his will. Prophecy had declared that the Papacy was to "think to change times and laws." Daniel 7:25. This work it was not slow to attempt. To afford converts from heathenism a substitute for the worship of idols, and thus to promote their nominal acceptance of Christianity, the adoration of images and relics was gradually introduced into the Christian worship. The decree of a general council finally established this system of popish idolatry. To complete the sacrilegious work, Rome presumed to expunge from the law of God the second commandment, forbidding image worship, and to divide the tenth commandment, in order to preserve the number.

The spirit of concession to paganism opened the way for a still further disregard of Heaven's authority. Satan tampered with the fourth commandment also, and essayed to set aside the ancient Sabbath, the day which God had blessed and sanctified, and in its stead to exalt the festival observed by the

224

heathen as "the venerable day of the sun." This change was not at first attempted openly. In the first centuries the true Sabbath had been kept by all Christians. They were jealous for the honor of God, and, believing that His law is immutable, they zealously guarded the sacredness of its precepts. But with great subtlety Satan worked through his agents to bring about his object. That the attention of the people might be called to the Sunday, it was made a festival in honor of the resurrection of Christ. Religious services were held on it; yet it was regarded as a day of recreation, the Sabbath being still sacredly observed.

Constantine, while still a heathen, issued a decree enjoining the general observance of Sunday as a public festival throughout the Roman Empire. After his conversion he remained a stanch advocate of Sunday, and his pagan edict was then enforced by him in the interests of his new faith. But the honor shown this day was not as yet sufficient to prevent Christians from regarding the true Sabbath as the holy of the Lord. Another step must be taken; the false sabbath must be exalted to an equality with the true. A few years after the issue of Constantine's decree, the Bishop of Rome conferred on the Sunday the title of Lord's day. Thus the people were gradually led to regard it as possessing a degree of sacredness. Still the original Sabbath was kept.

The archdeceiver had not completed his work. He was resolved to gather the Christian world under his banner, and to exercise his power through his vicegerent, the proud pontiff who claimed to be the representative of Christ. Through half-converted pagans, ambitious prelates, and world-loving churchmen he accomplished his purpose. Vast councils were held, from time to time, in which the dignitaries of the church were convened from all the world. In nearly every council the Sabbath which God had instituted was pressed down a little lower, while the Sunday was correspondingly exalted. Thus the pagan festival came finally to be honored as a divine institution, while the Bible Sabbath was pronounced a relic of Judaism, and its observers were declared to be accursed.

The great apostate had succeeded in exalting himself "above all that is called God, or that is worshipped." 2 Thessalonians 2:4. He had dared to change the only precept of the divine law that unmistakably points all mankind to the true and living God. In the fourth commandment God is revealed as the Creator of the heavens and the earth, and is thereby distinguished from all false gods. It was as a memorial of the work of creation that the seventh day was sanctified as a rest day for man. It was designed to keep the living God ever before the minds of men as the source of being and the object of reverence and worship. Satan strives to turn men from their allegiance to God and from rendering obedience to His law; therefore he directs his efforts especially against that commandment which points to God as the Creator.

Protestants now urge that the resurrection of Christ on Sunday made it the Christian Sabbath. But Scripture evidence is lacking. No such honor was given to the day by Christ or His apostles. The observance of Sunday as a Christian institution has its origin in that "mystery of lawlessness" which, even in Paul's day, had begun its work. Where and when did the Lord adopt this child of the Papacy? What valid reason can be given for a change concerning which the Scriptures are silent?

In the sixth century the Papacy had become firmly established. Its seat of power was fixed in the imperial city, and the Bishop of Rome was declared to be the head over the entire church. Paganism had given place to the Papacy. The dragon had given to the beast "his power, and his seat, and great authority." Revelation 13:2. And now began the 1260 years of papal oppression foretold in the prophecies of Daniel and John. (Daniel 7:25; Revelation 13:5-7.) Christians were forced to choose, either to yield their integrity and accept the papal ceremonies and worship, or to wear away their lives in dungeon cells, or suffer death by the rack, the fagot, or the headsman's ax. Now were fulfilled the words of Jesus, "Ye shall be betrayed both by parents, and brethren, and kinsfolks, and friends; and some of you shall they cause to be put to death. And ye shall be hated of all men for My name's sake." Luke 21:16, 17. Persecution opened upon the faithful with greater fury than ever before, and the world became a vast battlefield. For hundreds of years the church of Christ found refuge in seclusion and obscurity. Thus says the prophet: "The woman fled into the wilderness, where she hath a place prepared of God, that they should feed her there a thousand two hundred and threescore days." Revelation 12:6.

The Dark Ages

The accession of the Roman Church to power marked the beginning of the Dark Ages. As her power increased, the darkness deepened. Faith was transferred from Christ, the true foundation, to the pope of Rome. Instead of trusting in the Son of God for forgiveness of sins and for eternal salvation, the people looked to the pope and to the priests and prelates to whom he delegated authority. They were taught that the pope was their mediator, and that none could approach God except through him, and, further, that he stood in the place of God to them, and was therefore to be implicitly obeyed. A deviation from his requirements was sufficient cause for the severest punishment to be visited upon the bodies and souls of the offenders.

Thus the minds of the people were turned away from God to fallible, erring, and cruel men—nay, more, to the prince of darkness himself, who exercised his power through them. Sin was disguised in a garb of sanctity. When the Scriptures are suppressed, and man comes to regard himself as supreme, we need look only for fraud, deception, and debasing iniquity. With the elevation of human laws and traditions was manifest the corruption that ever results from setting aside the law of God.

Days of Peril

Those were days of peril for the church of Christ. The faithful standard-bearers were few indeed. Though the truth was not left without witnesses, yet at times it seemed that error and superstition would wholly prevail, and true religion would be banished from the earth. The gospel was lost sight of, but the forms of religion were multiplied, and the people were burdened with rigorous exactions.

They were taught not only to look to the pope as their mediator but to trust to works of their own to atone for sin. Long pilgrimages, acts of penance, the worship of relics, the erection of churches, shrines, and altars, the payment of large sums to the church—these and many similar acts were enjoined to appease the wrath of God or to secure his favor; as if God were like men, to be angered at trifles, or pacified by gifts or acts of penance!

The advancing centuries witnessed a constant increase of error in the doctrines put forth from Rome. Even before the establishment of the Papacy, the teachings of heathen philosophers had received attention and exerted an influence in the church. Many who professed conversion still clung to the tenets of their pagan philosophy, and not only continued its study themselves but urged it upon others as a means of extending their influence among the heathen. Thus were serious errors introduced into the Christian faith. Prominent among these was the belief in man's natural immortality and his consciousness in death. This doctrine laid the foundation upon which Rome established the invocation of saints and the adoration of the virgin Mary. From this sprung also the heresy of eternal torment for the finally impenitent, which was early incorporated into the papal faith.

Then the way was prepared for the introduction of still another invention of paganism, which Rome named purgatory, and employed to terrify the credulous and superstitious multitudes. By this heresy is affirmed the existence of a place of torment, in which the souls of such as have not merited eternal damnation are to suffer punishment for their sins, and from which, when freed from impurity, they are admitted to heaven.

Still another fabrication was needed to enable Rome to profit by the fears and the vices of her adherents. This was supplied by the doctrine of indulgences. Full remission of sins, past, present, and future, and release from all the pains and penalties incurred, were promised to all who would enlist in the pontiff's wars to extend his temporal dominion, to punish his enemies, or to exterminate those who dared deny his spiritual supremacy. The people were also taught that by the payment of money to the church they might free themselves from sin and also release the souls of their deceased friends who were confined in the tormenting flames. By such means did Rome fill her coffers and sustain the magnificence, luxury, and vice of the pretended representatives of Him who had not where to lay His head.

The Scriptural ordinance of the Lord's supper had been supplanted by the idolatrous sacrifice of the mass. Papist priests pretended, by their senseless mummery, to convert the simple bread and wine into the actual body and blood of Christ. With blasphemous presumption they openly claimed the power to "create their Creator." All Christians were required, on pain of death, to avow their faith in this horrible, Heaven-insulting heresy. Those who refused were given to the flames.

The noontide of the Papacy was the world's moral midnight. The Holy Scriptures were almost unknown, not only to the people, but to the priests. Like the Pharisees of old, the papist leaders hated the light which would reveal their sins. God's law, the standard of righteousness, having been removed, they exercised power without limit, and practiced vice without restraint. Fraud, avarice, and profligacy prevailed. Men shrank from no crime by which they could gain wealth or position. The palaces of popes and prelates were scenes of the vilest debauchery. Some of the reigning pontiffs were guilty of crimes so revolting that secular rulers endeavored to depose these dignitaries of the church as monsters too vile to be tolerated upon the throne. For centuries there was no progress in learning, arts, or civilization. A moral and intellectual paralysis had fallen upon Christendom.

Chapter 46—Early Reformers

Amid the gloom that settled upon the earth during the long period of papal supremacy, the light of truth could not be wholly extinguished. In every age there were witnesses for God—men who cherished faith in Christ as the only mediator between God and man, who held the Bible as the only rule of life, and who hallowed the true Sabbath. How much the world owes to these men, posterity will never know. They were branded as heretics, their motives impugned, their characters maligned, their writings suppressed, misrepresented, or mutilated. Yet they stood firm, and from age to age maintained their faith in its purity, as a sacred heritage for the generations to come.

So bitter had been the war waged upon the Bible that at times there were very few copies in existence; but God had not suffered His Word to be wholly destroyed. Its truths were not to be forever hidden. He could as easily unchain the words of life as He could open prison doors and unbolt iron gates to set His servants free. In the different countries of Europe men were moved by the Spirit of God to search for the truth as for hidden treasure. Providentially guided to the Holy Scriptures, they studied the sacred pages with intense interest. They were willing to accept the light at any cost to themselves. Though they did not see all things clearly, they were enabled to perceive many long-buried truths. As Heaven-sent messengers they went forth, rending asunder the chains of error and superstition, and calling upon those who had been so long enslaved to arise and assert their liberty.

The time had come for the Scriptures to be translated and given to the people of different lands in their native tongue. The world had passed its midnight. The hours of darkness were wearing away, and in many lands appeared tokens of the coming dawn.

The Morning Star of the Reformation

In the fourteenth century arose in England the "morning star of the Reformation." John Wycliffe was the herald of reform, not for England alone, but for all Christendom. He was the progenitor of the Puritans; his era was an oasis in the desert.

The Lord saw fit to entrust the work of reform to one whose intellectual ability would give character and dignity to his labors. This silenced the voice of contempt, and prevented the adversaries of truth from attempting to put discredit upon his cause by ridiculing the ignorance of the advocate. When Wycliffe had mastered the learning of the schools, he entered upon the study of the Scriptures. In the Scriptures he found that which he had before sought in vain. Here he saw the plan of salvation revealed, and Christ set forth as the only advocate for man. He saw that Rome had forsaken the Biblical paths for human traditions. He gave himself to the service of Christ, and determined to proclaim the truths which he had discovered.

The greatest work of his life was the translation of the Scriptures into the English language. This was the first complete English translation ever made. The art of printing being still unknown, it was only by slow and wearisome labor that copies of the work could be multiplied; yet this was done, and the people of England received the Bible in their own tongue. Thus the light of God's Word began to shed its bright beams athwart the darkness. A divine hand was preparing the way for the Great Reformation.

The appeal to men's reason aroused them from their passive submission to papal dogmas. The Scriptures were received with favor by the higher classes, who alone in that age possessed a knowledge of letters. Wycliffe now taught the distinctive doctrines of Protestantism—salvation through faith in Christ, and the sole infallibility of the Scriptures. Many priests joined him in circulating the Bible and in preaching the gospel; and so great was the effect of these labors and of Wycliffe's writings that the new faith was accepted by nearly one half of the people of England. The kingdom of darkness trembled.

The efforts of his enemies to stop his work and to destroy his life were alike unsuccessful, and in his sixty-first year he died in peace in the very service of the altar.

The Reformation Spreads

It was through the writings of Wycliffe that John Huss of Bohemia was led to renounce many of the errors of Romanism and to enter upon the work of reform. Like Wycliffe, Huss was a noble Christian, a man of learning and of unswerving devotion to the truth. His appeals to the Scriptures and his bold denunciations of the scandalous and immoral lives of the clergy awakened widespread interest, and thousands gladly accepted a purer faith. This excited the ire of pope and prelates, priests and friars, and Huss was summoned to appear before the Council of Constance to answer to the charge of heresy. A safe conduct was granted him by the German emperor, and upon his arrival at Constance he was personally assured by the pope that no injustice should be done him.

After a long trial, in which he maintained the truth, Huss was required to choose whether he would recant his doctrines or suffer death. He chose the martyr's fate, and after seeing his books given to the flames, he was himself burned at the stake. In the presence of the assembled dignitaries of church and state, the servant of God had uttered a solemn and faithful protest against the corruptions of the papal hierarchy. His execution, in shameless violation of the most solemn and public promise of protection, exhibited to the whole world the perfidious cruelty of Rome. The enemies of truth, though they knew it not, were furthering the cause which they sought vainly to destroy.

Notwithstanding the rage of persecution, a calm, devout, earnest, patient protest against the prevailing corruption of religious faith continued to be uttered after the death of Wycliffe. Like the believers in apostolic days, many freely sacrificed their worldly possessions for the cause of Christ.

Strenuous efforts were made to strengthen and extend the power of the papacy, but while the popes still claimed to be Christ's representatives, their lives were so corrupt as to disgust the people. By the aid of the invention of printing the Scriptures were more widely circulated, and many were led to see that the papal doctrines were not sustained by the Word of God.

When one witness was forced to let fall the torch of truth, another seized it from his hand and with undaunted courage held it aloft. The struggle had opened that was to result in the emancipation, not only of individuals and churches, but of nations. Across the gulf of a hundred years men stretched their hands to grasp the hands of the Lollards of the time of Wycliffe. Under Luther began the Reformation in Germany; Calvin preached the gospel in France, Zwingle in Switzerland. The world was awakened from the slumber of ages, as from land to land were sounded the magic words, "Religious Liberty."

Chapter 47—Luther and the Great Reformation

Foremost among those who were called to lead the church from the darkness of popery into the light of a purer faith, stood Martin Luther. Zealous, ardent, and devoted, knowing no fear but the fear of God, and acknowledging no foundation for religious faith but the Holy Scriptures, Luther was the man for his time; through him, God accomplished a great work for the reformation of the church and the enlightenment of the world.

While one day examining the books in the library of the university, Luther discovered a Latin Bible. He had before heard fragments of the Gospels and Epistles at public worship, and he thought that they were the whole of God's Word. Now, for the first time, he looked upon the whole Bible. With mingled awe and wonder he turned the sacred pages; with quickened pulse and throbbing heart he read for himself the words of life, pausing now and then to exclaim, "Oh, if God would give me such a book for my own!" Angels of heaven were by his side, and rays of light from the throne of God revealed the treasures of truth to his understanding. He had ever feared to offend God, but now the deep conviction of his condition as a sinner took hold upon him as never before. An earnest desire to be free from sin and to find peace with God led him at last to enter a cloister and devote himself to a monastic life.

Every moment that could be spared from his daily duties, he employed in study, robbing himself of sleep, and grudging even the moments spent at his humble meals. Above everything else he delighted in the study of God's Word. He had found a Bible chained to the convent wall, and to this he often repaired.

Luther was ordained a priest, and was called from the cloister to a professorship in the University of Wittenberg. Here he applied himself to the study of the Scriptures in the original tongues. He began to lecture upon the Bible; and the book of Psalms, the Gospels, and the Epistles were opened to the understanding of crowds of delighted listeners. He was mighty in the Scriptures, and the grace of God rested upon him. His eloquence captivated his hearers, the clearness and power with which he presented the truth convinced their understanding, and his deep fervor touched their hearts.

A Leader in Reforms

In the providence of God he decided to visit Rome. An indulgence had been promised by the pope to all who should ascend on their knees what was known as Pilate's staircase. Luther was one day performing this act, when suddenly a voice like thunder seemed to say to him, "The just shall live by faith!" He sprang upon his feet in shame and horror, and fled from the scene of his folly. That text never lost its power upon his soul. From that time he saw more clearly than ever before the fallacy of trusting to human works for salvation, and the necessity of constant faith in the merits of Christ. His eyes had been opened, and were never again to be closed, to the Satanic delusions of the Papacy. When he turned his face from Rome he had turned away also in heart, and from that time the separation grew wider, until he severed all connection with the papal church.

After his return from Rome, Luther received at the University of Wittenberg the degree of doctor of divinity. Now he was at liberty to devote himself, as never before, to the Scriptures that he loved. He had taken a solemn vow to study carefully and to preach with fidelity the Word of God, not the sayings and doctrines of the popes, all the days of his life. He was no longer the mere monk or professor, but the authorized herald of the Bible. He had been called as a shepherd to feed the flock of God, that were hungering and thirsting for the truth. He firmly declared that Christians should receive no other doctrines than those which rest on the authority of the Sacred Scriptures. These words struck at the very foundation of papal supremacy. They contained the vital principle of the Reformation.

Luther now entered boldly upon his work as a champion of the truth. His voice was heard from the pulpit in earnest, solemn warning. He set before the people the offensive character of sin, and taught them that it is impossible for man, by his own works, to lessen its guilt or evade its punishment. Nothing but repentance toward God and faith in Christ can save the sinner. The grace of Christ cannot be purchased; it is a free gift. He counseled the people not to buy indulgences, but to look in faith to a crucified Redeemer. He related his own painful experience in vainly seeking by humiliation and penance to secure salvation, and assured his hearers that it was by looking away from himself and believing in Christ that he found peace and joy.

Luther's teachings attracted the attention of thoughtful minds throughout all Germany. From his sermons and writings issued beams of light which awakened and illuminated thousands. A living faith was taking the place of the dead formalism in which the church had so long been held. The people were daily losing confidence in the superstitions of Romanism. The barriers of prejudice were giving way. The Word of God, by which Luther tested every doctrine and every claim, was like a two-edged sword, cutting its way to the hearts of the people. Everywhere there was awakening a desire for spiritual progress. Everywhere was such a hungering and thirsting after righteousness as had not been known for ages. The eyes of the people, so long directed to human rites and human mediators, were now turning, in penitence and faith, to Christ and Him crucified.

The Reformer's writings and his doctrine were extending to every nation in Christendom. The work spread to Switzerland and Holland. Copies of his writings found their way to France and Spain. In England his teachings were received as the word of life. To Belgium and Italy also the truth had extended. Thousands were awakening from their deathlike stupor to the joy and hope of a life of faith.

Luther Breaks With Rome

Rome was bent upon the destruction of Luther, but God was his defense. His doctrines were heard everywhere—in convents, in cottages, in the castles of the nobles, in the universities, in the palaces of kings; and noble men were rising on every hand to sustain his efforts.

In an appeal to the emperor and nobility of Germany in behalf of the Reformation of Christianity, Luther wrote concerning the pope: "It is a horrible thing to behold the man who styles himself Christ's vicegerent, displaying a magnificence that no emperor can equal. Is this being like the poor Jesus, or the humble Peter? He is, say they, the lord of the world! But Christ, whose vicar he boasts of being, has said, 'My kingdom is not of this world.' Can the dominions of a vicar extend beyond those of his superior?"

He wrote thus of the universities: "I am much afraid that the universities will prove to be the great gates of hell, unless they diligently labor in explaining the Holy Scriptures, and engraving them in the hearts of youth. I advise no one to place his child where the Scriptures do not reign paramount. Every institution in which men are not unceasingly occupied with the Word of God must become corrupt."

This appeal was rapidly circulated throughout Germany, and exerted a powerful influence upon the people. The whole nation was roused to rally around the standard of reform. Luther's opponents, burning with a desire for revenge, urged the pope to take decisive measures against him. It was decreed that his doctrines should be condemned immediately. Sixty days were granted the Reformer and his adherents, after which, if they did not recant, they were all to be excommunicated.

When the papal bull reached Luther, he said: "I despise and attack it, as impious, false.... It is Christ Himself who is condemned therein.... I rejoice in having to bear such ills for the best of causes. Already I feel greater liberty in my heart; for at last I know that the pope is antichrist, and that his throne is that of Satan himself."

Yet the word of the pontiff of Rome still had power. Prison, torture, and sword were weapons potent to enforce submission. Everything seemed to indicate that the Reformer's work was about to close. The weak and superstitious trembled before the decree of the pope, and while there was general sympathy for Luther, many felt that life was too dear to be risked in the cause of reform.

Chapter 48—Progress of the Reformation

A new emperor, Charles the Fifth, had ascended the throne of Germany, and the emissaries of Rome hastened to present their congratulations, and induce the monarch to employ his power against the Reformation. On the other hand, the Elector of Saxony, to whom Charles was in great degree indebted for his crown, entreated him to take no step against Luther until he should have granted him a hearing.

The attention of all parties was now directed to the assembly of the German States which convened at Worms soon after the accession of Charles to the empire. There were important political questions and interests to be considered by this national council; but these appeared of little moment when contrasted with the cause of the monk of Wittenberg.

Charles had previously directed the elector to bring Luther with him to the Diet, assuring him that the Reformer should be protected from all violence, and should be allowed a free conference with one competent to discuss the disputed points. Luther was anxious to appear before the emperor.

The friends of Luther were terrified and distressed. Knowing the prejudice and enmity against him, they feared that even his safe conduct would not be respected, and they entreated him not to imperil his life. He replied: "The papists do not desire my coming to Worms, but my condemnation and my death. It matters not. Pray not for me, but for the Word of God."

Luther Before the Council

At length Luther stood before the council. The emperor occupied the throne. He was surrounded by the most illustrious personages in the empire. Never had any man appeared in the presence of a more imposing assembly than that before which Martin Luther was to answer for his faith.

The very fact of that appearance was a signal victory for the truth. That a man whom the pope had condemned should be judged by another tribunal was virtually a denial of the pontiff's supreme authority. The Reformer, placed under ban, and denounced from human fellowship by the pope, had been assured protection, and was granted a hearing by the highest dignitaries of the nation. Rome had commanded him to be silent, but he was about to speak in the presence of thousands from all parts of Christendom. Calm and peaceful, yet grandly brave and noble, he stood as God's witness among the great ones of the earth. Luther made his answer in a subdued and humble tone, without violence or passion. His demeanor was diffident and respectful; yet he manifested a confidence and joy that surprised the assembly.

Those who stubbornly closed their eyes to the light, and determined not to be convinced of the truth, were enraged at the power of Luther's words. As he ceased speaking, the spokesman of the Diet said angrily, "You have not answered the question put to you.... You are required to give a clear and precise answer.... Will you, or will you not, retract?"

The Reformer answered: "Since your most serene majesty and your high mightinesses require from me a clear, simple, and precise answer, I will give you one, and it is this: I cannot submit my faith either to the pope or to the councils, because it is clear as the day that they have frequently erred and contradicted each other. Unless therefore I am convinced by the testimony of Scripture or by the clearest reasoning, unless I am persuaded by means of the passages I have quoted, and unless they thus render my conscience bound by the Word of God, I cannot and I will not retract, for it is unsafe for a Christian to speak against his conscience. Here I stand, I can do no other; may God help me. Amen."

Thus stood this righteous man, upon the sure foundation of the Word of God. The light of Heaven illuminated his countenance. His greatness and purity of character, his peace and joy of heart, were manifest to all as he testified against the power of error and witnessed to the superiority of that faith that overcomes the world.

Firm as a rock he stood, while the fiercest billows of worldly power beat harmlessly against him. The simple energy of his words, his fearless bearing, his calm, speaking eye, and the unalterable determination expressed in every word and act made a deep impression upon the assembly. It was evident that he could not be induced, either by promises or threats, to yield to the mandate of Rome.

Christ had spoken through Luther's testimony with a power and grandeur that for the time inspired both friends and foes with awe and wonder. The Spirit of God had been present in that council, impressing the hearts of the chiefs of the empire. Several of the princes openly acknowledged the justice of Luther's cause. Many were convinced of the truth, but with some the impressions received were not lasting. There was another class who did not at the time express their convictions, but who, having searched the Scriptures for themselves, at a future time declared with great boldness for the Reformation.

The elector Frederick had looked forward with anxiety to Luther's appearance before the Diet, and with deep emotion he listened to his speech. He rejoiced at the doctor's courage, firmness, and self-possession, and was proud of being his protector. He contrasted the parties in contest, and saw that the wisdom of popes, kings, and prelates had been brought to nought by the power of truth. The Papacy had sustained a defeat which would be felt among all nations and in all ages.

Had the Reformer yielded a single point, Satan and his hosts would have gained the victory. But his unwavering firmness was the means of emancipating the church and beginning a new and better era. The influence of this one man, who dared to think and act for himself in religious matters, was to affect the church and the world, not only in his own time, but in all future generations. His firmness and fidelity would strengthen all, to the close of time, who should pass through a similar experience. The power and majesty of God stood forth above the counsel of men, above the mighty power of Satan.

I saw that Luther was ardent and zealous, fearless and bold, in reproving sin and advocating the truth. He cared not for wicked men or devils; he knew that he had One with him mightier than they all. Luther possessed zeal, courage, and boldness, and at times was in danger of going to extremes. But God raised up Melancthon, who was just the opposite in character, to aid Luther in carrying on the work of reformation. Melancthon was timid, fearful, cautious, and possessed great patience. He was greatly beloved of God. His knowledge of the Scriptures was great, and his judgment and wisdom excellent. His love for the cause of God was equal to Luther's. The hearts of these men the Lord knit together; they were inseparable friends. Luther was a great help to Melancthon when in danger of being fearful and slow, and Melancthon in turn was a great help to Luther when in danger of moving too fast.

Melancthon's far-seeing caution often averted trouble which would have come upon the cause had the work been left alone to Luther; and ofttimes the work would not have been pushed forward had it been left to Melancthon alone. I was shown the wisdom of God in choosing these two men to carry on the work of reformation.

England and Scotland Enlightened

While Luther was opening a closed Bible to the people of Germany, Tyndale was impelled by the Spirit of God to do the same for England. He was a diligent student of the Scriptures, and fearlessly preached his convictions of truth, urging that all doctrines be brought to the test of God's Word. His zeal could but excite opposition from the papists. A learned Catholic doctor who engaged in controversy with him, exclaimed, "It were better for us to be without God's law than without the pope's." Tyndale replied, "I defy the pope and all his laws; and if God spare my life, ere many years I will cause a boy who driveth the plow to know more of the Scriptures than you do."

The purpose which he had begun to cherish, of giving to the people the New Testament Scriptures in their own language, was now confirmed, and he immediately applied himself to the work. All England seemed closed against him, and he resolved to seek shelter in Germany. Here he began the printing of the English New Testament. Three thousand copies of the New Testament were soon finished, and another edition followed in the same year.

He finally witnessed for his faith by a martyr's death, but the weapons which he prepared have enabled other soldiers to do battle through all the centuries even to our time.

In Scotland the gospel found a champion in the person of John Knox. This truehearted reformer feared not the face of man. The fires of martyrdom, blazing around him, served only to quicken his zeal to greater intensity. With the tyrant's ax held menacingly over his head, he stood his ground, striking sturdy blows on the right hand and on the left, to demolish idolatry. Thus he kept to his purpose, praying and fighting the battles of the Lord, until Scotland was free.

In England, Latimer maintained from the pulpit that the Bible ought to be read in the language of the people. The Author of Holy Scripture, said he, "is God Himself;" and this Scripture partakes of the might and eternity of its Author. "There is no king, emperor, magistrate, and ruler ... but are bound to obey ... His holy word." "Let us not take any by-walks, but let God's word direct us: let us not walk after ... our forefathers, nor seek not what they did, but what they should have done."

Barnes and Frith, the faithful friends of Tyndale, arose to defend the truth. The Ridleys and Cranmer followed. These leaders in the English Reformation were men of learning, and most of them had been highly esteemed for zeal or piety in the Romish communion. Their opposition to the Papacy was the result of their knowledge of the errors of the Holy See. Their acquaintance with the mysteries of Babylon gave greater power to their testimonies against her.

The grand principle maintained by Tyndale, Frith, Latimer, and the Ridleys was the divine authority and sufficiency of the sacred Scriptures. They rejected the assumed authority of popes, councils, fathers, and kings to rule the conscience in matters of religious faith. The Bible was their standard, and to this they brought all doctrines and all claims. Faith in God and His Word sustained these holy men as they yielded up their lives at the stake.

Chapter 49—Failure to Advance

The Reformation did not, as many suppose, end with Luther. It is to be continued to the close of this world's history. Luther had a great work to do in reflecting to others the light which God had permitted to shine upon him; yet he did not receive all the light which was to be given to the world. From that time to this, new light has been continually shining upon the Scriptures, and new truths have been constantly unfolding.

Luther and his co-laborers accomplished a noble work for God; but, coming as they did from the Roman Church, having themselves believed and advocated her doctrines, it was not to be expected that they would discern all these errors. It was their work to break the fetters of Rome and to give the Bible to the world; yet there were important truths which they failed to discover, and grave errors which they did not renounce. Most of them continued to observe the Sunday with other papal festivals. They did not, indeed, regard it as possessing divine authority, but believed that it should be observed as a generally accepted day of worship. There were some among them, however, who honored the Sabbath of the fourth commandment. Among the reformers of the church an honorable place should be given to those who stood in vindication of a truth generally ignored, even by Protestants—those who maintained the validity of the fourth commandment and the obligation of the Bible Sabbath. When the Reformation swept back the darkness that had rested down on all Christendom, Sabbathkeepers were brought to light in many lands.

Those who received the great blessings of the Reformation did not go forward in the path so nobly entered upon by Luther. A few faithful men arose from time to time to proclaim new truth and expose long-cherished error, but the majority, like the Jews in Christ's day, or the papists in the time of Luther, were content to believe as their fathers believed, and to live as they lived. Therefore religion again degenerated into formalism; and errors and superstitions which would have been cast aside had the church continued to walk in the light of God's Word, were retained and cherished. Thus the spirit inspired by the Reformation gradually died out, until there was almost as great need of reform in the Protestant churches as in the Roman Church in the time of Luther. There was the same spiritual stupor, the same respect for the opinions of men, the same spirit of worldliness, the same substitution of human theories for the teachings of God's Word. Pride and extravagance were fostered under the guise of religion. The churches became corrupted by allying themselves with the world. Thus were degraded the great principles for which Luther and his fellow laborers had done and suffered so much.

As Satan saw that he had failed to crush out the truth by persecution, he again resorted to the same plan of compromise which had led to the great apostasy and the formation of the church of Rome. He induced Christians to ally themselves, not now with pagans, but with those who, by their worship of the god of this world, as truly proved themselves idolaters.

Satan could no longer keep the Bible from the people; it had been placed within the reach of all. But he led thousands to accept false interpretations and unsound theories, without searching the Scriptures to learn the truth for themselves. He had corrupted the doctrines of the Bible, and traditions which were to ruin millions were taking deep root. The church was upholding and defending these traditions, instead of contending for the faith once delivered to the saints. And while wholly unconscious of their condition and their peril, the church and the world were rapidly approaching the most solemn and momentous period of earth's history—the period of the revelation of the Son of man.

Chapter 50—The First Angel's Message

The prophecy of the first angel's message, brought to view in Revelation 14, found its fulfillment in the advent movement of 1840 44. In both Europe and America, men of faith and prayer were deeply moved as their attention was called to the prophecies, and, tracing down the Inspired Record, they saw convincing evidence that the end of all things was at hand. The Spirit of God urged His servants to give the warning. Far and wide spread the message of the everlasting gospel, "Fear God, and give glory to Him; for the hour of His judgment is come." Revelation 14:7.

Wherever missionaries had penetrated, were sent the glad tidings of Christ's speedy return. In different lands were found isolated bodies of Christians, who, solely by the study of the Scriptures, had arrived at the belief that the Saviour's advent was near. In some portions of Europe, where the laws were so oppressive as to forbid the preaching of the advent doctrine, little children were impelled to declare it, and many listened to the solemn warning.

To William Miller and his co-laborers it was given to preach the message in America, and the light kindled by their labors shone out to distant lands. God sent His angel to move upon the heart of a farmer who had not believed the Bible, to lead him to search the prophecies. Angels of God repeatedly visited that chosen one, to guide his mind and open to his understanding prophecies which had ever been dark to God's people. The commencement of the chain of truth was given to him, and he was led on to search for link after link, until he looked with wonder and admiration upon the Word of God. He saw there a perfect chain of truth. That Word, which he had regarded as uninspired, now opened before his vision in its beauty and glory. He saw that one portion of Scripture explains another, and when one passage was closed to his understanding, he found in another part of the Word that which explained it. He regarded the sacred Word of God with joy, and with the deepest respect and awe.

As he followed down the prophecies he saw that the inhabitants of the earth were living in the closing scenes of this world's history; yet they knew it not. He looked at the churches, and saw that they were corrupt; they had taken their affections from Jesus and placed them on the world; they were seeking for worldly honor, instead of that honor which cometh from above; grasping for worldly riches, instead of laying up their treasure in heaven. He could see hypocrisy, darkness, and death everywhere. His spirit was stirred within him. God called him to leave his farm, as He called Elisha to leave his oxen and the field of his labor to follow Elijah.

With trembling, William Miller began to unfold to the people the mysteries of the kingdom of God, carrying his hearers down through the prophecies to the second advent of Christ. The testimony of the Scriptures pointing to the coming of Christ in 1843 awakened widespread interest. Many were convinced that the arguments from the prophetic periods were correct, and, sacrificing their pride of opinion, they joyfully received the truth. Some ministers laid aside their sectarian views and feelings, left their salaries and their churches, and united in proclaiming the coming of Jesus.

There were but few ministers, however, who would accept this message; therefore it was largely committed to humble laymen. Farmers left their fields, mechanics their tools, traders their merchandise, professional men their positions; and yet the number of workers was small in comparison with the work to be accomplished. The condition of an ungodly church and a world lying in wickedness burdened the souls of the true watchmen, and they willingly endured toil, privation, and suffering, that they might call men to repentance unto salvation. Though opposed by Satan, the work went steadily forward, and the advent truth was accepted by many thousands.

A Great Religious Revival

Everywhere was heard the searching testimony warning sinners, both worldlings and church members, to flee from the wrath to come. Like John the Baptist, the forerunner of Christ, the preachers laid the ax at the root of the tree and urged all to bring forth fruit meet for repentance. Their stirring appeals were in marked contrast to the assurances of peace and safety that were heard from popular pulpits, and wherever the message was given, it moved the people.

The simple, direct testimony of the Scriptures, set home by the power of the Holy Spirit, brought a weight of conviction which few were able wholly to resist. Professors of religion were roused from their false security. They saw their backslidings, their worldliness and unbelief, their pride and selfishness. Many sought the Lord with repentance and humiliation. The affections that had so long clung to earthly things they now fixed upon heaven. The Spirit of God rested upon them, and with hearts softened and subdued they joined to sound the cry, "Fear God, and give glory to Him; for the hour of His judgment is come." Revelation 14:7.

Sinners inquired with weeping, "What must I do to be saved?" Those whose lives had been marked with dishonesty were anxious to make restitution. All who found peace in Christ longed to see others share the blessing. The hearts of parents were turned to their children, and the hearts of children to their parents. The barriers of pride and reserve were swept away. Heartfelt confessions were made, and the members of the household labored for the salvation of those who were nearest and dearest.

Often was heard the sound of earnest intercession. Everywhere were souls in deep anguish, pleading with God. Many wrestled all night in prayer for the assurance that their own sins were pardoned, or for the conversion of their relatives or neighbors. That earnest, determined faith gained its object. Had the people of God continued to be thus importunate in prayer, pressing their petitions at the mercy seat, they would be in possession of a far richer experience than they now have. There is too little prayer, too little real conviction of sin; and the lack of living faith leaves many destitute of the grace so richly provided by our gracious Redeemer.

All classes flocked to the Adventist meetings. Rich and poor, high and low, were, from various causes, anxious to hear for themselves the doctrine of the second advent. The Lord held the spirit of opposition in check while His servants explained the reasons of their faith. Sometimes the instrument was feeble; but the Spirit of God gave power to His truth. The presence of holy angels was felt in these assemblies, and many were daily added to the believers. As the evidences of Christ's soon coming were repeated, vast crowds listened in breathless silence to the solemn words. Heaven and earth seemed to approach each other. The power of God would be felt upon old and young and middle-aged. Men sought their homes with praises upon their lips, and the glad sound rang out upon the still night air. None who attended those meetings can ever forget those scenes of deepest interest.

Opposition

The proclamation of a definite time for Christ's coming called forth great opposition from many of all classes, from the minister in the pulpit down to the most reckless, heaven-daring sinner. "No man knoweth the day nor the hour!" was heard alike from the hypocritical minister and the bold scoffer. They closed their ears to the clear and harmonious explanation of the text by those who were pointing to the close of the prophetic periods and to the signs which Christ Himself had foretold as tokens of His advent.

Many who professed to love the Saviour declared that they had no opposition to the preaching of His coming; they merely objected to the definite time. God's all-seeing eye read their hearts. They did not wish to hear of Christ's coming to judge the world in righteousness. They had been unfaithful servants, their works would not bear the inspection of the heart-searching God, and they feared to meet their Lord. Like the Jews at the time of Christ's first advent, they were not prepared to welcome Jesus. Satan and his angels exulted and flung the taunt in the face of Christ and holy angels, that His professed people had so little love for Him that they did not desire His appearing.

Unfaithful watchmen hindered the progress of the work of God. As the people were roused, and began to inquire the way of salvation, these leaders stepped in between them and the truth, seeking to quiet their fears by falsely interpreting the Word of God. In this work Satan and unconsecrated ministers united, crying, Peace, peace, when God had not spoken peace. Like the Pharisees in Christ's day, many refused to enter the kingdom of heaven themselves, and those who were entering in they hindered. The blood of these souls will be required at their hand.

Wherever the message of truth was proclaimed, the most humble and devoted in the churches were the first to receive it. Those who studied the Bible for themselves could but see the unscriptural character of the popular views of prophecy, and wherever the people were not deceived by the efforts of the clergy to misstate and pervert the faith, wherever they would search the Word of God for themselves, the advent doctrine needed only to be compared with the Scriptures to establish its divine authority.

Many were persecuted by their unbelieving brethren. In order to retain their position in the church, some consented to be silent in regard to their hope, but others felt that loyalty to God forbade them thus to hide the truths which He had committed to their trust. Not a few were cut off from the fellowship of the church for no other reason than expressing their belief in the coming of Christ. Very precious to those who bore the trial of their faith were the words of the prophet, "Your brethren that hated you, that cast you out for My name's sake, said, Let the Lord be glorified: but He shall appear to your joy, and they shall be ashamed." Isaiah 66:5.

Angels of God were watching with the deepest interest the result of the warning. When the churches as a body rejected the message, angels turned away from them in sadness. Yet there were in the churches many who had not yet been tested in regard to the advent truth. Many were deceived by husbands, wives, parents, or children, and were made to believe it a sin even to listen to such heresies as were taught by the Adventists. Angels were bidden to keep faithful watch over these souls; for another light was yet to shine upon them from the throne of God.

Preparing to Meet the Lord

With unspeakable desire those who had received the message watched for the coming of their Saviour. The time when they expected to meet Him was at hand. They approached this hour with a calm solemnity. They rested in sweet communion with God, an earnest of the peace that was to be theirs in the bright hereafter. None who experienced this hope and trust can forget those precious hours of waiting. Worldly business was for the most part laid aside for a few weeks. Believers carefully examined every thought and emotion of their hearts as if upon their deathbeds and in a few hours to close their eyes upon earthly scenes. There was no making of "ascension robes," but all felt the need of internal evidence that they were prepared to meet the Saviour; their white robes were purity of soul, characters cleansed from sin by the atoning blood of Christ.

God designed to prove His people. His hand covered a mistake in the reckoning of the prophetic periods. Adventists did not discover the error, nor was it discovered by the most learned of their opponents. The latter said, "Your reckoning of the prophetic periods is correct. Some great event is about to take place, but it is not what Mr. Miller predicts; it is the conversion of the world, and not the second advent of Christ."

The time of expectation passed, and Christ did not appear for the deliverance of His people. Those who with sincere faith and love had looked for their Saviour experienced a bitter disappointment. Yet the Lord had accomplished His purpose: He had tested the hearts of those who had professed to be waiting for His appearing. There were among them many who had been actuated by no higher motive than fear. Their profession of faith had not affected their hearts or their lives. When the expected event failed to take place, these persons declared that they were not disappointed; they had never believed that Christ would come. They were among the first to ridicule the sorrow of the true believers.

But Jesus and all the heavenly host looked with love and sympathy upon the tried and faithful yet disappointed ones. Could the veil separating the visible from the invisible world have been swept back, angels would have been seen drawing near to these steadfast souls and shielding them from the shafts of Satan.

Chapter 51—The Second Angel's Message

The churches that refused to receive the first angel's message rejected light from heaven. That message was sent in mercy to arouse them to see their true condition of worldliness and backsliding, and to seek a preparation to meet their Lord.

It was to separate the church of Christ from the corrupting influence of the world that the first angel's message was given. But with the multitude, even of professed Christians, the ties which bound them to earth were stronger than the attractions heavenward. They chose to listen to the voice of worldly wisdom, and turned away from the heart-searching message of truth.

God gives light to be cherished and obeyed, not to be despised and rejected. The light which He sends becomes darkness to those who disregard it. When the Spirit of God ceases to impress the truth upon the hearts of men, all hearing is vain, and all preaching also is vain.

When the churches spurned the counsel of God by rejecting the advent message, the Lord rejected them. The first angel was followed by a second, proclaiming, "Babylon is fallen, is fallen, that great city, because she made all nations drink of the wine of the wrath of her fornication." Revelation 14:8. This message was understood by Adventists to be an announcement of the moral fall of the churches in consequence of their rejection of the first message. The proclamation, "Babylon is fallen," was given in the summer of 1844, and as the result, about fifty thousand withdrew from these churches.

Those who preached the first message had no purpose or expectation of causing divisions in the churches, or of forming separate organizations. "In all my labors," said William Miller, "I never had the desire or thought to establish any separate interest from that of existing denominations, or to benefit one at the expense of another. I thought to benefit all. Supposing that all Christians would rejoice in the prospect of Christ's coming, and that those who could not see as I did would not love any the less those who should embrace this doctrine, I did not conceive there would ever be any necessity for separate meetings. My whole object was a desire to convert souls to God, to notify the world of a coming judgment, and to induce my fellow men to make that preparation of heart which will enable them to meet their God in peace. The great majority of those who were converted under my labors united with the various existing churches. When individuals came to me to inquire respecting their duty, I always told them to go where they would feel at home; and I never favored any one denomination in my advice to such."

For a time many of the churches welcomed his labors, but as they decided against the advent truth, they desired to suppress all agitation of the subject. Those who had accepted the doctrine were thus placed in a position of great trial and perplexity. They loved their churches, and were loth to separate from them; but as they were ridiculed and oppressed, denied the privilege of speaking of their hope, or of attending preaching upon the Lord's coming, many at last arose and cast off the yoke that had been imposed upon them.

Adventists, seeing that the churches rejected the testimony of God's Word, could no longer regard them as constituting the church of Christ, "the pillar and ground of the truth;" and as the message, "Babylon is fallen," began to be proclaimed, they felt themselves justified in separating from their former connection.

Since the rejection of the first message, a sad change has taken place in the churches. As truth is spurned, error is received and cherished. Love for God and faith in His Word have grown cold. The churches have grieved the Spirit of the Lord, and it has been in a great measure withdrawn.

The Tarrying Time

When the year 1843 entirely passed away unmarked by the advent of Jesus, those who had looked in faith for His appearing were for a time left in doubt and perplexity. But notwithstanding their disappointment, many continued to search the Scriptures, examining anew the evidences of their faith, and carefully studying the prophecies to obtain further light. The Bible testimony in support of their position seemed clear and conclusive. Signs which could not be mistaken pointed to the coming of Christ as near. The believers could not explain their disappointment; yet they felt assured that God had led them in their past experience.

Their faith was greatly strengthened by the direct and forcible application of those scriptures which set forth a tarrying time. As early as 1842, the Spirit of God had moved upon Charles Fitch to devise the prophetic chart, which was generally regarded by Adventists as a fulfillment of the command given by the prophet Habakkuk, to "write the vision, and make it plain upon tables." No one, however, then saw the tarrying time which was brought to view in the same prophecy. After the disappointment the full meaning of this scripture became apparent. Thus speaks the prophet: "Write the vision, and make it plain upon tables, that he may run that readeth it. For the vision is yet for an appointed time, but at the end it shall speak, and not lie: though it tarry, wait for it, because it will surely come, it will not tarry." Habakkuk 2:2, 3.

The waiting ones rejoiced that He who knows the end from the beginning had looked down through the ages, and, foreseeing their disappointment, had given them words of courage and hope. Had it not been for such portions of Scripture, showing that they were in the right path, their faith would have failed in that trying hour.

In the parable of the ten virgins, Matthew 25, the experience of Adventists is illustrated by the incidents of an Eastern marriage. "Then shall the kingdom of heaven be likened unto ten virgins, which took their lamps, and went forth to meet the bridegroom." "While the bridegroom tarried, they all slumbered and slept."

The widespread movement under the proclamation of the first message, answered to the going forth of the virgins, while the passing of the time of expectation, the disappointment, and the delay, were represented by the tarrying of the bridegroom. After the definite time had passed, the true believers were still united in the belief that the end of all things was at hand; but it soon became evident that they were losing, to some extent, their zeal and devotion, and were falling into the state denoted in the parable by the slumbering of the virgins during the tarrying time.

About this time fanaticism began to appear. Some who professed to be zealous believers in the message rejected the Word of God as the one infallible guide, and, claiming to be led by the Spirit, gave themselves up to the control of their own feelings, impressions, and imaginations. There were some who manifested a blind and bigoted zeal, denouncing all who would not sanction their course. Their fanatical ideas and exercises met with no sympathy from the great body of Adventists; yet they served to bring reproach upon the cause of truth.

The preaching of the first message in 1843, and of the midnight cry in 1844, tended directly to repress fanaticism and dissension. Those who participated in these solemn movements were in harmony; their hearts were filled with love for one another, and for Jesus, whom they expected soon to see. The one faith, the one blessed hope, lifted them above the control of any human influence and proved a shield against the assaults of Satan.

Chapter 52—The Midnight Cry

"While the bridegroom tarried, they all slumbered and slept. And at midnight there was a cry made, Behold, the bridegroom cometh; go ye out to meet him. Then all those virgins arose, and trimmed their lamps." Matthew 25:5-7.

In the summer of 1844 Adventists discovered the mistake in their former reckoning of the prophetic periods, and settled upon the correct position. The 2300 days of Daniel 8:14, which all believed to extend to the second coming of Christ, had been thought to end in the spring of 1844; but it was now seen that this period extended to the autumn of the same year, and the minds of Adventists were fixed upon this point as the time for the Lord's appearing. The proclamation of this time message was another step in the fulfillment of the parable of the marriage, whose application to the experience of Adventists had already been clearly seen.

As in the parable the cry was raised at midnight announcing the approach of the bridegroom, so in the fulfillment, midway between the spring of 1844, when it was first supposed that the 2300 days would close, and the autumn of 1844, at which time it was afterward found that they were really to close, such a cry was raised, in the very words of Scripture: "Behold, the Bridegroom cometh; go ye out to meet Him."

Like a tidal wave the movement swept over the land. From city to city, from village to village, and into remote country places it went, until the waiting people of God were fully aroused. Before this proclamation fanaticism disappeared, like early frost before the rising sun. Believers once more found their position, and hope and courage animated their hearts.

The work was free from those extremes which are ever manifested when there is human excitement without the controlling influence of the Word and Spirit of God. It was similar in character to those seasons of humiliation and returning unto the Lord which among ancient Israel followed messages of reproof from His servants. It bore the characteristics which mark the work of God in every age. There was little ecstatic joy, but rather deep searching of heart, confession of sin, and forsaking of the world. A preparation to meet the

Lord was the burden of agonizing spirits. There was persevering prayer and unreserved consecration to God.

The midnight cry was not so much carried by argument, though the Scripture proof was clear and conclusive. There went with it an impelling power that moved the soul. There was no doubt, no questioning. Upon the occasion of Christ's triumphal entry into Jerusalem, the people who were assembled from all parts of the land to keep the feast, flocked to the Mount of Olives, and as they joined the throng that were escorting Jesus, they caught the inspiration of the hour and helped to swell the shout, "Blessed is He that cometh in the name of the Lord." Matthew 21:9. In like manner did unbelievers who flocked to the Adventist meetings—some from curiosity, some merely to ridicule—feel the convincing power attending the message, "Behold, the Bridegroom cometh!"

At that time there was faith that brought answers to prayer—faith that had respect to the recompense of reward. Like showers of rain upon the thirsty earth, the Spirit of grace descended upon the earnest seekers. Those who expected soon to stand face to face with their Redeemer felt a solemn joy that was unutterable. The softening, subduing power of the Holy Spirit melted the heart, as wave after wave of the glory of God swept over the faithful, believing ones.

Carefully and solemnly those who received the message came up to the time when they hoped to meet their Lord. Every morning they felt that it was their first duty to secure the evidence of their acceptance with God. Their hearts were closely united, and they prayed much with and for one another. They often met together in secluded places to commune with God, and the voice of intercession ascended to heaven from the fields and groves. The assurance of the Saviour's approval was more necessary to them than their daily food, and if a cloud darkened their minds, they did not rest until it was swept away. As they felt the witness of pardoning grace, they longed to behold Him whom their souls loved.

Disappointed but Not Forsaken

But again they were destined to disappointment. The time of expectation passed, and their Saviour did not appear. With unwavering confidence they had looked forward to His coming, and now they felt as did Mary, when, coming to the Saviour's tomb and finding it empty, she exclaimed with weeping, "They have taken away my Lord, and I know not where they have laid Him." John 20:13.

A feeling of awe, a fear that the message might be true, had for a time served as a restraint upon the unbelieving world. After the passing of the time this did not at once disappear; they dared not triumph over the disappointed ones, but as no tokens of God's wrath were seen, they recovered from their fears and resumed their reproach and ridicule. A large class who had professed to believe in the Lord's soon coming renounced their faith. Some who had been very confident were so deeply wounded in their pride that they felt like fleeing from the world. Like Jonah, they complained of God, and chose death rather than life. Those who had based their faith upon the opinions of others, and not upon the Word of God, were now as ready to again exchange their views. The scoffers won the weak and cowardly to their ranks, and all united in declaring that there could be no more fears or expectations now. The time had passed, the Lord had not come, and the world might remain the same for thousands of years.

The earnest, sincere believers had given up all for Christ, and had shared His presence as never before. They had, as they believed, given their last warning to the world, and, expecting soon to be received into the society of their divine Master and the heavenly angels, they had, to a great extent, withdrawn from the unbelieving multitude. With intense desire they had prayed, "Come, Lord Jesus, and come quickly." But He had not come. And now to take up again the heavy burden of life's cares and perplexities, and to endure the taunts and sneers of a scoffing world, was indeed a terrible trial of faith and patience.

Yet this disappointment was not so great as was that experienced by the disciples at the time of Christ's first advent. When Jesus rode triumphantly into Jerusalem, His followers believed that He was about to ascend the throne of David and deliver Israel from her oppressors. With high hopes and joyful anticipations they vied with one another in showing honor to their King. Many spread out their garments as a carpet in His path, or strewed before Him the leafy branches of the palm. In their enthusiastic joy they united in the glad acclaim, "Hosanna to the Son of David!"

When the Pharisees, disturbed and angered by this outburst of rejoicing, wished Jesus to rebuke His disciples, He replied, "If these should hold their peace, the stones would immediately cry out." Luke 19:40. Prophecy must be fulfilled. The disciples were accomplishing the purpose of God; yet they were doomed to a bitter disappointment. But a few days had passed ere they witnessed the Saviour's agonizing death and laid Him in the tomb. Their expectations had not been realized in a single particular, and their hopes died with Jesus. Not till their Lord had come forth triumphant from the grave could they perceive that all had been foretold by prophecy, and "that Christ must needs have suffered, and risen again from the dead." Acts 17:3. In like manner was prophecy fulfilled in the first and second angels' messages. They were given at the right time and accomplished the work which God designed to accomplish by them.

The world had been looking on, expecting that if the time passed and Christ did not appear, the whole system of adventism would be given up. But while many, under strong temptation, yielded their faith, there were some who stood firm. They could detect no error in their reckoning of the prophetic periods. The ablest of their opponents had not succeeded in overthrowing their position. True, there had been a failure as to the expected event, but even this could not shake their faith in the Word of God.

God did not forsake His people; His Spirit still abode with those who did not rashly deny the light which they had received, and denounce the advent movement. The apostle Paul, looking down through the ages, had written words of encouragement and warning for the tried, waiting ones at this crisis: "Cast not away therefore your confidence, which hath great recompence of reward. For ye have need of patience, that, after ye have done the will of God, ye might receive the promise. For yet a little while, and He that shall come will come, and will not tarry. Now the just shall live by faith: but if any man draw back, My soul shall have no pleasure in him. But we are not of them who draw back unto perdition; but of them that believe to the saving of the soul." Hebrews 10:35-39.

Their only safe course was to cherish the light which they had already received of God, hold fast to His promises, and continue to search the Scriptures, and patiently wait and watch to receive further light.

Chapter 53—The Sanctuary

The scripture which above all others had been both the foundation and central pillar of the advent faith was the declaration, "Unto two thousand and three hundred days; then shall the sanctuary be cleansed." Daniel 8:14. These had been familiar words to all believers in the Lord's soon coming. By the lips of thousands was this prophecy joyfully repeated as the watchword of their faith. All felt that upon the events therein brought to view depended their brightest expectations and most cherished hopes. These prophetic days had been shown to terminate in the autumn of 1844. In common with the rest of the Christian world, Adventists then held that the earth, or some portion of it, was the sanctuary, and that the cleansing of the sanctuary was the purification of the earth by the fires of the last great day. This they understood would take place at the second coming of Christ. Hence the conclusion that Christ would return to the earth in 1844.

But the appointed time came, and the Lord did not appear. The believers knew that God's Word could not fail; their interpretation of the prophecy must be at fault; but where was the mistake? Many rashly cut the knot of difficulty by denying that the 2300 days ended in 1844. No reason could be given for this position, except that Christ had not come at the time of expectation. They argued that if the prophetic days had ended in 1844, Christ would then have come to cleanse the sanctuary by the purification of the earth by fire; and that since He had not come, the days could not have ended.

Though the majority of Adventists abandoned their former reckoning of the prophetic periods, and consequently denied the correctness of the movement based thereon, a few were unwilling to renounce points of faith and experience that were sustained by the Scriptures and by the special witness of the Spirit of God. They believed that they had adopted sound principles of interpretation in their study of the Scriptures, and that it was their duty to hold fast the truths already gained, and to still pursue the same course of Biblical research. With earnest prayer they reviewed their position, and studied the Scriptures to discover their mistake. As they could see no error in their explanation of the prophetic periods, they were led to examine more closely the subject of the sanctuary.

The Earthly and Heavenly Sanctuaries

In their investigation they learned that the earthly sanctuary, built by Moses at the command of God according to the pattern shown him in the mount, was "a figure for the time then present, in which were offered both gifts and sacrifices"; that its two holy places were "patterns of things in the heavens"; that Christ, our great High Priest, is "a minister of the sanctuary, and of the true tabernacle, which the Lord pitched, and not man"; that "Christ is not entered into the holy places made with hands, which are the figures of the true; but into heaven itself, now to appear in the presence of God for us." Hebrews 9:9, 23; 8:2; Hebrews 9:24.

The sanctuary in heaven, in which Jesus ministers in our behalf, is the great original, of which the sanctuary built by Moses was a copy. As the sanctuary on earth had two apartments, the holy and the most holy, so there are two holy places in the sanctuary in heaven. And the ark containing the law of God, the altar of incense, and other instruments of service found in the sanctuary below, have also their counterpart in the sanctuary above. In holy vision the apostle John was permitted to enter heaven, and he there beheld the candlestick and the altar of incense, and as "the temple of God was opened," he beheld also "the ark of His testament." Revelation 4:5; 8:3; Revelation 11:19.

Those who were seeking for the truth found indisputable proof of the existence of a sanctuary in heaven. Moses made the earthly sanctuary after a pattern which was shown him. Paul declared that that pattern was the true sanctuary which is in heaven. (Hebrews 8:2, 5.) John testified that he saw it in heaven.

At the termination of the 2300 days, in 1844, no sanctuary had existed on earth for many centuries; therefore the sanctuary in heaven must be the one brought to view in the declaration, "Unto two thousand and three hundred days; then shall the sanctuary be cleansed." But how could the sanctuary in heaven need cleansing? Turning again to the Scriptures, the students of prophecy learned that the cleansing was not a removal of physical impurities, for it was to be accomplished with blood, and therefore must be a cleansing from sin. Thus says the apostle: "It was therefore necessary that the patterns of things in the heavens should be purified with these [the blood of animals]; but the heavenly things themselves with better sacrifices than these [even the precious blood of Christ]." Hebrews 9:23.

To obtain a further knowledge of the cleansing to which the prophecy points, it was necessary to understand the ministration of the heavenly sanctuary. This could be learned only from the ministration of the earthly sanctuary; for Paul declares that the priests who officiated there served "unto the example and shadow of heavenly things." Hebrews 8:5.

The Cleansing of the Sanctuary

As the sins of the people were anciently transferred, in figure, to the earthly sanctuary by the blood of the sin offering, so our sins are, in fact, transferred to the heavenly sanctuary by the blood of Christ. And as the typical cleansing of the earthly was accomplished by the removal of the sins by which it had been polluted, so the actual cleansing of the heavenly is to be accomplished by the removal, or blotting out, of the sins which are there recorded. This necessitates an examination of the books of record to determine who, through repentance of sin and faith in Christ, are entitled to the benefits of His atonement. The cleansing of the sanctuary therefore involves a work of investigative judgment. This work must be performed prior to the coming of Christ to redeem His people, for when He comes, His reward is with Him to give to every man according to his works. (Revelation 22:12.)

Thus those who followed in the advancing light of the prophetic word saw that instead of coming to the earth at the termination of the 2300 days in 1844, Christ then entered the most holy place of the heavenly sanctuary, into the presence of God, to perform the closing work of atonement, preparatory to His coming.

Chapter 54—The Third Angel's Message

When Christ entered the most holy place of the heavenly sanctuary to perform the closing work of the atonement, He committed to His servants the last message of mercy to be given to the world. Such is the warning of the third angel of Revelation 14. Immediately following its proclamation, the Son of man is seen by the prophet coming in glory to reap the harvest of the earth.

As foretold in the Scriptures, the ministration of Christ in the most holy place began at the termination of the prophetic days in 1844. To this time apply the words of the Revelator, "The temple of God was opened in heaven, and there was seen in His temple the ark of His testament." Revelation 11:19. The ark of God's testament is in the second apartment of the sanctuary. As Christ entered there, to minister in the sinner's behalf, the inner temple was opened, and the ark of God was brought to view. To those who by faith beheld the Saviour in His work of intercession, God's majesty and power were revealed. As the train of His glory filled the temple, light from the holy of holies was shed upon His waiting people on the earth.

They had by faith followed their High Priest from the holy to the most holy, and they saw Him pleading His blood before the ark of God. Within that sacred ark is the Father's law, the same that was spoken by God Himself amid the thunders of Sinai, and written with His own finger on the tables of stone. Not one command has been annulled; not a jot or tittle has been changed. While God gave to Moses a copy of His law, He preserved the great original in the sanctuary above. Tracing down its holy precepts, the seekers for truth found, in the very bosom of the Decalogue, the fourth commandment, as it was first proclaimed: "Remember the Sabbath day, to keep it holy. Six days shalt thou labour, and do all thy work: but the seventh day is the Sabbath of the Lord thy God: in it thou shalt not do any work, thou, nor thy son, nor thy daughter, thy manservant, nor thy maidservant, nor thy cattle, nor thy stranger that is within thy gates: for in six days the Lord made heaven and earth, the sea, and all that in them is, and rested the seventh day: wherefore the Lord blessed the Sabbath day, and hallowed it." Exodus 20:8-11.

The Spirit of God impressed the hearts of these students of His Word. The conviction was urged upon them that they had ignorantly transgressed the fourth commandment by disregarding the Creator's rest day. They began to examine the reasons for observing the first day of the week instead of the day which God had sanctified. They could find no evidence in the Scriptures that the fourth commandment had been abolished, or that the Sabbath had been changed; the blessing which first hallowed the seventh day had never been removed. They had been honestly seeking to know and do God's will, and now, as they saw themselves transgressors of His law, sorrow filled their hearts. They at once evinced their loyalty to God by keeping His Sabbath holy.

Many and earnest were the efforts made to overthrow their faith. None could fail to see that if the earthly sanctuary was a figure or pattern of the heavenly, the law deposited in the ark on earth was an exact transcript of the law in the ark in heaven, and that an acceptance of the truth concerning the heavenly sanctuary involved an acknowledgment of the claims of God's law, and the obligation of the Sabbath of the fourth commandment.

Those who had accepted the light concerning the mediation of Christ and the perpetuity of the law of God, found that these were the truths brought to view in the third message. The angel declares, "Here are they that keep the commandments of God, and the faith of Jesus." Revelation 14:12. This statement is preceded by a solemn and fearful warning: "If any man worship the beast and his image, and receive his mark in his forehead, or in his hand, the same shall drink of the wine of the wrath of God, which is poured out without mixture into the cup of His indignation." Revelation 14:9, 10. An interpretation of the symbols employed was necessary to an understanding of this message. What was represented by the beast, the image, and the mark? Again those who were seeking for the truth returned to the study of the prophecies.

The Beast and Its Image

By this first beast is represented the Roman Church, an ecclesiastical body clothed with civil power, having authority to punish all dissenters. The image to the beast represents another religious body clothed with similar powers. The formation of this image is the work of that beast whose peaceful rise and mild professions render it so striking a symbol of the United States. Here is to be found an image of the Papacy. When the churches of our land, uniting upon such points of faith as are held by them in common, shall influence the State to enforce their decrees and sustain their institutions, then will Protestant America have formed an image of the Roman hierarchy. Then the true church will be assailed by persecution, as were God's ancient people.

The beast with lamblike horns commands "all, both small and great, rich and poor, free and bond, to receive a mark in their right hand, or in their foreheads: and that no man might buy or sell, save he that had the mark, or the name of the beast, or the number of his name." Revelation 13:16, 17. This is the mark concerning which the third angel utters his warning. It is the mark of the first beast, or the Papacy, and is therefore to be sought among the distinguishing characteristics of that power. The prophet Daniel declared that the Roman Church, symbolized by the little horn, was to think to change times and laws (Daniel 7:25), while Paul styled it the man of sin (2 Thessalonians 2:3, 4), who was to exalt himself above God. Only by changing God's law could the Papacy exalt itself above God; whoever should understandingly keep the law as thus changed would be giving supreme honor to that power by which the change was made.

The fourth commandment, which Rome has endeavored to set aside, is the only precept of the Decalogue that points to God as the Creator of the heavens and the earth, and thus distinguishes the true God from all false gods. The Sabbath was instituted to commemorate the work of creation, and thus to direct the minds of men to the true and living God. The fact of His creative power is cited throughout the Scriptures as proof that the God of Israel is superior to heathen deities. Had the Sabbath always been kept, man's thoughts and affections would have been led to his Maker as the object of reverence and worship, and there would never have been an idolater, an atheist, or an infidel.

That institution which points to God as the Creator is a sign of His rightful authority over the beings He has made. The change of the Sabbath is the sign, or mark, of the authority of the Romish Church. Those who, understanding the claims of the fourth commandment, choose to observe the false in place of the true Sabbath, are thereby paying homage to that power by which alone it is commanded.

A Solemn Message

The most fearful threatening ever addressed to mortals is contained in the third angel's message. That must be a terrible sin which calls down the wrath of God unmingled with mercy. Men are not to be left in darkness concerning this important matter; the warning against this sin is to be given to the world before the visitation of God's judgments, that all may know why they are to be inflicted, and have opportunity to escape them.

In the issue of the great contest, two distinct, opposite classes are developed. One class "worship the beast and his image, and receive his mark," and thus bring upon themselves the awful judgments threatened by the third angel. The other class, in marked contrast to the world, "keep the commandments of God, and the faith of Jesus." Revelation 14:9, 12.

Such were the momentous truths that opened before those who received the third angel's message. As they reviewed their experience from the first proclamation of the second advent to the passing of the time in 1844, they saw their disappointment explained, and hope and joy again animated their hearts. Light from the sanctuary illuminated the past, the present, and the future, and they knew that God had led them by His unerring providence. Now with new courage and firmer faith, they joined in giving the warning of the third angel. Since 1844, in fulfillment of the prophecy of the third angel's message, the attention of the world has been called to the true Sabbath, and a constantly increasing number are returning to the observance of God's holy day.

Chapter 55—A Firm Platform

I saw a company who stood well guarded and firm, giving no countenance to those who would unsettle the established faith of the body. God looked upon them with approbation. I was shown three steps—the first, second, and third angels' messages. Said my accompanying angel, "Woe to him who shall move a block or stir a pin of these messages. The true understanding of these messages is of vital importance. The destiny of souls hangs upon the manner in which they are received."

I was again brought down through these messages, and saw how dearly the people of God had purchased their experience. It had been obtained through much suffering and severe conflict. God had led them along step by step, until He had placed them upon a solid immovable platform. I saw individuals approach the platform and examine the foundation. Some with rejoicing immediately stepped upon it. Others commenced to find fault with the foundation. They wished improvements made, and then the platform would be more perfect and the people much happier.

Some stepped off the platform to examine it, and declared it to be laid wrong. But I saw that nearly all stood firm upon the platform and exhorted those who had stepped off to cease their complaints; for God was the Master Builder, and they were fighting against Him. They recounted the wonderful work of God, which had led them to the firm platform, and in union raised their eyes to heaven and with a loud voice glorified God. This affected some of those who had complained and left the platform, and they with humble look again stepped upon it.

Experience of Jews Repeated

I was pointed back to the proclamation of the first advent of Christ. John was sent in the spirit and power of Elijah to prepare the way for Jesus. Those who rejected the testimony of John were not benefited by the teachings of Jesus. Their opposition to the message that foretold His coming placed them where they could not readily receive the strongest evidence that He was the Messiah. Satan led on those who rejected the message of John to go still farther, to reject and crucify Christ. In doing this they placed themselves where they could not receive the blessing on the day of Pentecost, which would have taught them the way into the heavenly sanctuary.

The rending of the veil of the temple showed that the Jewish sacrifices and ordinances would no longer be received. The great Sacrifice had been offered and had been accepted, and the Holy Spirit which descended on the day of Pentecost carried the minds of the disciples from the earthly sanctuary to the heavenly, where Jesus had entered by His own blood, to shed upon His disciples the benefits of His atonement. But the Jews were left in total darkness. They lost all the light which they might have had upon the plan of salvation, and still trusted in their useless sacrifices and offerings. The heavenly sanctuary had taken the place of the earthly, yet they had no knowledge of the change. Therefore they could not be benefited by the mediation of Christ in the holy place.

Many look with horror at the course of the Jews in rejecting and crucifying Christ; and as they read the history of His shameful abuse, they think they love Him, and would not have denied Him as did Peter, or crucified Him as did the Jews. But God, who reads the hearts of all, has brought to the test that love for Jesus which they professed to feel.

All heaven watched with the deepest interest the reception of the first angel's message. But many who professed to love Jesus, and who shed tears as they read the story of the cross, derided the good news of His coming. Instead of receiving the message with gladness, they declared it to be a delusion. They hated those who loved His appearing and shut them out of the churches. Those who rejected the first message could not be benefited by the second; neither were they benefited by the midnight cry, which was to prepare them to enter with Jesus by faith into the most holy place of the heavenly sanctuary. And by rejecting the two former messages, they have so darkened their understanding that they can see no light in the third angel's message, which shows the way into the most holy place.

Chapter 56—Satan's Delusions

Satan commenced his deception in Eden. He said to Eve, "Ye shall not surely die." This was Satan's first lesson upon the immortality of the soul, and he has carried on this deception from that time to the present, and will carry it on until the captivity of God's children shall be turned. I was pointed to Adam and Eve in Eden. They partook of the forbidden tree, and then the flaming sword was placed around the tree of life, and they were driven from the garden, lest they should partake of the tree of life, and be immortal sinners. The fruit of this tree was to perpetuate immortality. I heard an angel ask, "Who of the family of Adam have passed that flaming sword and have partaken of the tree of life?" I heard another angel answer, "Not one of the family of Adam has passed that flaming sword and partaken of that tree; therefore there is not an immortal sinner." The soul that sinneth, it shall die an everlasting death—a death from which there will be no hope of a resurrection; and then the wrath of God will be appeased.

It was a marvel to me that Satan could succeed so well in making men believe that the words of God, "The soul that sinneth, it shall die" (Ezekiel 18:4), mean that the soul that sinneth it shall not die, but live eternally in misery. Said the angel, "Life is life, whether it is in pain or happiness. Death is without pain, without joy, without hatred."

Satan told his angels to make a special effort to spread the lie first repeated to Eve in Eden, "Ye shall not surely die." And as the error was received by the people, and they were led to believe that man was immortal, Satan led them on to believe that the sinner would live in eternal misery. Then the way was prepared for Satan to work through his representatives and hold up God before the people as a revengeful tyrant—one who plunges all those into hell who do not please Him, and causes them ever to feel His wrath; and while they suffer unutterable anguish, and writhe in the eternal flames, He is represented as looking down upon them with satisfaction. Satan knew that if this error should be received, God would be hated by many, instead of being loved and adored; and that many would be led to believe that the threatenings of God's Word would not be literally fulfilled, for it would be against His character of benevolence and love to plunge into eternal torments the beings whom He had created.

Another extreme which Satan has led the people to adopt is entirely to overlook the justice of God and the threatenings of His Word, and to represent Him as being all mercy, so that not one will perish, but that all, both saint and sinner, will at last be saved in His kingdom.

In consequence of the popular errors of the immortality of the soul and endless misery, Satan takes advantage of another class and leads them to regard the Bible as an uninspired book. They think it teaches many good things, but they cannot rely upon it and love it, because they have been taught that it declares the doctrine of eternal misery.

Another class Satan leads on still further, even to deny the existence of God. They can see no consistency in the character of the God of the Bible, if He will inflict horrible tortures upon a portion of the human family to all eternity. Therefore they deny the Bible and its Author, and regard death as an eternal sleep.

There is still another class who are fearful and timid. These Satan tempts to commit sin, and after they have sinned, he holds up before them that the wages of sin is not death but life in horrible torments, to be endured throughout the endless ages of eternity. By thus magnifying before their feeble minds the horrors of an endless hell, he takes possession of their minds, and they lose their reason. Then Satan and his angels exult, and the infidel and atheist join in casting reproach upon Christianity. They claim that these evils are the natural results of believing in the Bible and its Author, whereas they are the results of the reception of popular heresy.

The Scriptures a Safeguard

I saw that the heavenly host were filled with indignation at this bold work of Satan. I inquired why all these delusions should be suffered to take effect upon the minds of men when the angels of God were powerful, and if commissioned, could easily break the enemy's power. Then I saw that God knew that Satan would try every art to destroy man; therefore He had caused His word to be written out, and had made His purposes in regard to the human race so plain that the weakest need not err. After having given His word to man, He had carefully preserved it from destruction by Satan or his angels, or by any of his agents or representatives. While other books might be destroyed, this was to be immortal. And near the close of time, when the delusions of Satan should increase, it was to be so multiplied that all who desired might have a copy, and, if they would, might arm themselves against the deceptions and lying wonders of Satan.

I saw that God had especially guarded the Bible; yet when copies of it were few, learned men had in some instances changed the words, thinking that they were making it more plain, when in reality they were mystifying that which was plain, by causing it to lean to their established views, which were governed by tradition. But I saw that the Word of God, as a whole, is a perfect chain, one portion linking into and explaining another. True seekers for truth need not err, for not only is the Word of God plain and simple in declaring the way of life, but the Holy Spirit is given as a guide in understanding the way to life therein revealed.

I saw that the angels of God are never to control the will. God sets before man life and death. He can have his choice. Many desire life, but still continue to walk in the broad road. They choose to rebel against God's government, notwithstanding His great mercy and compassion in giving His Son to die for them. Those who do not choose to accept of the salvation so dearly purchased, must be punished. But I saw that God would not shut them up in hell to endure endless misery, neither will He take them to heaven; for to bring them into the company of the pure and holy would make them exceedingly miserable. But He will destroy them utterly and cause them to be as if they had not been; then His justice will be satisfied. He formed man out of the dust of the earth, and the disobedient and unholy will be consumed by fire and return to dust again. I saw that the benevolence and compassion of God in this matter should lead all to admire His character and to adore His holy name. After the wicked are destroyed from off the earth, all the heavenly host will say, "Amen!"

Satan looks with great satisfaction upon those who profess the name of Christ, yet closely adhere to the delusions which he himself has originated. His work is still to devise new delusions, and his power and art in this direction continually increase. He led his representatives, the popes and the priests, to exalt themselves, and to stir up the people to bitterly persecute and destroy those who were not willing to accept his delusions. Oh, the sufferings and agony which the precious followers of Christ were made to endure! Angels have kept a faithful record of it all. Satan and his evil angels exultingly told the angels who ministered to these suffering saints that they were all to be killed, so that there would not be left a true Christian upon the earth. I saw that the church of God was then pure. There was no danger of men with corrupt hearts coming into it, for the true Christian, who dared to declare his faith, was in danger of the rack, the stake, and every torture which Satan and his evil angels could invent or inspire in the mind of man.

Chapter 57—Spiritualism

The doctrine of natural immortality has prepared the way for modern Spiritualism. If the dead are admitted to the presence of God and holy angels, and privileged with knowledge far exceeding what they before possessed, why should they not return to the earth to enlighten and instruct the living? How can those who believe in man's consciousness in death reject what comes to them as divine light communicated by glorified spirits? Here is a channel regarded as sacred, through which Satan works for the accomplishment of his purposes. The fallen angels who do his bidding appear as messengers from the spirit world. While professing to bring the living into communication with the dead, Satan exercises his bewitching influence upon their minds.

He has power even to bring before men the appearance of their departed friends. The counterfeit is perfect; the familiar look, the words, the tone, are reproduced with marvelous distinctness. Many are comforted with the assurance that their loved ones are enjoying the bliss of heaven, and without suspicion of danger they give ear to seducing spirits and doctrines of devils.

When they have been led to believe that the dead actually return to communicate with them, Satan causes those to appear who went into the grave unprepared. They claim to be happy in heaven, and even to occupy exalted positions there; and thus the error is widely taught that no difference is made between the righteous and the wicked. The pretended visitants from the world of spirits sometimes utter cautions and warnings which prove to be correct. Then, as confidence is gained, they present doctrines which directly undermine faith in the Scriptures. With an appearance of deep interest in the well-being of their friends on earth, they insinuate the most dangerous errors. The fact that they state some truths, and are able at times to foretell future events, gives to their statements an appearance of reliability; and their false teachings are accepted by the multitudes as readily, and believed as implicitly, as if they were the most sacred truths of the Bible. The law of God is set aside, the Spirit of grace despised, the blood of the covenant counted an unholy thing. The spirits deny the divinity of Christ and place even the Creator on a level with themselves. Thus under a new disguise the great rebel still carries forward his warfare against God, begun in heaven and for nearly six thousand years continued upon the earth.

Many endeavor to account for spiritual manifestations by attributing them wholly to fraud and sleight of hand on the part of the medium. While it is true that the results of trickery have often been palmed off as genuine manifestations, there have been, also, marked exhibitions of supernatural power. The mysterious rapping with which modern Spiritualism began was not the result of human trickery or cunning, but the direct work of evil angels, who thus introduced one of the most successful of soul-destroying delusions. Many will be ensnared through the belief that Spiritualism is a merely human imposture; when brought face to face with manifestations which they can but regard as supernatural, they will be deceived, and will be led to accept them as the great power of God.

These persons overlook the testimony of the Scriptures concerning the wonders wrought by Satan and his agents. It was by Satanic aid that Pharaoh's magicians were enabled to counterfeit the work of God. The apostle John, describing the miracle-working power that will be manifested in the last days, declares: "He doeth great wonders, so that he maketh fire come down from heaven on the earth in the sight of men, and deceiveth them that dwell on the earth by the means of those miracles which he had power to do." Revelation 13:13, 14. No mere impostures are here brought to view. Men are deceived by the miracles which Satan's agents have power to do, not which they pretend to do.

Witchcraft in Modern Form

The very name of witchcraft is now held in contempt. The claim that men can hold intercourse with evil spirits is regarded as a fable of the Dark Ages. But Spiritualism, which numbers its converts by hundreds of thousands, yea, by millions, which has made its way into scientific circles, which has invaded churches and has found favor in legislative bodies, and even in the courts of kings—this mammoth deception is but a revival in a new disguise of the witchcraft condemned and prohibited of old.

Satan beguiles men now, as he beguiled Eve in Eden, by exciting a desire to obtain forbidden knowledge. "Ye shall be as gods," he declares, "knowing good and evil." Genesis 3:5. But the wisdom which Spiritualism imparts is that described by the apostle James, which "descendeth not from above, but is earthly, sensual, devilish." James 3:15.

271

The prince of darkness has a masterly mind, and he skillfully adapts his temptations to men of every variety of condition and culture. He works "with all deceivableness of unrighteousness" to gain control of the children of men, but he can accomplish his object only as they voluntarily yield to his temptations. Those who place themselves in his power by indulging their evil traits of character, little realize where their course will end. The tempter accomplishes their ruin, and then employs them to ruin others.

None Need Be Deceived

But none need be deceived by the lying claims of Spiritualism. God has given the world sufficient light to enable them to discover the snare. If there were no other evidence, it should be enough for the Christian that the spirits make no difference between righteousness and sin, between the noblest and purest of the apostles of Christ and the most corrupt of the servants of Satan. By representing the basest of men as in heaven, and highly exalted there, Satan virtually declares to the world, No matter how wicked you are; no matter whether you believe or disbelieve God and the Bible. Live as you please; heaven is your home. Moreover, the apostles, as personated by these lying spirits, are made to contradict what they wrote at the dictation of the Holy Spirit when on earth. They deny the divine origin of the Bible, and thus tear away the foundation of the Christian's hope, and put out the light that reveals the way to heaven.

Satan is making the world believe that the Bible is a mere fiction, or at least a book suited to the infancy of the race, but now to be lightly regarded or cast aside as obsolete. And to take the place of the Word of God he holds out spiritual manifestations. Here is a channel wholly under his control; by this means he can make the world believe what he will. The Book that is to judge him and his followers he puts into the shade, just where he wants it; the Saviour of the world he makes to be no more than a common man. And as the Roman guard that watched the tomb of Jesus spread the lying report which the priests and elders put into their mouths to disprove His resurrection, so do the believers in spiritual manifestations try to make it appear that there is nothing miraculous in the circumstances of our Saviour's life. After thus seeking to put Jesus in the background, they call attention to their own miracles, declaring that these far exceed the works of Christ.

Says the prophet Isaiah: "When they shall say unto you, Seek unto them that have familiar spirits, and unto wizards that peep, and that mutter: should not a people seek unto their God? for the living to the dead? To the law and to the testimony: if they speak not according to this word, it is because there is no light in them." Isaiah 8:19, 20. If men had been willing to receive the truth so plainly stated in the Scriptures, that the dead know not anything, they would see in the claims and manifestations of Spiritualism the working of Satan with power and signs and lying wonders. But rather than yield the liberty so agreeable to the carnal heart, and renounce the sins which they love, the multitudes close their eyes to the light, and walk straight on, regardless of warnings, while Satan weaves his snares about them, and they become his prey. "Because they received not the love of the truth, that they might be saved," therefore "God shall send them strong delusion, that they should believe a lie." 2 Thessalonians 2:10, 11.

Those who oppose the teachings of Spiritualism are assailing, not men alone, but Satan and his angels. They have entered upon a contest against principalities and powers and wicked spirits in high places. Satan will not yield one inch of ground except as he is driven back by the power of heavenly messengers. The people of God should be able to meet him, as did our Saviour, with the words, "It is written." Satan can quote Scripture now as in the days of Christ, and he will pervert its teachings to sustain his delusions. But the plain statements of the Bible will furnish weapons powerful in every conflict.

Those who would stand in the time of peril must understand the testimony of the Scriptures concerning the nature of man and the state of the dead, for in the near future many will be confronted by the spirits of devils personating beloved relatives or friends and declaring the most dangerous heresies. These visitants will appeal to our tenderest sympathies and will work miracles to sustain their pretensions. We must be prepared to withstand them with the Bible truth that the dead know not anything, and that they who thus appear are the spirits of devils. Long has Satan been preparing for his final effort to deceive the world. The foundation of his work was laid by the assurance given to Eve in Eden, "Ye shall not surely die: ... in the day ye eat thereof, then your eyes shall be opened, and ye shall be as gods, knowing good and evil." Genesis 3:4, 5. Little by little he has prepared the way for his masterpiece of deception in the development of Spiritualism. He has not yet reached the full accomplishment of his designs; but it will be reached in the last remnant of time, and the world will be swept into the ranks of this delusion. They are fast being lulled into a fatal security, to be awakened only by the outpouring of the wrath of God.

Chapter 58—The Loud Cry

I saw angels hurrying to and fro in heaven, descending to the earth, and again ascending to heaven, preparing for the fulfillment of some important event. Then I saw another mighty angel commissioned to descend to the earth, to unite his voice with the third angel, and give power and force to his message. Great power and glory were imparted to the angel, and as he descended, the earth was lightened with his glory. The light which attended this angel penetrated everywhere, as he cried mightily, with a strong voice, "Babylon the great is fallen, is fallen, and is become the habitation of devils, and the hold of every foul spirit, and a cage of every unclean and hateful bird." Revelation 18:2.

The message of the fall of Babylon, as given by the second angel, is repeated, with the additional mention of the corruptions which have been entering the churches since 1844. The work of this angel comes in at the right time to join in the last great work of the third angel's message as it swells to a loud cry. And the people of God are thus prepared to stand in the hour of temptation, which they are soon to meet. I saw a great light resting upon them, and they united to fearlessly proclaim the third angel's message.

Angels were sent to aid the mighty angel from heaven, and I heard voices which seemed to sound everywhere, "Come out of her, My people, that ye be not partakers of her sins, and that ye receive not of her plagues. For her sins have reached unto heaven, and God hath remembered her iniquities." Revelation 18:4, 5. This message seemed to be an addition to the third message, joining it as the midnight cry joined the second angel's message in 1844. The glory of God rested upon the patient, waiting saints, and they fearlessly gave the last solemn warning, proclaiming the fall of Babylon and calling upon God's people to come out of her, that they might escape her fearful doom.

The light that was shed upon the waiting ones penetrated everywhere, and those in the churches who had any light, who had not heard and rejected the three messages, obeyed the call and left the fallen churches. Many had come to years of accountability since these messages had been given, and the light shone upon them, and they were privileged to choose life or death. Some chose life and took their stand with those who were looking for their Lord and keeping all His commandments. The third message was to do its work; all were to be tested upon it, and the precious ones were to be called out from the religious bodies.

A compelling power moved the honest, while the manifestation of the power of God brought a fear and restraint upon their unbelieving relatives and friends so that they dared not, neither had they the power to, hinder those who felt the work of the Spirit of God upon them. The last call was carried even to the poor slaves; and the pious among them poured forth their songs of rapturous joy at the prospect of their happy deliverance. [Note.—That there will be slavery at the time of the second advent is made clear by the prophet John in Revelation 6:15, 16, in his vivid description of "every bondman, and every free man" calling for the "mountains and rocks" to fall on them and hide them "from the face of Him that sitteth on the throne."—Compilers.] Their masters could not check them; fear and astonishment kept them silent. Mighty miracles were wrought, the sick were healed, and signs and wonders followed the believers. God was in the work, and every saint, fearless of consequences, followed the convictions of his own conscience and united with those who were keeping all the commandments of God; and with power they sounded abroad the third message. I saw that this message will close with power and strength far exceeding the midnight cry.

Servants of God, endowed with power from on high, with their faces lighted up, and shining with holy consecration, went forth to proclaim the message from heaven. Souls that were scattered all through the religious bodies answered to the call, and the precious were hurried out of the doomed churches, as Lot was hurried out of Sodom before her destruction. God's people were strengthened by the excellent glory which rested upon them in rich abundance and prepared them to endure the hour of temptation. I heard everywhere a multitude of voices saying, "Here is the patience of the saints: here are they that keep the commandments of God, and the faith of Jesus." Revelation 14:12.

Chapter 59—The Close of Probation

I was pointed down to the time when the third angel's message was closing. The power of God had rested upon His people; they had accomplished their work and were prepared for the trying hour before them. They had received the latter rain, or refreshing from the presence of the Lord, and the living testimony had been revived. The last great warning had sounded everywhere, and it had stirred up and enraged the inhabitants of the earth who would not receive the message.

I saw angels hurrying to and for in heaven. An angel with a writer's inkhorn by his side returned from the earth and reported to Jesus that his work was done, and the saints were numbered and sealed. Then I saw Jesus, who had been ministering before the ark containing the Ten Commandments, throw down the censer. He raised His hands, and with a loud voice said, "It is done." And all the angelic host laid off their crowns as Jesus made the solemn declaration, "He that is unjust, let him be unjust still: and he which is filthy, let him be filthy still: and he that is righteous, let him be righteous still: and he that is holy, let him be holy still." Revelation 22:11.

Every case had been decided for life or death. While Jesus had been ministering in the sanctuary, the judgment had been going on for the righteous dead, and then for the righteous living. Christ had received His kingdom, having made the atonement for His people and blotted out their sins. The subjects of the kingdom were made up. The marriage of the Lamb was consummated. And the kingdom, and the greatness of the kingdom under the whole heaven, was given to Jesus and the heirs of salvation, and Jesus was to reign as King of kings and Lord of lords.

As Jesus moved out of the most holy place, I heard the tinkling of the bells upon His garment; and as He left, a cloud of darkness covered the inhabitants of the earth. There was then no mediator between guilty man and an offended God. While Jesus had been standing between God and guilty man, a restraint was upon the people; but when He stepped out from between man and the Father, the restraint was removed and Satan had entire control of the finally impenitent.

It was impossible for the plagues to be poured out while Jesus officiated in the sanctuary; but as His work there is finished, and His intercession closes, there is nothing to stay the wrath of God, and it breaks with fury upon the shelterless head of the guilty sinner, who has slighted salvation and hated reproof. In that fearful time, after the close of Jesus' mediation, the saints were living in the sight of a holy God without an intercessor. Every case was decided, every jewel numbered. Jesus tarried a moment in the outer apartment of the heavenly sanctuary, and the sins which had been confessed while He was in the most holy place were placed upon Satan, the originator of sin, who must suffer their punishment. [Note.—This suffering of Satan is in no sense a vicarious atonement. As indicated in a previous chapter: "As man's substitute and surety, the iniquity of men was laid upon Christ." (See p. 225.) But after those who accept Christ's sacrifice have been redeemed, it is certainly just that Satan, the originator of sin, should suffer the final punishment. As Mrs. White has said elsewhere, "When the work of atonement in the heavenly sanctuary has been completed, then in the presence of God and heavenly angels, and the host of the redeemed, the sins of God's people will be placed upon Satan; he will be declared guilty of all the evil which he has caused them to commit."—The Great Controversy, 658.—Compilers.]

Too Late! Too Late!

Then I saw Jesus lay off His priestly attire and clothe Himself with His most kingly robes. Upon His head were many crowns, a crown within a crown. Surrounded by the angelic host, He left heaven. The plagues were falling upon the inhabitants of the earth. Some were denouncing God and cursing Him. Others rushed to the people of God and begged to be taught how they might escape His judgments. But the saints had nothing for them. The last tear for sinners had been shed, the last agonizing prayer offered, the last burden borne, the last warning given. The sweet voice of mercy was no more to invite them. When the saints, and all heaven, were interested for their salvation, they had no interest for themselves. Life and death had been set before them. Many desired life, but made no effort to obtain it. They did not choose life, and now there was no atoning blood to cleanse the guilty, no compassionate Saviour to plead for them and cry, "Spare, spare the sinner a little longer." All heaven had united with Jesus, as they heard the fearful words, "It is done. It is finished." The plan of salvation had been accomplished, but few had chosen to accept it. And as mercy's sweet voice died away, fear and horror seized the wicked. With terrible distinctness they heard the words, "Too late! too late!"

Those who had not prized God's Word were hurrying to and fro, wandering from sea to sea, and from the north to the east, to seek the Word of the Lord. Said the angel, "They shall not find it. There is a famine in the land; not a famine of bread, nor a thirst for water, but for hearing the words of the Lord. What would they not give for one word of approval from God! but no, they must hunger and thirst on. Day after day have they slighted salvation, prizing earthly riches and earthly pleasure higher than any heavenly treasure or inducement. They have rejected Jesus and despised His saints. The filthy must remain filthy forever."

Many of the wicked were greatly enraged as they suffered the effects of the plagues. It was a scene of fearful agony. Parents were bitterly reproaching their children, and children their parents, brothers their sisters, and sisters their brothers. Loud, wailing cries were heard in every direction, "It was you who kept me from receiving the truth which would have saved me from this awful hour." The people turned upon their ministers with bitter hate and reproached them, saying, "You have not warned us. You told us that all the world was to be converted, and cried, Peace, peace, to quiet every fear that was aroused. You have not told us of this hour; and those who warned us of it you declared to be fanatics and evil men, who would ruin us." But I saw that the ministers did not escape the wrath of God. Their suffering was tenfold greater than that of their people.

Chapter 60—The Time of Jacob's Trouble

I saw the saints leaving the cities and villages, and associating together in companies, and living in the most solitary places. Angels provided them food and water, while the wicked were suffering from hunger and thirst. Then I saw the leading men of the earth consulting together, and Satan and his angels busy around them. I saw a writing, copies of which were scattered in different parts of the land, giving orders that unless the saints should yield their peculiar faith, give up the Sabbath, and observe the first day of the week, the people were at liberty after a certain time to put them to death. But in this hour of trial the saints were calm and composed, trusting in God and leaning upon His promise that a way of escape would be made for them.

In some places, before the time for the decree to be executed, the wicked rushed upon the saints to slay them; but angels in the form of men of war fought for them. Satan wished to have the privilege of destroying the saints of the Most High, but Jesus bade His angels watch over them. God would be honored by making a covenant with those who had kept His law, in the sight of the heathen round about them; and Jesus would be honored by translating, without their seeing death, the faithful, waiting ones who had so long expected Him.

Soon I saw the saints suffering great mental anguish. They seemed to be surrounded by the wicked inhabitants of the earth. Every appearance was against them. Some began to fear that God had at last left them to perish by the hand of the wicked. But if their eyes could have been opened, they would have seen themselves surrounded by angels of God. Next came the multitude of the angry wicked, and next a mass of evil angels, hurrying on the wicked to slay the saints. But before they could approach God's people, the wicked must first pass this company of mighty, holy angels. This was impossible. The angels of God were causing them to recede and also causing the evil angels who were pressing around them to fall back.

The Cry for Deliverance

It was an hour of fearful, terrible agony to the saints. Day and night they cried unto God for deliverance. To outward appearance, there was no possibility of their escape. The wicked had already begun to triumph, crying out, "Why doesn't your God deliver you out of our hands? Why don't you go up and save your lives?" But the saints heeded them not. Like Jacob, they were wrestling with God. The angels longed to deliver them, but they must wait a little longer; the people of God must drink of the cup and be baptized with the baptism. The angels, faithful to their trust, continued their watch. God would not suffer His name to be reproached among the heathen. The time had nearly come when He was to manifest His mighty power and gloriously deliver His saints. For His name's glory He would deliver every one of those who had patiently waited for Him and whose names were written in the book.

I was pointed back to faithful Noah. When the rain descended and the Flood came, Noah and his family had entered the ark, and God had shut them in. Noah had faithfully warned the inhabitants of the antediluvian world, while they had mocked and derided him. And as the waters descended upon the earth, and one after another was drowning, they beheld that ark, of which they had made so much sport, riding safely upon the waters, preserving the faithful Noah and his family. So I saw that the people of God, who had faithfully warned the world of His coming wrath, would be delivered. God would not suffer the wicked to destroy those who were expecting translation and who would not bow to the decree of the beast or receive his mark. I saw that if the wicked were permitted to slay the saints, Satan and all his evil host, and all who hate God, would be gratified. And oh, what a triumph it would be for his satanic majesty to have power, in the last closing struggle, over those who had so long waited to behold Him whom they loved! Those who have mocked at the idea of the saints' going up will witness the care of God for His people and behold their glorious deliverance.

As the saints left the cities and villages, they were pursued by the wicked, who sought to slay them. But the swords that were raised to kill God's people broke and fell as powerless as straw. Angels of God shielded the saints. As they cried day and night for deliverance, their cry came up before the Lord.

Chapter 61—Deliverance of the Saints

It was at midnight that God chose to deliver His people. As the wicked were mocking around them, suddenly the sun appeared, shining in his strength, and the moon stood still. The wicked looked upon the scene with amazement, while the saints beheld with solemn joy the tokens of their deliverance. Signs and wonders followed in quick succession. Everything seemed turned out of its natural course. The streams ceased to flow. Dark, heavy clouds came up and clashed against each other. But there was one clear place of settled glory, whence came the voice of God like many waters, shaking the heavens and the earth. There was a mighty earthquake. The graves were opened, and those who had died in faith under the third angel's message, keeping the Sabbath, came forth from their dusty beds, glorified, to hear the covenant of peace that God was to make with those who had kept His law.

The sky opened and shut and was in commotion. The mountains shook like a reed in the wind and cast out ragged rocks all around. The sea boiled like a pot and cast out stones upon the land. And as God spoke the day and the hour of Jesus' coming and delivered the everlasting covenant to His people, He spoke one sentence, and then paused, while the words were rolling through the earth. The Israel of God stood with their eyes fixed upward, listening to the words as they came from the mouth of Jehovah and rolled through the earth like peals of loudest thunder. It was awfully solemn. At the end of every sentence the saints shouted, "Glory! Hallelujah!" Their countenances were lighted up with the glory of God, and they shone with glory as did the face of Moses when he came down from Sinai. The wicked could not look upon them for the glory. And when the never-ending blessing was pronounced on those who had honored God in keeping His Sabbath holy, there was a mighty shout of victory over the beast and over his image.

Then commenced the jubilee, when the land should rest. I saw the pious slave rise in victory and triumph, and shake off the chains that bound him, while his wicked master was in confusion and knew not what to do, for the wicked could not understand the words of the voice of God.

The Second Advent of Christ

Soon appeared the great white cloud, upon which sat the Son of man. When it first appeared in the distance, this cloud looked very small. The angel said that it was the sign of the Son of man. As it drew nearer the earth, we could behold the excellent glory and majesty of Jesus as He rode forth to conquer. A retinue of holy angels, with bright, glittering crowns upon their heads, escorted Him on His way.

No language can describe the glory of the scene. The living cloud of majesty and unsurpassed glory came still nearer, and we could clearly behold the lovely person of Jesus. He did not wear a crown of thorns, but a crown of glory rested upon His holy brow. Upon His vesture and thigh was a name written, King of kings, and Lord of lords. His countenance was as bright as the noonday sun, His eyes were as a flame of fire, and His feet had the appearance of fine brass. His voice sounded like many musical instruments. The earth trembled before Him, the heavens departed as a scroll when it is rolled together, and every mountain and island were moved out of their places. "And the kings of the earth, and the great men, and the rich men, and the chief captains, and the mighty men, and every bondman, and every free man, hid themselves in the dens and in the rocks of the mountains; and said to the mountains and rocks, Fall on us, and hide us from the face of Him that sitteth on the throne, and from the wrath of the Lamb: for the great day of His wrath is come; and who shall be able to stand?" Revelation 6:15-17.

Those who a short time before would have destroyed God's faithful children from the earth, now witnessed the glory of God which rested upon them. And amid all their terror they heard the voices of the saints in joyful strains, saying, "Lo, this is our God; we have waited for Him, and He will save us." Isaiah 25:9.

The First Resurrection

The earth mightily shook as the voice of the Son of God called forth the sleeping saints. They responded to the call and came forth clothed with glorious immortality, crying, "Victory, victory, over death and the grave! O death, where is thy sting? O grave, where is thy victory?" (See 1 Corinthians 15:55.) Then the living saints and the risen ones raised their voices in a long transporting shout of victory. Those bodies that had gone down into the grave bearing the marks of disease and death came up in immortal health and vigor. The living saints are changed in a moment, in the twinkling of an eye, and caught up with the risen ones, and together they meet their Lord in the air. Oh, what a glorious meeting! Friends whom death had separated were united, never more to part.

On each side of the cloudy chariot were wings, and beneath it were living wheels; and as the chariot rolled upward, the wheels cried, "Holy," and the wings, as they moved, cried, "Holy," and the retinue of holy angels around the cloud cried, "Holy, holy, holy, Lord God Almighty!" And the saints in the cloud cried, "Glory! Alleluia!" And the chariot rolled upward to the Holy City. Before entering the city, the saints were arranged in a perfect square, with Jesus in the midst. He stood head and shoulders above the saints and above the angels. His majestic form and lovely countenance could be seen by all in the square.

Chapter 62—The Saints' Reward

Then I saw a very great number of angels bring from the city glorious crowns—a crown for every saint, with his name written thereon. As Jesus called for the crowns, angels presented them to Him, and with His own right hand the lovely Jesus placed the crowns on the heads of the saints. In the same manner the angels brought the harps, and Jesus presented them also to the saints. The commanding angels first struck the note, and then every voice was raised in grateful, happy praise, and every hand skillfully swept over the strings of the harp, sending forth melodious music in rich and perfect strains.

Then I saw Jesus lead the redeemed company to the gate of the city. He laid hold of the gate and swung it back on its glittering hinges and bade the nations that had kept the truth enter in. Within the city there was everything to feast the eye. Rich glory they beheld everywhere. Then Jesus looked upon His redeemed saints; their countenances were radiant with glory; and as He fixed His loving eyes upon them, He said, with His rich, musical voice, "I behold the travail of My soul, and am satisfied. This rich glory is yours to enjoy eternally. Your sorrows are ended. There shall be no more death, neither sorrow nor crying, neither shall there be any more pain." I saw the redeemed host bow and cast their glittering crowns at the feet of Jesus, and then, as His lovely hand raised them up, they touched their golden harps and filled all heaven with their rich music and songs to the Lamb.

I then saw Jesus leading His people to the tree of life, and again we heard His lovely voice, richer than any music that ever fell on mortal ear, saying, "The leaves of this tree are for the healing of the nations. Eat ye all of it." Upon the tree of life was most beautiful fruit, of which the saints could partake freely. In the city was a most glorious throne, from which proceeded a pure river of water of life, clear as crystal. On each side of this river was the tree of life, and on the banks of the river were other beautiful trees bearing fruit which was good for food. Language is altogether too feeble to attempt a description of heaven. As the scene rises before me, I am lost in amazement. Carried away with the surpassing splendor and excellent glory, I lay down the pen, and exclaim, "Oh, what love! what wondrous love!" The most exalted language fails to describe the glory of heaven or the matchless depths of a Saviour's love.

Chapter 63—The Millennium

My attention was again directed to the earth. The wicked had been destroyed, and their dead bodies were lying on its surface. The wrath of God in the seven last plagues had been visited upon the inhabitants of the earth, causing them to gnaw their tongues from pain and to curse God. The false shepherds had been the signal objects of Jehovah's wrath. Their eyes had consumed away in their holes, and their tongues in their mouths, while they stood upon their feet. After the saints had been delivered by the voice of God, the wicked multitude turned their rage upon one another. The earth seemed to be deluged with blood, and dead bodies were from one end of it to the other.

The earth looked like a desolate wilderness. Cities and villages, shaken down by the earthquake, lay in heaps. Mountains had been moved out of their places, leaving large caverns. Ragged rocks, thrown out by the sea, or torn out of the earth itself, were scattered all over its surface. Large trees had been uprooted and were strewn over the land. Here is to be the home of Satan with his evil angels for a thousand years. Here he will be confined, to wander up and down over the broken surface of the earth and see the effects of his rebellion against God's law. For a thousand years he can enjoy the fruit of the curse which he has caused.

Limited alone to the earth, he will not have the privilege of ranging to other planets, to tempt and annoy those who have not fallen. During this time Satan suffers extremely. Since his fall his evil traits have been in constant exercise. But he is then to be deprived of his power and left to reflect upon the part which he has acted since his fall, and to look forward with trembling and terror to the dreadful future, when he must suffer for all the evil that he has done and be punished for all the sins that he has caused to be committed.

I heard shouts of triumph from the angels and from the redeemed saints which sounded like ten thousand musical instruments, because they were to be no more annoyed and tempted by Satan and because the inhabitants of other worlds were delivered from his presence and his temptations.

Then I saw thrones, and Jesus and the redeemed saints sat upon them; and the saints reigned as kings and priests unto God. Christ, in union with His people, judged the wicked dead, comparing their acts with the Statute Book, the Word of God, and deciding every case according to the deeds done in the body. Then they meted out to the wicked the portion which they must suffer, according to their works; and it was written against their names in the book of death. Satan also and his angels were judged by Jesus and the saints. Satan's punishment was to be far greater than that of those whom he had deceived. His suffering would so far exceed theirs as to bear no comparison with it. After all those whom he had deceived had perished, Satan was still to live and suffer on much longer.

After the judgment of the wicked dead had been finished, at the end of the one thousand years, Jesus left the city, and the saints and a train of the angelic host followed Him. Jesus descended upon a great mountain, which, as soon as His feet touched it, parted asunder and became a mighty plain. Then we looked up and saw the great and beautiful city, with twelve foundations and twelve gates, three on each side, and an angel at each gate. We cried out, "The city! the great city! It is coming down from God out of heaven!" And it came down in all its splendor and dazzling glory, and settled in the mighty plain which Jesus had prepared for it.

Chapter 64—The Second Resurrection

Then Jesus and all the retinue of holy angels, and all the redeemed saints, left the city. The angels surrounded their Commander and escorted Him on His way, and the train of redeemed saints followed. Then, in terrible, fearful majesty, Jesus called forth the wicked dead; and they came up with the same feeble, sickly bodies that went into the grave. What a spectacle! What a scene! At the first resurrection all came forth in immortal bloom, but at the second the marks of the curse are visible on all. The kings and noblemen of the earth, the mean and low, the learned and unlearned, come forth together. All behold the Son of man; and those very men who despised and mocked Him, who put the crown of thorns upon His sacred brow and smote Him with the reed, behold Him in all His kingly majesty. Those who spat upon Him in the hour of His trial now turn from His piercing gaze and from the glory of His countenance. Those who drove the nails through His hands and feet now look upon the marks of His crucifixion. Those who thrust the spear into His side behold the marks of their cruelty on His body. And they know that He is the very one whom they crucified and derided in His expiring agony. And then there arises one long protracted wail of agony, as they flee to hide from the presence of the King of kings and Lord of lords.

All are seeking to hide in the rocks, to shield themselves from the terrible glory of Him whom they once despised. And, overwhelmed and pained with His majesty and exceeding glory, they with one accord raise their voices, and with terrible distinctness exclaim, "Blessed is He that cometh in the name of the Lord!"

Then Jesus and the holy angels, accompanied by all the saints, again go to the city, and the bitter lamentations and wailings of the doomed wicked fill the air. Then I saw that Satan again commenced his work. He passed around among his subjects and made the weak and feeble strong, and told them that he and his angels were powerful. He pointed to the countless millions who had been raised. There were mighty warriors and kings who were well skilled in battle and who had conquered kingdoms. And there were mighty giants and valiant men who had never lost a battle. There was the proud, ambitious Napoleon, whose approach had caused kingdoms to tremble. There stood men of lofty stature and dignified bearing, who had fallen in battle while thirsting to conquer.

As they come forth from their graves, they resume the current of their thoughts where it ceased in death. They possess the same desire to conquer which ruled when they fell. Satan consults with his angels, and then with those kings and conquerors and mighty men. Then he looks over the vast army, and tells them that the company in the city is small and feeble, and that they can go up and take it, and cast out its inhabitants, and possess its riches and glory themselves.

Satan succeeds in deceiving them, and all immediately begin to prepare themselves for battle. There are many skillful men in that vast army, and they construct all kinds of implements of war. Then with Satan at their head, the multitude move on. Kings and warriors follow close after Satan, and the multitude follow after in companies. Each company has its leader, and order is observed as they march over the broken surface of the earth to the Holy City. Jesus closes the gates of the city, and this vast army surround it, and place themselves in battle array, expecting a fierce conflict.

Chapter 65—The Coronation of Christ

Now Christ again appears to the view of His enemies. Far above the city, upon a foundation of burnished gold, is a throne, high and lifted up. Upon this throne sits the Son of God, and around Him are the subjects of His kingdom. The power and majesty of Christ no language can describe, no pen portray. The glory of the Eternal Father is enshrouding His Son. The brightness of His presence fills the city of God and flows out beyond the gates, flooding the whole earth with its radiance.

Nearest the throne are those who were once zealous in the cause of Satan, but who, plucked as brands from the burning, have followed their Saviour with deep, intense devotion. Next are those who perfected Christian characters in the midst of falsehood and infidelity, those who honored the law of God when the Christian world declared it void, and the millions, of all ages, who were martyred for their faith. And beyond is the "great multitude, which no man could number, of all nations, and kindreds, and people, and tongues, … before the throne, and before the Lamb, clothed with white robes, and palms in their hands." Revelation 7:9. Their warfare is ended, their victory won. They have run the race and reached the prize. The palm branch in their hands is a symbol of their triumph, the white robe an emblem of the spotless righteousness of Christ, which now is theirs.

The redeemed raise a song of praise that echoes and re-echoes through the vaults of heaven, "Salvation to our God which sitteth upon the throne, and unto the Lamb." And angel and seraph unite their voices in adoration. As the redeemed have beheld the power and malignity of Satan, they have seen, as never before, that no power but that of Christ could have made them conquerors. In all that shining throng there are none to ascribe salvation to themselves, as if they had prevailed by their own power and goodness. Nothing is said of what they have done or suffered; but the burden of every song, the keynote of every anthem, is, "Salvation to our God … and unto the Lamb." Revelation 7:10.

In the presence of the assembled inhabitants of earth and heaven takes place the final coronation of the Son of God. And now, invested with supreme majesty and power, the King of kings pronounces sentence upon the rebels against His government, and executes justice upon those who have transgressed His law and oppressed His people. Says the prophet of God: "I saw a great white throne, and Him that sat on it, from whose face the earth and the heaven fled away; and there was found no place for them. And I saw the dead, small and great, stand before God; and the books were opened: and another book was opened, which is the book of life: and the dead were judged out of those things which were written in the books, according to their works." Revelation 20:11, 12.

As soon as the books of record are opened, and the eye of Jesus looks upon the wicked, they are conscious of every sin which they have ever committed. They see just where their feet diverged from the path of purity and holiness, just how far pride and rebellion have carried them in the violation of the law of God. The seductive temptations which they encouraged by indulgence in sin, the blessings perverted, the waves of mercy beaten back by the stubborn, unrepentant heart—all appear as if written in letters of fire.

Panorama of the Great Conflict

Above the throne is revealed the cross; and like a panoramic view appear the scenes of Adam's temptation and fall, and the successive steps in the great plan of redemption. The Saviour's lowly birth; His early life of simplicity and obedience; His baptism in Jordan; the fast and temptation in the wilderness; His public ministry, unfolding to men heaven's most precious blessings; the days crowded with deeds of love and mercy, the nights of prayer and watching in the solitude of the mountains; the plottings of envy, hate, and malice which repaid His benefits; the awful mysterious agony in Gethsemane, beneath the crushing weight of the sins of the whole world; His betrayal into the hands of the murderous mob; the fearful events of that night of horror: the unresisting prisoner, forsaken by His best-loved disciples, rudely hurried through the streets of Jerusalem; the Son of God exultingly displayed before Annas, arraigned in the high priest's palace, in the judgment hall of Pilate, before the cowardly and cruel Herod, mocked, insulted, tortured, and condemned to die—all are vividly portrayed.

And now before the swaying multitude are revealed the final scenes: the patient Sufferer treading the path to Calvary; the Prince of heaven hanging upon the cross; the haughty priests and the jeering rabble deriding His expiring agony; the supernatural darkness; the heaving earth, the rent rocks, the open graves, marking the moment when the world's Redeemer yielded up His life.

The awful spectacle appears just as it was. Satan, his angels, and his subjects have no power to turn from the picture of their own work. Each actor recalls the part which he performed. Herod, who slew the innocent children of Bethlehem that he might destroy the King of Israel; the base Herodias, upon whose guilty soul rests the blood of John the Baptist; the weak, time-serving Pilate; the mocking soldiers; the priests and rulers and the maddened throng who cried, "His blood be on us, and on our children"—all behold the enormity of their guilt. They vainly seek to hide from the divine majesty of His countenance, outshining the glory of the sun, while the redeemed cast their crowns at the Saviour's feet, exclaiming, "He died for me!"

Amid the ransomed throng are the apostles of Christ, the heroic Paul, the ardent Peter, the loved and loving John, and their truehearted brethren, and with them the vast host of martyrs; while outside the walls, with every vile and abominable thing, are those by whom they were persecuted, imprisoned, and slain. There is Nero, that monster of cruelty and vice, beholding the joy and exaltation of those whom he once tortured, and in whose extremest anguish he found Satanic delight. His mother is there to witness the result of her own work; to see how the evil stamp of character transmitted to her son, the passions encouraged and developed by her influence and example, have borne fruit in crimes that caused the world to shudder.

There are papist priests and prelates, who claimed to be Christ's ambassadors, yet employed the rack, the dungeon, and the stake to control the consciences of His people. There are the proud pontiffs who exalted themselves above God and presumed to change the law of the Most High. Those pretended fathers of the church have an account to render to God from which they would fain be excused. Too late they are made to see that the Omniscient One is jealous of His law, and that He will in no wise clear the guilty. They learn now that Christ identifies His interest with that of His suffering people; and they feel the force of His own words, "Inasmuch as ye have done it unto one of the least of these My brethren, ye have done it unto Me." Matthew 25:40.

At the Bar of Judgment

The whole wicked world stand arraigned at the bar of God, on the charge of high treason against the government of heaven. They have none to plead their cause; they are without excuse; and the sentence of eternal death is pronounced against them.

It is now evident to all that the wages of sin is not noble independence and eternal life, but slavery, ruin, and death. The wicked see what they have forfeited by their life of rebellion. The far more exceeding and eternal weight of glory was despised when offered them; but how desirable it now appears. "All this," cries the lost soul, "I might have had, but I chose to put these things far from me. Oh, strange infatuation! I have exchanged peace, happiness, and honor for wretchedness, infamy, and despair." All see that their exclusion from heaven is just. In their lives they declared, We will not have this Jesus to reign over us.

As if entranced, the wicked have looked upon the coronation of the Son of God. They see in His hands the tables of the divine law, the statutes which they have despised and transgressed. They witness the outburst of wonder, rapture, and adoration from the saved; and as the wave of melody sweeps over the multitudes without the city, all with one voice exclaim, "Marvellous are Thy works, Lord God Almighty; just and true are Thy ways, Thou King of saints" (Revelation 15:3), and falling prostrate, they worship the Prince of life.

Chapter 66—The Second Death

Satan seems paralyzed as he beholds the glory and majesty of Christ. He who was once a covering cherub remembers whence he has fallen. A shining seraph, "son of the morning"; how changed, how degraded!

Satan sees that his voluntary rebellion has unfitted him for heaven. He has trained his powers to war against God; the purity, peace, and harmony of heaven would be to him supreme torture. His accusations against the mercy and justice of God are now silenced. The reproach which he has endeavored to cast upon Jehovah rests wholly upon himself. And now Satan bows down and confesses the justice of his sentence.

Every question of truth and error in the longstanding controversy is made plain. God's justice stands fully vindicated. Before the whole world is clearly presented the great sacrifice made by the Father and the Son in man's behalf. The hour has come when Christ occupies His rightful position, and is glorified above principalities and powers and every name that is named.

Notwithstanding Satan has been constrained to acknowledge God's justice, and to bow to the supremacy of Christ, his character remains unchanged. The spirit of rebellion, like a mighty torrent, again bursts forth. Filled with frenzy, he determines not to yield the great controversy. The time has come for a last desperate struggle against the King of heaven. He rushes into the midst of his subjects and endeavors to inspire them with his own fury and arouse them to instant battle. But of all the countless millions whom he has allured into rebellion, there are none now to acknowledge his supremacy. His power is at an end. The wicked are filled with the same hatred of God that inspires Satan; but they see that their case is hopeless, that they cannot prevail against Jehovah. Their rage is kindled against Satan and those who have been his agents in deception. With the fury of demons they turn upon them, and there follows a scene of universal strife.

Fire From Heaven

Then are fulfilled the words of the prophet: "The indignation of the Lord is upon all nations, and His fury upon all their armies: He hath utterly destroyed them, He hath delivered them to the slaughter." Isaiah 34:2. "Upon the wicked

He shall rain quick burning coals, fire and brimstone, and an horrible tempest: this shall be the portion of their cup." Psalm 11:6, margin. Fire comes down from God out of heaven. The earth is broken up. The weapons concealed in its depths are drawn forth. Devouring flames burst from every yawning chasm. The very rocks are on fire. The day has come that "shall burn as an oven." Malachi 4:1. The elements melt with fervent heat, the earth also and the works that are therein are burned up. (2 Peter 3:10.) The fire of Tophet is prepared for the king, the chief of rebellion; the pile thereof is deep and large, and "the breath of the Lord, like a stream of brimstone, doth kindle it." Isaiah 30:33. The earth's surface seems one molten mass—a vast, seething lake of fire. It is the time of the judgment and perdition of ungodly men —"the day of the Lord's vengeance, and the year of recompences for the controversy of Zion." Isaiah 34:8.

The wicked receive their recompense in the earth. They "shall be stubble: and the day that cometh shall burn them up, saith the Lord of hosts." Malachi 4:1. Some are destroyed as in a moment, while others suffer many days. All are punished according to their deeds. The sins of the righteous have been transferred to Satan, the originator of evil, who must bear their penalty. [See footnote p. 403.] Thus he is made to suffer, not only for his own rebellion, but for all the sins which he has caused God's people to commit. His punishment is to be far greater than that of those whom he has deceived. After all have perished who fell by his deceptions, he is still to live and suffer on. In the cleansing flames the wicked are at last destroyed, root and branch—Satan the root, his followers the branches. The justice of God is satisfied, and the saints and all the angelic host say with a loud voice, Amen.

While the earth is wrapped in the fire of God's vengeance, the righteous abide safely in the Holy City. Upon those that had part in the first resurrection, the second death has no power. (Revelation 20:6.) While God is to the wicked a consuming fire, He is to His people both a sun and a shield. (Psalm 84:11.)

Chapter 67—The New Earth

"And I saw a new heaven and a new earth: for the first heaven and the first earth were passed away." Revelation 21:1. The fire that consumes the wicked purifies the earth. Every trace of the curse is swept away. No eternally burning hell will keep before the ransomed the fearful consequences of sin. One reminder alone remains: our Redeemer will ever bear the marks of His crucifixion. Upon His wounded head, His hands and feet, are the only traces of the cruel work that sin has wrought.

"O Tower of the flock, the strong hold of the daughter of Zion, unto thee shall it come, even the first dominion." Micah 4:8. The kingdom forfeited by sin, Christ has regained, and the redeemed are to possess it with Him. "The righteous shall inherit the land, and dwell therein for ever." Psalm 37:29. A fear of making the saints' inheritance seem too material has led many to spiritualize away the very truths which lead us to look upon the new earth as our home. Christ assured His disciples that He went to prepare mansions for them. Those who accept the teachings of God's Word will not be wholly ignorant concerning the heavenly abode. And yet the apostle Paul declares, "Eye hath not seen, nor ear heard, neither have entered into the heart of man, the things which God hath prepared for them that love Him." 1 Corinthians 2:9. Human language is inadequate to describe the reward of the righteous. It will be known only to those who behold it. No finite mind can comprehend the glory of the Paradise of God.

In the Bible the inheritance of the saved is called a country. (Hebrews 11:14-16.) There the great Shepherd leads His flock to fountains of living waters. The tree of life yields its fruit every month, and the leaves of the tree are for the service of the nations. There are ever-flowing streams, clear as crystal, and beside them waving trees cast their shadows upon the paths prepared for the ransomed of the Lord. There the wide-spreading plains swell into hills of beauty, and the mountains of God rear their lofty summits. On those peaceful plains, beside those living streams, God's people, so long pilgrims and wanderers, shall find a home.

The New Jerusalem

There is the New Jerusalem, "having the glory of God," her light "like unto a stone most precious, even like a jasper stone, clear as crystal." Revelation 21:11. Saith the Lord, "I will rejoice in Jerusalem, and joy in My people." Isaiah 65:19. "The tabernacle of God is with men, and He will dwell with them, and they shall be His people, and God Himself shall be with them, and be their God. And God shall wipe away all tears from their eyes; and there shall be no more death, neither sorrow, nor crying, neither shall there be any more pain: for the former things are passed away." Revelation 21:3, 4.

In the city of God "there shall be no night." None will need or desire repose. There will be no weariness in doing the will of God and offering praise to His name. We shall ever feel the freshness of the morning, and shall ever be far from its close. "And they need no candle, neither light of the sun; for the Lord God giveth them light." Revelation 22:5. The light of the sun will be superseded by a radiance which is not painfully dazzling, yet which immeasurably surpasses the brightness of our noontide. The glory of God and the Lamb floods the holy city with unfading light. The redeemed walk in the sunless glory of perpetual day.

"I saw no temple therein: for the Lord God Almighty and the Lamb are the temple of it." Revelation 21:22. The people of God are privileged to hold open communion with the Father and the Son. Now we "see through a glass, darkly." 1 Corinthians 13:12. We behold the image of God reflected, as in a mirror, in the works of nature and in His dealings with men; but then we shall see Him face to face, without a dimming veil between. We shall stand in His presence and gaze upon the glory of His countenance.

There immortal minds will study with never-failing delight the wonders of creative power, the mysteries of redeeming love. There is no cruel, deceiving foe to tempt to forgetfulness of God. Every faculty will be developed, every capacity increased. The acquirement of knowledge will not weary the mind or exhaust the energies. There the grandest enterprises may be carried forward, the loftiest aspirations reached, the highest ambitions realized; and still there will arise new heights to surmount, new wonders to admire, new truths to comprehend, fresh objects to call forth the powers of mind and soul and body.

And as the years of eternity roll, they will bring richer and more glorious revelations of God and of Christ. As knowledge is progressive, so will love, reverence, and happiness increase. The more men learn of God, the greater will be their admiration of His character. As Jesus opens before them the riches of redemption and the amazing achievements in the great controversy with Satan, the hearts of the ransomed beat with a stronger devotion, and they sweep the harps of gold with a firmer hand; and ten thousand times ten thousand and thousands of thousands of voices unite to swell the mighty chorus of praise.

"And every creature which is in heaven, and on earth, and under the earth, and such as are in the sea, and all that are in them, heard I saying, Blessing, and honour, and glory, and power, be unto Him that sitteth upon the throne, and unto the Lamb for ever and ever." Revelation 5:13.

Sin and sinners are no more, God's entire universe is clean, and the great controversy is forever ended.

New Books Available

Someones are in Amazon
*Spanish and English

1. Comentario Exhaustivo de los Escritos de Elena G de White sobre Génesis.
2. Guía de Estudio: Fundamentos de la Biblia Volumen 1.
3. Comentario Exhaustivo sobre el libro de Apocalipsis Volumen 1.
4. Serie: El Gran Conflicto en Tapa Dura Rojo.

English

5. Revelation: Bible Study Guide Volume 1 (with Ellen white quotes)

NEW BOOKS COMING SOON

6. Guía de Estudio: Fundamentos de la Biblia Volumen 2.
7. Guía de Estudio: Fundamentos de la Biblia Volumen 3.
8. Comentario Exhaustivo de sus Escritos sobre el libro de Daniel.
9. Historia de los Profetas y Reyes en letra Grande.
10. El Deseado de todas las Gentes en letra Grande.
11. Patriarchs and Prophets Big Print Edition *like this copy*.
12. Desire of Ages Big Print Edition
13. The Great Controversy Big Print Edition

¡And much more will coming!

Contact us by email for bulk prices per boxes:
*kalhelministries21@gmail.com

CPSIA information can be obtained
at www.ICGtesting.com
Printed in the USA
BVHW050215100221
599682BV00010B/289